To my very senior brother & friend,

Sir Brian E. Urquhart,

with my deepest appreciation
for your kind support & encouragement
and with pleasant memories of
those difficult times in the
Middle East.

God bless.

Author,
Accra.
1st October 1989

MISSION WITH UNIFIL

The author in 1975, on his appointment as Chief of Staff of the United Nations Truce Supervision Organization in Palestine (UNTSO).

LIEUTENANT-GENERAL
EMMANUEL A. ERSKINE

Mission with
UNIFIL
An African Soldier's Reflections

WITH A FOREWORD BY SIR BRIAN URQUHART

HURST & COMPANY, LONDON

First published in the United Kingdom
by C. Hurst & Co. (Publishers) Ltd.,
38 King Street, London WC2E 8JT
© Lieutenant-General Emmanuel A. Erskine, 1989
ISBN 1-85065-048-9
Printed in England on long-life paper

This book is dedicated to all the officers and men of UNIFIL, the Military Observers of UNTSO and the supporting Field Service Officers who serve the cause of peace in the Middle East

FOREWORD

by Sir Brian Urquhart

General Erskine's reflections on his time as a United Nations peace-keeper in the Middle East give a human and thoughtful account of some very difficult assignments. General Erskine was the Commander of the Army of Ghana when he was assigned to the United Nations as Chief of Staff and Deputy Commander of the newly set up peace-keeping force in Egypt and Sinai (UNEF II) in 1974. His military bearing, his knowledge of his trade and his capacity for getting on with subordinates and superiors alike were matched by a generous and outgoing personality.

After two years with UNEF II, General Erskine became Chief of Staff of the United Nations Truce Supervision Organization (UNTSO) based in Jerusalem. UNTSO is the oldest UN peace-keeping operation, dating from 1948, and apart from its field duties it serves as a sort of depot for new peace-keeping operations in the Middle East and elsewhere.

As Chief of Staff, General Erskine had to run his observers and their supporting organization, and also keep in touch with the governments — Syria, Lebanon, Israel, Jordan and Egypt — on whose territory they were operating.

In the crisis which arose over Israel's invasion of Lebanon in March 1978, General Erskine was appointed commander of the newly-established United Nations Interim Force in Lebanon (UNIFIL) and remained in this exacting post for nearly three years. This nerve-racking and often violent job required exceptional qualities of resilience, improvisation, leadership and humour. General Erskine's detailed account of his time with UNIFIL gives a perceptive, and often poignant, insight into the challenges and dilemmas of peace-keeping in a violent area where government authority has vanished and has been replaced by a factional struggle with important international overtones. Erskine carried out this complicated and in some ways unfulfillable task with style and understanding until he returned to his old post at UNTSO early in 1981. He remained there until 1986.

General Erskine comments with refreshing frankness on his international service. Especially in his account of UNIFIL, the great and complex problems of peace-keeping emerge vividly as seen by a responsible insider. UNIFIL was, and is, with the exception of the Congo operation, probably the most difficult peace-keeping operation the United Nations has yet undertaken, and its first commander's account is therefore particularly valuable and original.

Throughout his international service General Erskine showed unswerving loyalty to, and understanding of, the United Nations. His observations on the nature, problems and techniques of peace-keeping reflect this loyalty, and highlight the problem of staying above the conflict while at the same time exercising a restraining influence on those engaged it.

UN peace-keeping is now beginning to be recognized as a valuable weapon in the arsenal of peace. There is an increasing demand for peace-keeping operations, but there is still not too much general understanding of their character, limitations, and the necessary pre-conditions for success. General Erskine's reflections will be of parti-cular value on this score, both to the soldiers who follow him as commanders of these operations and to governments who have to con-sider, and make, the necessary decisions.

This book by a distinguished and respected African soldier breaks some new ground in the growing literature on peace-keeping. It is a valuable contribution to this still novel but increasingly vital activity.

AUTHOR'S PREFACE & ACKNOWLEDGMENTS

My main preoccupation since returning home from my UN assignments in the Middle East on 9 May 1986 has been to work on this book.
I have been prompted and encouraged to do so for four principal
reasons. First, we officers in the Ghana armed forces have woefully
failed to put on record important international military operations in
which we have been major participants. It is a great pity that even
though Ghana was one of the first countries to send a contingent to the
UN peacekeeping operations in the Congo where the troops acquitted
themselves creditably, and we continued operations until the end of
ONUC, not one of the many books written on UN operations in the
Congo has been by a member of our armed forces. In this book, I have
devoted some attention to the role of the Ghana armed forces in UNEF
2 and UNIFIL, with the object of partly redressing this deficiency.

Again, since my return home, I have given one public lecture on UN
peacekeeping activities and the political situation in the Middle East. I
think the lecture went off well, and some members of the audience
appealed to me to give more similar lectures. They made me feel that I
have insights on this subject which they wanted me to share with them,
and I have the feeling too that some of it should also be shared with a
wider international readership. Hence the convergence of public and
personal motives which forms my second reason for writing this book.

As with those members of the audience at my public lecture, and my
wife and children whose interest is perhaps natural, many friends and
colleagues, Ghanaian and non-Ghanaian, have urged me to share an
account of my twelve years' experience in the Middle East with the
world community. Twelve years in any theatre of operations, and by
any measure of judgement, is a long time, and participation in UNEF
2 in Sinai, UNDOF on the Golan, UNIFIL in Lebanon, and UNTSO
spread over the entire mission area provides a goldmine of experience
for any good professional soldier. It would be selfish to keep this varied
experience to myself.

My fourth reason is rather practical. As the result of participating in
peacekeeping seminars and giving lectures since 1979, I have accumu-
lated a great amount of written material. I have often asked myself if I
have not wasted my time if I do not put some of it into more lasting
form.

I have tried as best I could to be original. It seems to me that there is
no point in delving into the Bible and history to explain why chaos persists in the Middle East. There are many books on the market on this
topic. However, personal records of the situation are rather scanty and
I feel that the public may like to read my uninfluenced thoughts at
first-hand.

Acknowledgments

Writing this book would scarcely have been possible without the assistance and encouragement of some of my staff and friends.

While serving as the Force Commander of UNIFIL, my Personal Assistant and Secretary, Field Service Officer (FSO) Prathip Rochanapruk, helped me to maintain a personal diary which has been an invaluable source of reference. I am profoundly grateful to Prathip. A similar diary was kept for me when I moved to UNTSO in February 1981 by my then Personal Assistant and Secretary, Miss Sonya Morris. Most unfortunately, Sonya later died in her home country, South Africa. She was a highly professional secretary and extremely helpful to me, and I wish to pay her my posthumous respect. To Miss Margaret Strang who succeeded Sonya, and to FSO Michael Onyekpe who took over from Margaret following her transfer to Geneva; to my Military Assistants and Aides-de-camp Commandants Brian O'Sullivan, John Ryan, John Joe Ryan, Paul O'Donnell and Noel Kelly (all Irish); Captain Peter Cosgrove (New Zealand); Captains Stan Pilbrow and Geoff Bell (Australia); Captains Panaya and Mosey (Fiji) and Captain Doug Mair (Canada), I wish to express my profound gratitude and appreciation for maintaining my newspaper files, which have been extremely useful.

Equally helpful to me has been the periodical *UNTSO News*, successively edited and published by selected Military Observers. Here I am particularly obliged to two former editors, Commandant Harry Smith (Ireland) and Captain Jari Lohi (Finland).

I wish to express special gratitude to Professor Adu Boahen, former head of the Department of History, University of Ghana, Legon, for assisting with the title for the book and to Professor Paul A.V. Ansah, head of the Communications Department at Legon, for patiently giving his time to read through the entire manuscript. And to Major George Sarpong, Lt-Colonel Kadri Abdulai, Colonel Henry Anyidoho and Colonel Joe Odei, all of the Ghana Army and colleagues of mine serving with me on the Commission inquiring into the Structure of the Ghana Armed Forces, my gratitude for their invaluable assistance in reading through the galley proofs.

Writing this book has demanded a lot from me mentally and physically, and for this reason, I have particularly appreciated the encouragement given me by a few friends and my family, notably Philip Lythcott of the UN HQ, New York; Eugene Kweku Forson; Ghana News Agency representative to the UN; Colonel V. Coker-Appiah, a colleague in the army; Lt.-Col. Samuel Brew-Graves; Ted Bernasko;

Samuel Oscar Erskine, Managing Director of Wang, Ghana; K.O. Sackey; and my eldest son Alex.

Special acknowledgement is also due to the President of the International Peace Academy in New York, veteran peacekeeper Major-General Indar Jit Rikhye, Indian Army (retired), for much-valued advice and help.

To Sir Brian Urquhart, unfailing source of support to so many peacekeepers during his years as the UN's Under Secretary-General for Special Political Affairs, I acknowledge deep gratitude for the foreword he has so kindly agreed to write for this book.

Finally, my dearest thanks and appreciation go to my wife Rose. Her encouragement and moral support have been immeasurable, and throughout the late and long hours of writing she was always, as ever, good company.

Accra, Ghana   E.A. ERSKINE
January 1989

CONTENTS

PART TWO

PLATES

The author in 1975, on his appointment as Chief of Staff of the United
Nations Truce Supervision Organization in Palestine (UNTSO)
frontispiece

between pages 98 and 99

Soon after the establishment of UNIFIL, Senegalese soldiers arrive to
take over positions from the withdrawing Israeli forces.
Refugees returning to their homes in Southern Lebanon after UNIFIL
had been set up.
Destruction resulting from the Israeli invasion of Southern Lebanon
from March 1978.
The deserted town of Khiam, Southern Lebanon.
UNIFIL troops conducting a routine check for arms and explosives at
a checkpoint.
Dutch troops on patrol in their area of responsibility.
One of the UNTSO observation posts on the Lebanese-Israeli border.
Norwegian medical team bringing a wounded civilian from the
UNIFIL area of operations for treatment at the Base Hospital in
Naqoura.
French engineers preparing a position for the construction of shelters
for troops.
Troops' quarters in Naqoura destroyed by shelling from Major
Haddad's De Facto Forces, April 1980.
The author as UNIFIL force commander and his deputy Brigadier-
General Jean Cuq, with Major-General Ben-Gal and an IDF section
commander at the taking over of the Abbassiya sector from the IDF
on 14 April 1978.
Meeting on 28 March 1978 between UN representatives and the PLO.
The author inspecting the Nigeria contingent during their medal
parade at Nibatt HQ, Tayr Zibua, on 7 September 1979.
The author, as Chief of Staff, UNTSO, at a medal parade for UNTSO
military observers.
The author's successor as UNIFIL force commander, Lt.-Gen.
William Callaghan, presents him with a set of crystal glasses.
Troops of the Fiji battalion entertaining their guests with a national
dance, following their medal parade.

MAPS

xv

PRINCIPAL ABBREVIATIONS

ADF	Arab Deterrent Force
ADL	Armistice Demarcation Line (1949)
AE	Armed Element
ALA	Arab Lebanese Army
DEF	De Facto Forces (South Lebanon)
EIMAC	Egypt Israel Mixed Armistice Commission
FMR	Force Mobile Reserve
FSF	Forces of the South Front
HKJIMAC	Hashemite Kingdom of Jordan and Israel Mixed Armistice Commission
IDF	Israel Defence Forces
ILMAC	Israel Lebanon Mixed Armistice Commission
ISMAC	Israel Syria Mixed Armistice Commission
MNF	Multinational Force (Beirut)
MNO	Multinational Force and Observers
OAU	Organization of African Unity
OGB, OGE, OGG, OGJ, OGL, OGS	Observer Group Beirut, —Egypt, —Golan, —Jerusalem, —Lebanon, —Sinai
ONUC	Opération des Nations Unies au Congo
OUSGSPA	Office of the Under Secretary-General for Political Affairs
PFLP	Popular Front for the Liberation of Palestine
PLO	Palestine Liberation Organisation
UN	United Nations
UNDOF	UN Disengagement Observation Force (Syria)
UNEF	UN Emergency Force (Sinai)
UNFICYP	UN Peacekeeping Force in Cyprus
UNIFIL	UN Interim Force in Lebanon
UNMO	UN Military Observer
UNTSO	UN Treaty Supervision Organisation (Palestine)
UNTAG	UN Transition Assistance Group (Namibia)

PART ONE
1
BECOMING A MAKER AND KEEPER OF PEACE

The only international combat exposure to which Ghanaian soldiers, both officers and men, who were on active service in the early 1960s could lay claim was their participation in the United Nations Operations in the Congo, ONUC. Ghana Contingent was one of the first to arrive in the Congo, on 15 July 1960, but since its participation came to an end on 25 September 1963, service personnel of the Ghana army have mainly stayed at home, with the exception of a few troop exchange programmes with the British army.

ONUC brought considerable experience to the Ghana army. Its timing could not have been more opportune to Ghana. On 23 September 1961, Dr Kwame Nkrumah, Ghana's first President, decided to implement his policy to 'Ghananise' the armed forces with the removal of the British commanders and principal staff and their replacement by Ghanaian officers. Fortunately, thanks to ONUC, there were a reasonable number of mature, seasoned and professional Ghanaian officers immediately available to fill the vacuum.

The Ghana army has been fortunate in having the British to build it up to high standards of efficiency and professionalism, equal to their own though of course within certain limits. The need to sustain these standards was uppermost in the minds of the Ghana government and all ranks of the armed forces. Experience was essential. We had participated in ONUC; we knew and appreciated its great value and yearned for another UN-sponsored peacekeeping exposure. The quest for further international exposure had become insatiable by the time I returned to Flagstaff House in January 1973 to resume my previous appointment as Army Commander.

In October 1973 the opportunity unveiled itself. The UN Security Council had passed its Resolution 338 which, among other demands, called for a ceasefire in the Middle Eastern war then raging, and requested the Secretary-General to set up a peacekeeping force to supervise the implementation of its resolution. Ghana was invited by the Secretary-General to provide an infantry battalion and staff officers to participate in UNEF 2.

The request was received with great pleasure. In November 1973 I led a delegation — including Colonel Edwin Sam, Director General of Operations and Plans, and Smyly C.A. Chinery, Principal Secretary, Ministry of Defence — to UN headquarters in New York to discuss the terms for our participation. On 3 January 1974, Ghana's first contingent to UNEF 2, commanded by Lt.-Col. W. Bruce-Konuah, left Accra for Cairo on what we term 'Operation Sunrise', i.e. UN peacekeeping operations in the Middle East.

According to UN peacekeeping practice, not only are the participating troops drawn from a broad geographical spread, but each contributing country is also allotted one senior staff appointment at the Force HQ. In March 1974 Ghana was offered the appointment of Chief of Staff of UNEF 2, then headquartered at Heliopolis in Cairo. This appointment fell to me.

I flew again to UN HQ on 14 April 1974 for briefing by the Secretary-General's staff responsible for UN peacekeeping operations. It was on this visit that I established a warm rapport with Brian Urquhart, then Under Secretary-General for Special Political Affairs; his was the Secretariat responsible to the Secretary-General for the efficient conduct of all UN peacekeeping missions. It was through him that I received my training in peacemaking and peacekeeping techniques, and he has always enjoyed my great respect and admiration. I returned home a week later, and on 1 May 1974 left Accra to begin my new career as a maker and keeper of peace.

UNEF 2 was only six months old when I joined it and, like all other peacekeeping operations mounted by the UN, it was having teething problems. The administrative and logistical machinery required to give full support to the operations in Sinai was still being established. When the contingents that were less experienced in UN peacekeeping techniques — like those of Panama, Peru, Nepal and Senegal — arrived in the mission area with little contingent-owned equipment, we had immense difficulty in sustaining them logistically in their operational duties. This state of affairs was compounded by the fact that there was little material available for purchase in Cairo, and most had to be obtained from outside markets and brought in by sea through Alexandria and Port Said.

As Chief of Staff, I was responsible for coordinating the activities of the headquarters, whose principal task was to ensure the effective operational functioning of the force. It was in UNEF 2 that I learnt that gathering troops from different parts of the world to operate together as a force in peacekeeping — despite differences in language, cultural background and religion — presents no difficulty whatsoever. What is difficult and no less important is to sustain them logistically. I was fortunate to learn this vital lesson in Sinai in 1974 and not in South Lebanon in 1978. Additionally, I was extremely fortunate to have had, as my Force Commander and boss, Lieut.-General

Ensio Siilasvuo of Finland, who preferred to handle the political aspects of the operations while entrusting the military aspects to my professional hands. I could not have had a better base to start my peacekeeping career.

UNEF 2 was involved in two principal operations and as Chief of Staff, and later Deputy Force Commander as an additional function, I was deeply involved in both of them. The first was the establishment of the United Nations Disengagement Force, UNDOF, which was mounted in June 1974 with all its infantry units and administrative and logistical support drawn from UNEF 2 resources. This meant a certain amount of shuttling between Cairo/Sinai and Damascus/Golan for myself and the Force Commander. Brigadier-General Briceno (Peru), my Deputy, was posted to UNDOF as its first Force Commander.

The other principal operation was the second disengagement of forces between Egypt and Israel in August – September 1975. By the terms of the Disengagement Agreement, the Israel Defence Forces (IDF) withdrew further to the east, thereby facilitating to the maximum the operations of the Suez Canal. As the IDF pulled back, UNEF 2 redeployed into the vacated areas. This was an interesting period in the history of the mission. The Sinai Field Mission, as part of the Agreement, was established on the hills in the area of the Giddi pass to monitor possible Egyptian troop movements which could be considered as violating the Agreement. With the full implementation of the Disengagement of Forces Agreement, it was time for me to leave for my new assignment.

On 8 September 1975, I was offered the appointment of Chief of Staff, United Nations Truce Supervision Organisation (UNTSO), through this message received from the Secretary-General, Dr Kurt Waldheim: 'It is my intention to appoint you as Chief of Staff of UNTSO. I very much hope you will accept this important appointment. In view of your responsibilities in UNEF at this crucial stage, it would be my intention that you should not take up your appointment with UNTSO until about end October or mid-November. I should appreciate your reaction to these proposals before proceeding further.' I do not think that many commanders would have turned down such an offer, and with the agreement of my government, I accepted it with great pleasure. However, I asked to stay in UNEF 2 until the troops had been fully redeployed to meet the terms of the Disengagement Agreement. On 6 January 1976, I drove to Jerusalem, the headquarters of UNTSO, the oldest UN observer mission, to assume my new appointment as its executive head.

UNEF 2 served as the base for my training in field command as it related to peacekeeping. UNTSO, on the other hand, was to train me in peacemaking. As its Chief of Staff, I was accredited to the governments of Israel, Syria, Lebanon, Egypt and Jordan. Holding meetings with their respective Defence and Foreign Ministers, commanders of their armed forces and other senior officials to discuss political and military issues related to the region and affecting the operations of UNTSO, became part of my normal function.

UNTSO, with its military observers drawn from seventeen countries, attracted frequent visits from parliamentarians, senior government officials and army commanders from participating countries. My staff and I received and briefed them as best we could on the political and military situation in the general area, and made projections of possible future trends.

It was on 19 March 1978 that I moved to South Lebanon to establish the United Nations Interim Force in Lebanon (UNIFIL) as its first Force Commander. If UNEF 2 and UNTSO were my training institutions, UNIFIL was to be the institution for practical application. All the field techniques learnt in keeping the peace in UNEF 2 and the negotiating techniques learnt in peacemaking in UNTSO had to be put into practice in UNIFIL.

The subject of this book is what I learnt and applied in my twelve years of peacemaking and peacekeeping in the Middle East.

2

THE SITUATION IMMEDIATELY BEFORE
UNIFIL WAS ESTABLISHED

The October 1973 Middle East war drew much public attention because it was fought in an area of the world where there is intense political and military activity involving the world's two major powers, the United States and the Soviet Union. Wars in the Middle East have put to the test the technological prowess of each superpower through the effectiveness or otherwise of its hardware used by one or the other of the combatants. The United States is the major supplier of arms and aircraft to Israel while the Soviets have fulfilled that role towards Syria, Jordan and Egypt. The superpowers' military and technological secrets have often been exposed in the Middle East through both the competent and the incompetent use of their equipment by combatants in the field.

The Americans were excited when, in the 1982 air battle between Syria and Israel (a byproduct of the Israeli invasion of Lebanon), the Israeli Air Force (IAF) was able to destroy about a quarter of the total Syrian combat air capability. The IAF was able to retrieve and take into Israel two of the latest model of Soviet-made combat aircraft which they had shot down, and the Israeli Defence Forces (IDF) captured some of the latest models of Soviet-made tanks. Technologists from the US military and civilian war establishment paid a special visit to Israel to examine them. Soviet technologists showed a similar interest in captured Israeli equipment. In the absence of direct major armed confrontation between the two superpowers, these wars, and sporadic fighting between the Jews and Arabs, have helped both the United States and the Soviet Union to obtain good information about the quality and technique of each other's arms, combat aircraft, ground missiles, weapon control systems and associated war equipment.

Again the Middle East region provokes intense public interest worldwide because it is the focus, not only of the Palestine and Arab problems, but of the Jewish problem. The on-going Lebanese crisis, compounded by the PLO's quest for a state on Lebanese soil, which affects Israel's security interests and had provoked it into armed hostilities, also draws the world's attention regularly to the region.

For these reasons, what has been happening in the Middle East has always been highlighted in the international media. The world public was thus fully informed of the situation in the region immediately before, during and after the war which started on 6 October 1973.

I will therefore only briefly mention a few important aspects of the situation in the post-war days as I saw them on arriving in Cairo on 3 May 1974 to assume my duties as Chief of Staff of UNEF 2. It should be noted that UNEF 1 was established in 1956 following the Suez crisis. The unilateral withdrawal of the force on the insistence of President Nasser of Egypt early in 1967 was the catalyst for the June 1967 war, pre-empted by Israel.

Yom Kippur, the day of atonement, is considered the holiest of all days in the Jewish calendar. The day is wholly dedicated to prayers, and the devout spend much of the time in the synagogues. Workaday life comes to a total halt, and no vehicular movements whatsoever are permitted. Until the October 1973 war, Israel's national security was also apparently relaxed on Yom Kippur, and this explains why President Anwar Sadat of Egypt and President Hafez el Assad of Syria decided to declare war against Israel on that day. The fact that the Egyptian forces were able to cross the Suez Canal and overrun the 'Bar Lev line' of defence, and that the Syrian forces were able to overrun the Golan Heights, both with little resistance from the IDF, under-scored the strategic wisdom of Sadat and Assad in declaring war on Israel on the Jewish day of atonement. The Bar Lev line, named after the general commanding Israel's Southern Front at the time of the war, who developed the concept, consisted of a series of heavily-defended and well-built positions running parallel to the Canal on its eastern side.

While Egypt, after Israel had defeated it along with its Arab neigh-bours in 1948 and 1967, was rejoicing at crossing the Canal despite the presence of the IDF and the Bar Lev line, Syria was not in such an ecstatic mood, because the war still raged on. In Israel the politicians were trying to find scapegoats for the country having been caught with its pants down.

Morale in the Arab world had fallen very low following the Six Day War in June 1967. The West Bank of the River Jordan had been totally overrun by the Israelis, thereby terminating Jordanian administration over the area with its West Bank Palestinians; Gaza had been overrun along with the Palestinians living in the strip, terminating Egyptian administration; Sinai had been overrun, with the oilfields of Abu Rudeis falling into Israeli hands; and the Suez Canal had been blocked, stopping all ship movements through it. The cessation of operations of the Abu Rudeis oilfields and the Suez Canal, which generated a large income for the Egyptian economy, was a major factor contributing to the depression which struck Egypt after the June 1967 war. Subsidies from Saudi Arabia, Kuwait and other oil-rich Arab states were not enough to feed, clothe and house the Egyptian people or pay for Egypt's war debts to the Soviet Union.

On 6 October 1973, President Sadat reversed the trend. For the first few days after the Egyptian army crossed the canal, the IDF was on the defensive. Egypt was jubilant, and its morale was high. The Suez Canal was almost in its hands again, and retrieving the Southern Sinai oilfields in Abu Rudeis was in sight, or at least that possibility now existed. There was hope. The mental breakdown brought about by the total destruction of a high percentage of the Egyptian air force on its tarmacs in Cairo in 1967 had been overcome. The myth of Israeli military invincibility had been broken. Israel eventually won the battle, but Egypt won the war.

Suez City, Ismailia and El Kantara were a few of the areas badly hit as the result of the war. Evidence of severe fighting was readily discernible in all these areas, with many destroyed buildings. By May, when I arrived in the country, the population in Suez City was scanty, but Ismailia, once a beautiful and active city on the Canal, was virtually empty: it had been declared a war zone and out of bounds to all civilians. Heliopolis, especially the parts of it immediately bordering Cairo's international airport, had been fully prepared with air defence multiple rockets, and the 110- and 130-km. stretches of desert between Heliopolis and Ismailia and Suez City respectively were military zones, well prepared militarily to meet any ground or air approaches from the east.

However, rehabilitation was soon to start. With the establishment of UNEF 2 and its effective operations, strengthened by the agreement between Egypt and Israel signed at Geneva on 18 January 1974, the environment in Egypt was peaceful and conducive to a rehabilitation programme aimed at reactivating the economy and bringing Egyptian life back to normal. Special funds were provided by Saudi Arabia and Kuwait to rehabilitate Ismailia and Suez City, not only by repairing damaged buildings but also by constructing completely new neighbourhoods for the two cities. Today they are a beautiful sight.

The major economic rehabilitation activity consisted of the efforts by international consortia to re-open the Suez Canal. Not only did passage through the Suez Canal reduce sailing time between European and eastern seaports, but it also meant hard cash for the Egyptian government, a scarce and much-needed commodity at that time, especially after a war. Japanese, French and British companies were contracted to recover the wrecked and sunken ships and sea-mines deliberately laid there. It was a joy for us, even those who were not Egyptians, to see the Canal reopened personally by President Sadat in June 1975. The President, dressed in naval uniform, followed the opening ceremony in Port Said by sailing through in one of his naval frigates. It was both a moving and a happy occasion. The light of peace between Egypt and Israel could already be seen at the end of the tunnel.

The situation inside Israel was always more political than military. Israel has fought its wars outside its territory, and therefore there was nothing visible to suggest that a war had been fought only eight months earlier. Social life was normal, but the political life seethed with anger. Prime Minister Golda Meir's Labour government was in serious trouble: the question being asked was whether the Israeli intelligence agencies — Shin Beit, Mossad and the general security services — were aware that Presidents Sadat and Assad were planning to launch their attacks on Yom Kippur.

The Israeli commission of inquiry, set up under Chief Justice Agranat to investigate how the country had fallen victim to Sadat's surprise-attack on 6 October, reported that two main issues had contributed to Israeli's initial lapses. The first was that Israeli intelligence agencies had believed that Egypt would not attack Israel unless it had full air superiority. Secondly, the agencies, particularly the military intelligence, were confident that they would be able to give enough advance warning of an Egyptian attack to enable the IDF to mobilise. As a result the information received at the Israeli General Headquarters in Tel Aviv on Egyptian war activities was wrongly interpreted as 'exercise' and not 'war'. One of the effects of Israel's initial fiasco in the Yom Kippur war was a radical review of mobilisation techniques by the IDF. New mobilisation procedures, evolved as Standing Operating Procedures (SOPs), continue to be rehearsed periodically throughout Israel.

Syria was still in the grip of the war on the Golan, although it was not as intense as before the Security Council was able to arrange a ceasefire by virtue of Security Council Resolution 338. The IDF had overcome the initial Syrian success and pushed the Syrians back beyond the village of Sasa, a few kilometres from Damascus, and were holding a line, in a bulge, with Sasa as their Forward Defended Locality (FDL). Shooting was intermittent and controlled. It continued until the ceasefire agreement between the two countries was signed at the end of May 1975, thereby permitting the establishment and operation of the United Nations Disengagement Observer Force (UNDOF), which effectively disengaged the two armies and stabilised the Golan.

Jordan looked quite normal. It had not participated in the October 1973 war. The bitter experiences of 1967 had served as a deterrent; in that conflict it had lost its administration and control of the West Bank and, with that loss, all political influence over the West Bank Palestinians. The loss of any empire is a hard experience, and so it was with the Hashemite kingdom of Jordan.

3

THE CAMP DAVID ACCORD AND UNIFIL

The political activity in the area which was the most significant factor leading to the establishment of UNIFIL was the peacemaking process which culminated in the 1979 peace treaty between Egypt and Israel. This process had its earliest origin on 6 October 1973 when President Sadat, in concert with President Assad of Syria, declared war on Israel.

The separation of Egyptian and Israeli forces by the interpositioning of the advance party of UNEF troops detached from the UN Forces in Cyprus (UNFICYP) marked the first disengagement of warring forces following the October 1973 war. The line of separation ran from Kilometre 101 on the Cairo-Suez highway northwards to a line about 10 km. from Ismailia. This interpositioning between the two opposing forces facilitated the negotiations that were going on concurrently at Kilometre 101 to accomplish three particular tasks: working out a formula for the administration of the Egyptian Third Army which had been cut off by the IDF on the Eastern side of the Suez Canal; arranging for hostilities to cease in consonance with the Security Council demands for a ceasefire in its Resolution 338; and agreeing on a *modus operandi* for UNEF operations. This agreement was eventually concluded and signed in Geneva on 18 January 1974. Lieutenant-General Ensio Siilasvuo, Force Commander UNEF 2, chaired these negotiations, assisted by Dr James O.C. Jonah (Sierra Leone) from UN HQ New York.

UNEF 2 effectively stabilised Sinai and reduced tension between Egypt and Israel, making it possible for the peacemaking process to gain momentum. In August – September 1975, the Second Disengagement of Forces became effective. For this much credit has to go to Dr Henry Kissinger, then US Secretary of State, whose strenuous and pioneering 'shuttle diplomacy' had earlier brought about the ceasefire arrangements and the first disengagement of forces agreement between Egypt and Israel.

By the terms of the Second Disengagement of Forces Agreement, the IDF pulled further to the east. In the northern sector, it shared a common boundary with the Swedish battalion and in the south with the Finnish battalion, headquartered in Abu Rudeis. The Ghana battalion took over the important task in the Sinai Middle Sector of controlling all movements to and from the sensitive Giddi and Mitla passes, which had been vital for Israeli troop movements during the

June 1967 war. It is essential to note that as a condition for Israel conceding this Second Disengagement Agreement, the US government was obliged to agree that it would not engage in any kind of direct discussion or negotiation with the PLO until the PLO accepted Security Council Resolutions 242 and 338, which accord *de facto* recognition to the state of Israel. This is the basis of the US government's subsequent position in refusing to negotiate with the PLO. The Second Disengagement Agreement of 1975 could be effectively viewed as the forerunner of the Camp David Accord, which culminated in the 1979 peace treaty between Egypt and Israel. By this agreement, the oilfields of Abu Rudeis were handed over to Egypt by Israel.

President Sadat defied the wishes of his major war ally, President Assad of Syria, and most of his Arab colleagues in the twenty-one-member Arab League when he visited Israel on 11 November 1977. It was a historic and emotional visit to the Holy Land, combining pilgrimage and peacemaking. I watched President Sadat's arrival at Ben Gurion airport in Tel Aviv on television in my residence in Jerusalem. A considerable time passed after his entourage had disembarked before he emerged on to the gangway of the aircraft that had brought him from Cairo. At one stage, the Israeli dignitaries and the diplomatic corps waiting to receive him with the appropriate formal presidential courtesies feared that he had had a sudden change of mind and decided to go back to Cairo. I shared those apprehensions with them. But eventually the Egyptian President, who four years earlier had declared war against his host, emerged dignified but tense. Most Israelis and people like myself remained sceptical about the visit ever coming off until the plane actually touched down. And then both Israeli and Palestinian friends with whom I spoke during the visit hoped that it signalled the end of the crisis in the region. It did indeed bring a 'cold peace' between the two, but the crisis has continued unabated up till the present. President Sadat was able to find time out of his congested schedule to pray in the Al Aqsa mosque in the old city of Jerusalem, the third holiest mosque in the Islamic world after Mecca and Medina. This was the pilgrimage side to his visit.

The subdued nervous tension which preceded Sadat's visit had given way to a relaxed atmosphere and cautious optimism by the time it ended. At a social get-together, Mrs Meir, Prime Minister of Israel at the time of the October 1973 war, sat side by side with Sadat, and the two exchanged gifts, with Mrs Meir giving the President a present for his new grandchild. No communiqué could have done better than the refrain of 'No more war' pledged by President Sadat, with Prime Minister Begin responding 'No more bloodshed'. This refrain continued to be broadcast by the Israel national broadcasting corporation long after the visit.

The visit gave the necessary momentum for the Camp David Accord brokered by the US President Jimmy Carter, who became personally involved in the peacemaking efforts. He was determined to see the peace between Egypt and Israel through to a successful conclusion. When President Carter left the White House in 1981 after only one presidential term, he had an indelible international achievement to his credit, comparable to that of his elected predecessor, President Nixon, in successfully restoring the severely strained American relations with mainland China.

With most of the Arab countries intensely opposed to President Sadat's peace initiatives, it was imperative for Israel not to antagonise its Arab neighbours unless its national security interests were under severe threat. For it to do so would make Sadat's peace initiatives extremely difficult to pursue. President Carter would have been a major beneficiary, if the peace objective were achieved. A massive Israeli presence in Lebanon therefore had to be avoided, but if it did happen, a formula had to be evolved for getting the Israeli forces out again as quickly as possible, principally to avoid embarrassing Sadat before his Arab brothers and thus further jeopardising his peace initiative. Was UNIFIL that formula?

Before beginning this survey let us see briefly how the UN was disposed in its peacekeeping activities in the area. Military observers of the UN Truce Supervision Organisation (UNTSO) were already performing their observation and reporting functions in Sinai and on the Golan, and they actually remained *in situ* in both places, albeit in shelters, throughout the duration of the war. Military observers serving in Sinai used to talk of the years between the June 1967 and October 1973 conflicts when, during daytime, troops from both the Israeli and Egyptian sides would sit and drink coffee together while at night they turned their guns on each other. This was the period, especially just before October 1973, which has always been referred to as the war of attrition. UNEF 2 had been operational since late October 1973 when the Security Council imposed a ceasefire on Egypt and Israel in Sinai, and UNDOF began its operations on the Golan immediately after Syria and Israel had concluded their disengagement agreement in Geneva at the end of May 1974.

Lebanon before UNIFIL — the general situation

I went to Lebanon relatively late, in 1976, on taking up the appointment as Chief of Staff UNTSO. In that capacity, I had my unarmed UN observers manning the five UNTSO observation posts (OPs) – Lab, Hin, Ras, Mar, Khiam – along the 1949 Armistice

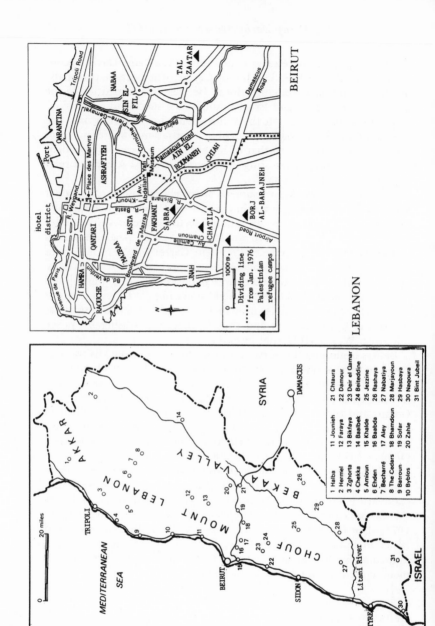

BEIRUT

LEBANON

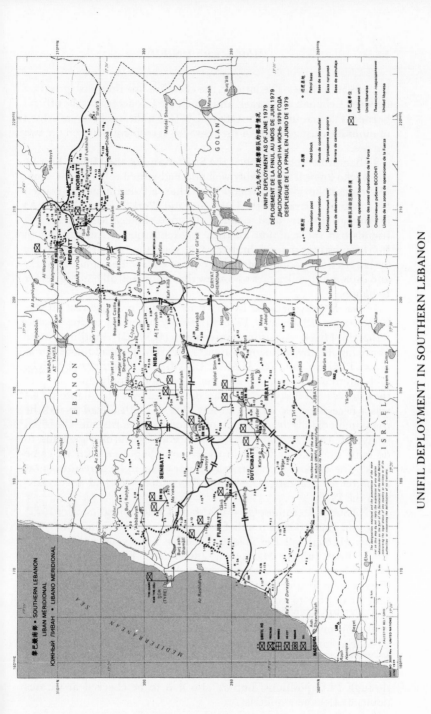

UNIFIL DEPLOYMENT IN SOUTHERN LEBANON

Demarcation Line. The latter is the ceasefire line that was agreed on between Lebanon and Israel, and which the UN accepts as the official border. The manning of the OPs by UNTSO military observers helped to monitor infringements of the ceasefire agreement between the two parties.

Lebanon had been dubbed the Switzerland of the Middle East by those who knew it reasonably well and had visited it before my time. My tennis colleague and friend Elias Elias, a Palestinian who started his career as a clerk with the UN Relief and Works Agency (UNRWA) in Amman, Jordan, used to talk of the good old days when he and his friends had spent almost all their weekends not in Amman but in Beirut, mostly at that celebrated rendezvous, the St George Hotel. My Syrian friends also spoke of their frequent visits to Beirut just to relax, and diplomatic colleagues who knew the region well all had praises for Lebanon.

I was unlucky because by the time I paid my first visit to Ras Naqoura on 13 January 1976 to see my observers of the Israeli-Lebanon Mixed Armistice Agreement (ILMAC), hostilities were poisoning the environment. Naqoura, the ILMAC headquarters, was under PLO control, and ILMAC UN Military Observers (UNMOs) and international civilian staff on relief and supply duty visits to the Observation Posts had to be accompanied by a PLO fighter. This was a necessity if we wanted to stay alive. The PLO had mined the road immediately leading out of Naqoura towards the Christian village of Alma Achaab; hence, we needed this armed guerrilla to de-mine the road and wait in the surrounding area until we came back. The departure and arrival timings had to be agreed upon as a matter of Standing Operating Procedure. We had to co-exist with the PLO.

UNTSO's easternmost OP was Khiam. Until the beginning of 1977, we could undertake our relief and supply runs, driving along the border through all the villages, notable among which were Ayn Abel, Bent Jubail, Marjayoun and finally Khiam. From early 1977, Marjayoun was closed to us by Major Saad Haddad and his Christrian militia for their own security reasons. It is important to note that what were to become the Christian enclave and the De Facto Forces (DFF) in 1978 when UNIFIL was established had already been operating on the ground as early as 1976. With the closing to us of Marjayoun, our relief and supply base had to be shifted from Naqoura to Beirut. Driving from Beirut through the Arkoub was scenically, beautiful but frightening. Not only did we have to go through PLO positions, but we also had to be checked at various points by Lebanese militias.

I undertook the relief and supply trip once in the company of my observers. The chairman of ILMAC, Lt.-Col. Jean Espinassy (French), was with me. The previous evening, I had joined some of the observers for a drink and dined at a restaurant in West Beirut called the Captain's Cabin. In the course of that evening, a concerned observer tried to advise me not to undertake the pending relief trip. That was to be expected, but I asked him why I should not join the team. He was frank: 'Sir, it is too dangerous for you.' I thanked him for his concern and added that if it was dangerous for me, it was equally so for them and if I had to send them there on duty, there was no excuse or any earthly reason to stop me from undertaking the same trip. My stand was fully appreciated by all ranks of ILMAC, and I am confident that most commanders in the field would have taken the same decision.

We were stopped as we moved along by the PLO, the Progressive Socialist Party (PSP), the Communists and a few others. Some who knew our UN flag and were sufficiently confident just waved us on. At such checkpoints we slowed down, said 'hello' or '*marhaba*', and then pushed on. At Kaukaba we stopped to dress properly — for the real unknown. Colonel Espinassy donned his flak jacket and steel helmet, and helped me to put on mine. Then we proceeded under PLO control to Ebel es Saki. The most dangerous part of the journey was still ahead: it was the no-man's-land, the 2 km. stretch between Ebel as Saki and Khiam, both of which were under PLO control. The Christian militia headquartered in Marjayoun frequently bombarded this stretch of land to disrupt PLO movements of reinforcements and supplies reaching the two townships. Fortunately we made it to Khiam, and what relief and satisfaction I felt after being with my men in such a God-forsaken enclave.

With the heavy fighting through most of 1977 between the PLO entrenched in Khiam, on the one side, and Haddad and his men in Marjayoun, on the other, the inhabitants of Khiam had to be driven out of the town, and the victorious Christian militias could not allow them to return till after the 1982 Israeli invasion of Lebanon. It was during one of these bouts of heavy fighting that the two observers in OP Khiam could not be relieved for seventeen days, the longest OP duty in all my time with UNTSO. At one stage my principal staff and I were seriously concerned for the safety of the two (the officers were French and American respectively). The OP antenna had been destroyed, thus cutting off communications; the main building had also been destroyed and the UNMOs spent all day and all night in their well-protected shelters. They had dry rations to live on for a month, but I was most concerned about their water supply. At one point, we thought of evacuating them, but how? The two might come out with the UN flag, but we suspected that the ground immediately surrounding the OP had been mined, and so this idea had to be abandoned. But after seventeen days of continuous heavy fighting with Haddad and his forces, who were supported by the IDF, the PLO fighters were driven out of Khiam and Ebel es Saki. Had we known that Chairman Arafat had instructed his Khiam commander to take care of our men, including the provision of water, we would still have worried but certainly less.

What the PLO had desired but could not fulfil in Jordan was precisely what was gradually shaping up in Lebanon. It was the establishment of an autonomous presence in West Beirut — much to the anger and opposition of the Lebanese, particularly the Christians of East Beirut. Concurrently with their endeavours to establish their power-base in Lebanon, the PLO increased their hostile activities against Israel, principally from South Lebanon. The PLO struck more frequently and much harder at the Israelis, provoking ever more forceful Israeli retaliation. There was great consternation in Lebanon among the men of power. Some felt that the government should use force to get the PLO out, and that if this failed, they should put clamps on their hostilities against Israel to forestall Israeli counter-attacks, which invariably hurt the indigenous Shiite Lebanese population of the south more than they hurt the Palestinians.

By late 1975, confrontations between the Lebanese Christians and the PLO had escalated into major armed hostilities, ushering in the Lebanese civil war. The government ceased to function effectively, and Lebanon became a country of warlords. The army split into two main confessional communities, Christian and Muslim, thereby increasing its ineffectiveness as a national army and an instrument of authority. With the continuing absence of law and order, and severe fighting between Lebanese Christians and the PLO, the Lebanese President, Suleiman Franjieh, asked Syria for military support. President Assad responded favourably by sending in over 25,000 troops, whose presence within the context of the Arab Deterrent Force (ADF) was later formalised by the Arab League in Cairo.

The military situation in South Lebanon before the PLO attack and IDF invasion
.

As could be observed, the PLO fighters were extremely active in South Lebanon, from where they frequently mounted hostile activities across the 1949 Armistice Demarcation Line against townships in the north of Israel. The PLO was reasonably strong in Naqoura, Tyre, Bent Jubail, Khiam and Nabatiya, all of which were Muslim-dominated towns and villages. PLO arms caches were abundant throughout South Lebanon.

The strongest PLO base was in Beaufort Castle, an ancient Crusader fortress which dominates most of eastern South Lebanon, and from the surroundings of which Katyusha rockets have frequently been fired by the PLO at the Israeli border-towns of Metulla and Kiryat Shemona. These attacks indeed made life extremely uncomfortable for the inhabitants of both towns, and families, including children, had to spend long hours in underground bomb shelters during the attacks. They had become a challenge to Israeli military might.

PLO Katyusha attacks also triggered off political questions as to the capabilities of Israeli governments to deal with PLO 'terrorism'. So it should not be surprising that both Israeli invasions, in March 1978 and June 1982, had as their objectives the destruction of PLO fighting power in South Lebanon. Also, fighting between the PLO entrenched in Beaufort and the DFF from their HQ in Marjayoun had been frequent and heavy.

The response of the IDF to PLO attacks was prompt and heavy. Known PLO bases and Palestinian refugee camps were the first targets of its relatiatory air raids. Lebanese villages known or considered to be safe havens for the PLO were the secondary targets. Also, Rashadiya refugee camp and the ancient town of Tyre became regular targets — it is amazing to see the ruins of ancient Tyre still in fair condition, despite the hundreds of artillery and mortar shells and the air and naval bombardments that Israel has unleashed on the town over the years. Beaufort and Nabatiya also took severe shelling and air strikes from the IDF. As late as 1985, I paid a visit to Beaufort during my inspection visit to UNTSO OP 'Chateau' (Castle) which is only 700 metres away from it. OP 'Chateau' was established after Israel's Operation 'Litani' to monitor IDF activities in that area and to facilitate ceasefire negotiations whenever they become necessary. Amazingly, Beaufort looked strong, with little damage to its structure.

As a measure to control encroachment of its northern townships by PLO fighters close to the border, and thereby reduce the possibility of direct attacks against those townships, the Israeli authorities had started nursing the concept of a security belt, which in later years was to play a major part in preventing UNIFIL from carrying out its mandate to the full. An area varying in depth from 1 to 5 km. inland from the Armistice Demarcation Line, and stretching from the Christian village of Alma Achaab eastwards to Chebaa, had been commandeered by Major Saad Haddad and Major Sami Chidiak. Both were regular officers in the Lebanese army and were on legitimate military duty in the south with their regular troops until they got cut off from their headquarters in Yarze, Beirut, during the civil war. Whether the cut-off from Yarze was accidental, deliberate or externally inspired is a question I cannot answer. However, by the time I arrived on the scene in January 1976, Haddad and Chidiak were receiving all the hardware they needed for their combat activities against the PLO from the Israeli authorities. Chidiak controlled the western sector of the belt while Haddad took the eastern sector with Marjayoun as his HQ.

Further north towards Sidon at the oil refinery and port of Zahrani, there was a small detachment of Syrian soldiers. These were part of the Syrian army contingent participating in the Arab Deterrent Force based in Greater Beirut. The activities of this Syrian detachment were never extended south beyond Zahrani, thereby insulating Syria from direct involvement in the confrontation between Israel and the PLO.

As a direct result of the ongoing civil war, the Lebanese army had also split into two major confessional identities, Christian and Muslim. Most of the Christians had moved into the fighting camps of Pierre Gemayel's 'Kataeb', while others had gone to Camille Chamoun's 'Tigers' and yet others to Suleiman Franjieh's 'Marauders'. At this stage in Lebanon's history, the Shiite Amal movement had yet to be born. I would imagine that a small portion of the breakaway Muslims must have gone to the camps of the various armed elements within the Lebanese National Movement, but the majority of them went into the newly-formed Arab Lebanese Army (ALA), under the command of Lieutenant Khatib. The ALA controlled the Kasmiya bridge, the main bridge on the coastal road linking Tyre and South Lebanon with the north. The bridge was of such great strategic importance to the Lebanese, both for economic activities and military operations, that its control by the ALA and not the PLO was significant.

PLO attack and the launching of 'Operation Litani'

The upshot of this fighting and confusion was that the PLO had increased freedom to conduct armed action both in Beirut and in South Lebanon. It took advantage of this freedom to increase its attacks on Israel.

On 11 March 1978 an event took place which had a direct bearing on the establishment of UNIFIL. This was a daring attack mounted by PLO fighters against Israel. Moving by sea and coming ashore near the Israeli coastal city of Herzliya, about 8 km. from Tel Aviv, they commandeered an Israel tourist bus. The original plan, as reported in the press, was to move to Tel Aviv, take over a hotel, secure the guests as hostages, and impose demands on Israel. However, the passengers in the bus reacted, and got the driver to stop at a police roadblock. In the ensuing shoot-out, some thirty Israelis were killed and over seventy were wounded. Palestinian losses were ten dead.

I was in Cairo on a visit to my UNTSO outstation, Observer Group

Sinai, when the news of the PLO attack was announced by the BBC. I knew all too well that Israel would retaliate almost immediately — it was a standing operating procedure. Hence I decided to terminate my programme and return immediately to my HQ in Jerusalem.

Throughout the entire six-hour journey from Cairo to Jerusalem, my wife Rose, who was with me on this visit, and I discussed the possibility of massive Israeli retaliation on Lebanon, as had always happened before. It was expected by the diplomatic corps based in Israel and by all Israelis; the only question was when it would come. The weather during the next 2 – 3 days was bad with poor visibility, making air attacks almost impossible. Then it came, as we had all anticipated. On the night of 14/15 March 1978, the IDF, with massive force, launched 'Operation Litani' — the code-name for the invasion of South Lebanon.

4

THE ESTABLISHMENT OF UNIFIL

The UNIFIL mandate

The Security Council, the sole authority charged with the responsibility for the maintenance of international peace and security as enshrined in the United Nations Charter, was convened to discuss the grave situation in South Lebanon. The outcome of the meeting was the passing of Security Council Resolution 425 authorising the setting up of the United Nations Interim Force in Lebanon (UNIFIL). Secco Res 425 further requested the Secretary-General to submit a report to the Council within twenty-four hours on its implementation. This report was duly submitted and approved for implementation by Secco Res 426.*

The Secretary-General in his report gave the general outline of how he planned to implement Secco res 425 in the setting-up of UNIFIL. The report dealt with the principal objectives for the force, spelling out its terms of reference in full and defining the chain of command. As the highest body, the Security Council was to exercise its authority through the Secretary-General, whose responsibility it was to keep it fully informed on all important matters relating to UNIFIL's operations. The legal status of the force in terms of its immunities in its operations within the host-countries, the force level and, most important, the running cost were all covered in the report.

The operative points of UNIFIL's terms of reference can be summarised as follows:

(*a*) to determine cessation of hostilities by Israel;
(*b*) to confirm Israeli withdrawal;
(*c*) to restore international peace and security;
(*d*) to assist the Lebanese government to restore its authority in the area; and
(*e*) to establish and maintain itself in an area of operations to be defined through negotiations with the parties.

---

* Security Council Resolutions 425 and 426 and the Secretary-General's report are reproduced in Appendixes A, B and C.

Setting up the Force: The mechanism as we applied it

Immediately on receiving the Secretary-General's instructions, I assembled my principal staff officers from UNTSO: the Senior Staff Officer, Colonel W. Callaghan (Ireland), later to succeed me as Force Commander UNIFIL in 1981 and as Chief of Staff UNTSO in 1986; the Chief Operations Officer, J. Potter (United States); and the Chief UN Military Observer, Observer Group Sinai (OGS), Cairo, Lt.-Col N.C. Peck (Australia). This was in order to study Secco Res 425 and the Secretary-General's instructions, discuss our moves and take appropriate decisions.

I also put Observer Group Jerusalem (OGJ) on stand-by to move at twelve hours' notice to augment the Israel-Lebanon Mixed Armistice Commission (ILMAC), which was already in South Lebanon operating its five observation posts on the 1949 Armistice Demarcation Line. The twelve-hour stand-by turned out to be a wait of two and half days. Augmentation of the Blue Berets was not in the interest of the Israeli Defence Force who at that time were in their mopping-up, ground-consolidating stages following the attack.

I then summoned a senior UN Military Observer (UNMO) from Observer Group Sinai, Lt.-Col. Tom E. Leverette (United States), to move to Naqoura as officer-in-charge of operations, and he was on the ground and in full charge within twenty-four hours. On 20 March, I tasked the Chief Administraive Officer UNTSO, Gerry Dunn, to look into the administrative and logistical support aspect for the force. Maximum use was to be made of UNTSO resources, and maximum support was to be sought from UNEF in Sinai and UNDOF in the Golan. These were given on an impressive scale.

I reorganised ILMAC to serve two main functions. The first was to serve as HQ staff in all sections, namely Chief Engineer Officer, Chief Signals Officer, Movement Control, Air Liaison Officer, Operations Officers, Chief Logistics Officer, Chief Humanitarian Officer, Camp Commandant, Senior Medical Staff Officer, Force Welfare Officer and so on. This was most helpful considering that we did not receive UNIFIL permanent staff from contributing countries till the latter half of the following month. The second function was to serve as escorts and guides for the initial two companies (a Swedish company from UNEF and an Iranian one from UNDOF) and later for the battalions. ILMAC observers put their experience and knowledge of the area at the disposal of the battalion commanders. The Observer Group Lebanon (OGL) Teams concept had its origin from this arrangement.

For all operational, administrative and logistical planning purposes, UNTSO HQ was reorganised to serve as Rear HQ for UNIFIL.

This arrangement was of great use in putting to full use the expert skill and knowledge of UNTSO staff, both military and civilian, and the excellent existing communication facilities.

Political shuttles

At the same time as the operational, administrative and logistical matters were being undertaken, political shuttles were being run with the parties.

The next morning, 20 March 1978, Lt.-Gen. Siilasvuo, the Chief Coordinator, and I held meetings with Israeli officials, including Mr Weizman, the Minister of Defence, and General Gur, IDF Chief of Staff. Our main objective was to plan the operation — withdrawal of the IDF and deployment of UNIFIL troops; the timing of the IDF's withdrawal; the ceasefire arrangements; establishing a common base of understanding of Secco res 425 and the Secretary-General's report; and securing full Israeli support and cooperation for our mission.

Meetings were held in Beirut the following day with the Lebanese Prime Minister Selim el Hoss, the Foreign Minister Fuad Butros, and the Defence Minister and army commander, Brigadier Victor Khoury. Our objectives were to discuss the points raised with the Israelis, and to brief the Lebanese authorities on the views held by the Israelis and seek their views also. Briefing each side in a dispute on what the other side is thinking has been a continuing function of peacemaking. Meetings were held with the Syrians to solicit their support for UNIFIL operations, and especially on problems associated with the PLO.

Dr James Jonah represented the office of the Under-Secretary-General for Special Political Affairs, Brian Urquhart. (This office, as already mentioned, was the Secretary-General's secretariat directly responsible to him for the day-to-day operations of all UN peace-keeping missions.) Dr Jonah and I had a meeting with Chairman Arafat on the morning of 28 March to discuss the points outlined above. Arafat gave us a lecture lasting forty-five minutes on how the PLO had stood up to the IDF during the invasion. We left the meeting in no doubt over the PLO's position on Secco res 425, as we shall see later. Dr Jonah, with his keen intelligence and knowledge of the region's politics, made a great contribution to the peace process and to the effectiveness of the UN as a whole. He had been tasked by Brian Urquhart to represent the Secretariat at the negotiations between Egypt and Israel, both at Kilometre 101 in Egypt and in Geneva on the establishment of UNEF 2, following the cessation of the October 1973 hostilities called for by Secco res 338; he was involved in similar polit-ical negotiations leading to the establishment of UNDOF in May 1974 and participated fully in the discussion that led to the setting up of UNIFIL in March 1978. These shuttles, vital for the launching of the force, still continue at the present time, within the framework of the peacemaking process.

First move towards the main UNIFIL presence in South Lebanon

The principle and practice of establishing a UN presence in the area of operations concerned *immediately* after a Security Council Resolution has been passed authorising the Secretary-General to establish a peacekeeping force have always had a beneficial psychological impact on the parties to a conflict, the opposing troops on the ground, and the population living in the area affected by the hostilities. Thus company detachments of Norwegian, Austrian, Swedish and Irish troops had to be flown from the UN Force in Cyprus (UNFICYP) into Sinai directly after the passing of Secco res 338, which established UNEF 2. The same principle and practice were observed in the establishment of UNDOF, with Austrian, Peruvian, Canadian and Polish contingents being drafted in from UNEF 2.

The first major UN presence in South Lebanon could not be established till 21 March 1978, when we had twenty-two additional observers to reinforce the ILMAC UNMOs already operating there. On 22 March, two reinforced companies, IranCoy from UNDOF and SwedCoy from UNEF (respectively Iranian and Swedish companies) arrived. These formed the nucleus of UNIFIL.

Of the main UNIFIL contingents the French arrived first — at Beirut's international airport on 23 March. The Norwegians arrived next, at Tel Aviv on 25 March. Last came the Iranians on 9 June, after the Security Council had approved an increase in the Force from its starting level of 4,000 to 6,000. (The Secretary-General had visited the area in April, and we discussed the inadequacy of the Force's manpower. As the result of our proposals, he recommended to the Security Council an increase to 6,000.) The nine countries contributing to UNIFIL at this time were Canada, Fiji, France, Iran, Ireland, Nepal, Nigeria, Norway and Senegal. Canada withdrew its communications contingent on 1 October 1978.

Initial deployment of troops

The IDF deployment on the ground following the invasion was planned to cover the PLO's main infiltration routes and lines of supply and its potential base camps for attacks against Israel. The main threats were from the north-eastern sector and the port of Tyre. IDF deployment therefore stretched from the high ridges along the Tyre pocket, with a reinforced detachment in Bazuriyah, north to the western edges of the Litani river, and expanding east and south into the Christian enclave. The main bridges on the Litani were heavily guarded: Kasmiya from the high ground in the area of Abbassiya, and Khardala from the high ground bordering Marjayoun and Al Qualayah. The IDF physically sat on Akiya bridge.

Our terms of reference — that the Force would use its best efforts to prevent the recurrence of fighting and to prevent its area of operation from being utilised for hostile activities of any kind — imposed on us arduous and in fact impossible task of insulating the indigenous population of South Lebanon, the PLO, the IDF and Israel itself from any form of armed hostilities. I felt that to stop the PLO from moving into the evacuated areas was a possible means of achieving that objective. For our strategic considerations, and because the IDF withdrawals were from the Litani southwards, it was only too logical that UNIFIL's deployment should follow the IDF's withdrawal pattern. These considerations, coupled with the requirement that we should check the infiltration routes of the PLO and contain their fighters in their potential base camps, formed the basis for my concept in the initial deployment of UNIFIL troops into their areas of operations. The mental picture I had formed was that as the IDF withdrew from a sector, UNIFIL troops would simultaneously take it over, deploy into it and control it. When the IDF had completed its withdrawal exercises, in phases, from its forward defended localities along the Litani river south to the Armistice Demarcation Line of 1949 (i.e. to the Israeli-Lebanese border), and the corresponding deployment of UNIFIL troops into those evacuated areas had taken place, the Lebanese army, gendarmerie and other national security organisations would be helped to deploy into these areas, and once governmental authority was being effectively exercised, UNIFIL could withdraw. Secco Res 425 would have been fulfilled and the force could be disbanded.

However, subsequent events showed that I was too optimistic. I did not anticipate the hardline attitudes of the Israelis, which were to determine the progress, or lack of it, in the fulfilment of our mission. In reply to a question from Lieutenant-General Mordechai Gur, then IDF Chief of Staff, at our first meeting with him on 20 March 1978 (also attended by General Siilasvuo, the UN's Chief Coordinator) when we discussed UNIFIL's *modus operandi*, I briefed him according to my concept outlined above. I do not know what General Gur and his staff thought as they listened to a brief which ran completely counter to Israeli political and military intentions, which were to precipitate a prolonged stay for UNIFIL in South Lebanon.

In the early days following 'Operation Litani', the Israeli authorities, both politicians and generals, publicly stated that they had no
objection to the Lebanese army finally taking over South Lebanon.
General Gur said this to me at our meeting on 24 March, adding that
Israel's main fear was that a vacuum would be created in South
Lebanon following its final withdrawal, which could permit the return
of the PLO whose hostile activities towards Israeli settlements in the
north posed both political and military difficulties for them. General
Gur talked in a relaxed mood of the IDF's readiness to pull out at any
time, provided that UNIFIL and the Lebanese army were fully
deployed in the area; at the same time he emphasised that the dis-
arming of the Christian militias was unthinkable and that Israel could
not let them down after their close cooperation over the past three
years. Was there any hint then that the IDF was going to stay in South
Lebanon? Was he indicating this to General Siilasvuo and me when he
strongly suggested that UNIFIL should not be deployed 'at this time'
in the Christian enclave and Marjayoun, since the Christians were very
sensitive and needed time before they could trust the UN presence in
the area?

As we got to know the thinking of the Israelis generally and the IDF
in particular, it became clear that the concept of the so-called
'Christian enclave' (security zone) was the strategic basis for the invasion of South Lebanon on 14/15 March. Little did the Security
Council, meeting on 19 March to decide the establishment of UNIFIL
realise that Israel was in South Lebanon to stay. Hence my false
optimism, based on inadequate intelligence, about the IDF's intentions. General Gur knew what they were planning, and I had interpreted his words to mean acceptance of the Lebanese army in the area.
UNIFIL, the Lebanese army and the indigenous Lebanese population
of South Lebanon were to pay with their blood for this false impression
given by the IDF. If there was any one individual who at this very early
stage knew that the IDF had no intention whatever of disengaging
completely from South Lebanon, it was Chairman Yasir Arafat.

On the morning of 28 March, accompanied by Dr James Jonah and
Colonel Jean Espinassy, the UNTSO representative with ILMAC in
Beirut, I drove to one of the exclusively Palestinian areas of Beirut.
This heavily populated residential area, not far from the Sabra and
Chatila refugee camp complex, was one of many hideouts which, for
obvious security reasons, Yasir Arafat had to maintain. After inspect-
ing a guard of honour made up of young Palestinian guerrillas, in
clean camouflage uniforms and armed with their customary Russian
Kalashnikov (AK47) rifles, I was led to a lift which was reserved for me
and my team of officials. The passageway leading to the meeting room

was jammed to capacity, mostly by international press and television journalists and by the security men detailed by Arafat for our protection while we were in the building. Having pushed our way through the congestion, we finally came face to face with the Chairman of the Executive Committee of the Palestine Liberation Organisation, Yasir Arafat. Chairman Arafat is very bald; consequently his head is covered by the Arab *kafir* most of the time. Abu Ammar ('Father of Ammar'), as he is called by those close to him, looked older than his age. With the pressures and responsibilities that weigh on him, this was not surprising.

The reception accorded us was extremely cordial. After a quick exchange of pleasantaries, we plunged into serious talking. Our main mission was to convey to Arafat the Secretary-General's appeal for the PLO's cooperation in a ceasefire in South Lebanon. This appeal had been made in the Security Council the previous day. The PLO was the major party to the conflict in the south, and if it did not cooperate in the strict observance of the ceasefire and cessation of hostilities, there was no way that the IDF could be persuaded to stop fighting and thus enable UNIFIL to start the execution of its mission. We briefed Arafat on Security Council Resolutions 425 and 426, and appealed for his help in our efforts to get the IDF out of the area. If UNIFIL was to carry out its mission to establish international peace and security, and get the Lebanese government to re-establish its authority in the region, it was imperative for the IDF to withdraw. Chairman Arafat fully shared our views, but he was sceptical about UNIFIL being able to achieve its objective because he felt that the Israelis would not pull out completely from the south. He was to be proved right. At this meeting, we also appealed to him to stop firing Katyushas into Kiryat Shemona and other settlements in northern Israel, since such hostile activities only provoked counterblasts from the IDF, thus making our operations extremely difficult and endangering the lives of the local indigenous population.

Arafat was a good listener and a good talker too. He spent the first part of his reply lecturing us on how the PLO had withstood the Israelis in their invasion of South Lebanon. He was proud of his men who had fought heroically and forced the IDF to fight both by day and by night — the first time, by his evaluation, that it had had to do so. He then talked of the Palestinian struggle and why this should continue. This took over forty-five minutes, but despite being irrelevant to our mission, it was interesting and good fun to listen to the 'chief terrorist and head of a terrorist organisation', as he has sometimes been labelled. In a subsequent meeting, he asked rhetorically: 'Who is the better terrorist, myself or Mr Begin, the chief of the Israeli terrorists?'

When the French contingent arrived on 23 March, it was initially deployed in the Tyre pocket, and the Norwegians were deployed in the north-eastern sector of UNIFIL's area of operations. The deployment of the French and Norwegians ('Frenchbatt' and 'Norbatt') into these two sensitive sectors was to check PLO infiltration and their potential base camps, both of which constituted the major threats to UNIFIL. The deployments of Nigerian, Iranian, Irish, Senegalese, Fiji and Nepalese followed the IDF withdrawals on 11, 14 and 30 April.

Critical arrivals and deployment into the area of operation

There had been considerable pressure on Prime Minister Menachem Begin from the UN Secretary-General Kurt Waldheim to withdraw his troops back into Israel and hand over the evacuated areas to UNIFIL. Obviously there was also pressure on the Secretary-General to ensure some progress on Secco res 425. He personally visited Israel in April, met Mr Begin and appealed for his support and cooperation to get the IDF out of South Lebanon. This effort presumably continued after his return to UN headquarters in New York.

On 11 April 1978, the first IDF withdrawal began. The area to be evacuated consisted of the north-eastern sector and part of the eastern sector, and in a formal ceremony at Rachaya el Foukhar I took over the evacuated areas from the IDF. Norbatt was available to exercise control over these areas, but it had to be thinly spread out on the ground because of its inadequate strength. Vital and sensitive areas like Kaukaba, Blate and the Khardala bridge, separating Marjayoun from Beaufort castle, were held in reasonably good strength. It was in the area of the Khardala bridge that UNIFIL suffered its first fatal casualty with the killing of Master Warrant Officer Karl Oskar Johansson on 29 March through a mine accident. He was a member of the Swedish company detached from UNEF, along with an Iranian company, to assist UNIFIL as its first armed troops.

The second IDF withdrawal on 14 April from areas bordering the Litani and to the south-east of it went off without much difficulty. However, the third withdrawal in the western and eastern areas on 30 April was critical. The handover ceremony was held at Abbasiyah in the Senbatt (Senegalese battalion) area of responsibility. Senegalese detachments arrived in the mission area via Damascus, and, avoiding the Golan and Israel, had to come through Beirut into South Lebanon. One Senbatt detachment managed to arrive at the area of evacuation just in time to occupy the ground as the IDF were pulling out. On the same critical day, 30 April, we were also fortunate to have a Nepalese detachment arriving punctually to occupy Ett Taibe and the surrounding areas from which the IDF were withdrawing. Maybe God was on our side.

Concept of deployment of troops

The deployment of particular units into particular areas of responsibilities has never been based on any special national military considerations or political biases, but purely on strategic considerations and other exigencies on the ground.

With the uncertainty as to when troops would be arriving, and even whether they would be arriving at all, the question of which battalion should go where, and where it should not go, did not arise. At this very preliminary stage in our deployment, political sensitivity in deploying units had, fortunately, not dawned on me. Considering the high sensitivity of the Palestinian issue, and the differing national political biases in relation to the Jews, the Palestinians and, to a less extent, the Lebanese, one would expect such political biases to be taken into account in the deployments. But throughout our deployment I avoided doing this in the best interests of our mission and of the UN.

As mentioned earlier, ability to meet the main threats was UNIFIL's overriding concern. Fortunately for us, the first two contingents to arrive, the French and the Norwegians, were well equipped in manpower, communications, battalion transport with good cross-country performance, and surveillance devices to enhance detection of movement at long ranges. They were thus respectively deployed into the Tyre pocket and the north-eastern sectors of the area of operations, which represented our major threats. The Tyre pocket was the main PLO infiltration route from the western sector, while the north-eastern sector was not only a major infiltration area, but contained some of the PLO's large base-camps. Furthermore, the north-eastern sector was completely cut off from the main UNIFIL area of operations by the Christian enclave, and a well-equipped and highly mobile contingent such as Norbatt, with its professional peacekeeping experience, was best suited to being deployed in that sector.

The north-eastern sector was considered too large an area for Norbatt alone to control, and Nepbatt had to be redeployed from Ett Taibe into Blate to take some of the pressure from the Norwegians. The Nepalese, although they are highly professional soldiers, lacked equipment at the initial stages of the operations. Hence their deployment close to Norbatt was based on the assessment that in a situation of extreme emergency, Norbatt would be available to give them support.

From time to time, minor deployment adjustments were made to meet and contain certain contingencies and exigencies. Iranbatt's withdrawal in November 1978 on the eve of the Iranian revolution, and the temporary withdrawals of Frenchbatt in March 1979 and

Nepbatt in June 1980, all made it necessary for us to readjust deployment on the ground.

Administration and logistics

While political shuttles were in progress and troops were being deployed, administrative and logistics staff, both military and civilian, were also busily engaged in planning the support for the force. Administration and logistics cells were established at UNTSO HQ in Government House, Jerusalem. Both military observers and civilian staff were drawn principally from UNTSO, UNEF and UNDOF. Our initial preoccupations were as follows:

Receiving troops. Troops were arriving through three main points of entry: Tel Aviv, Damascus and Beirut. Various facilities had to be prepared and services made available to receive arriving contingents. There had to be the usual transit facilities — sleeping accommodation, feeding, washing, toilets, physical training and resting; facilities for briefings on operations and administration; familiarisation training on the newly-supplied German trucks (especially important for the Nepalese); movement control — this was handled expertly by the UNTSO observers and a Canadian movement control detachment already in Tel Aviv (Damascus was handled by UNDOF staff and Beirut by ILMAC staff) — and an area for holding vehicles and stores.

Rations. Troops had been requested to bring not less than thirty days' dry ('C') rations. Fortunately, with the assistance of UNTSO, UNIFIL was able to provide contingents with fresh rations within seven days on arrival in the mission area.

Petrol, oil and lubricants. Contracts for their supply were established immediately. This was no major problem, since existing UNTSO contracts were extended to cover UNIFIL.

Transport. Apart from the Nepalese battalion, which was equipped by West Germany, all other battalions arrived in the mission area with a number of their contingent-owned vehicles, later to be supplemented by the UN. Thus transport difficulties were minimal in the initial stages.

Clothing and *communications* were both national responsibilities, and no initial difficulties were encountered.

Accommodation. A large number of tents were required and this presented no difficulty since UNEF was readily available to help.

Maj.-Gen. Rais Abin (Indonesia), Force Commander UNEF, and his Chief Logistics Officer, Colonel Leech (Canada), rendered great assistance.

There had to be a structure for handling national matters, particularly in discipline, contingent personnel matters and troops' evaluation reports. Discipline is a national issue, since practices vary from one contributing country to the other. However, in serious cases of indiscipline and misconduct, the Force Commander normally reports to the UN HQ, which takes the matters up with the contributing country concerned. There is an arrangement among the contingent commanders, purely on a national basis, to deal with these functions.

5

OPERATIONAL ACTIVITIES

Evolution of Standing Operating Procedures

Generally, the concept of operations for UNIFIL was based on the terms of reference contained in the 'Report of the Secgen on the implementation of Secco Res 425 (1978)' (approved by Secco Res 426). From this we developed the Force Standing Operating Procedures for operations. From these were developed battalion SOPs, which were fully coordinated by Force HQ, Naqoura.

However, certain vital procedures had to be developed in response to the practicalities and realities of the situation on the ground. Significant among these were:

Returning confiscated weapons to armed elements* after a certain period of time. This practice provoked much criticism — from, among others, some of my principal staff and battalion commanders who came to UNIFIL later. I had to listen patiently to their views and explain why UNIFIL had no choice in the matter. In the arms-infested area of South Lebanon, UNIFIL troops were grossly exposed because they did not operate in buffer zones or within exclusive corridors but had to use the same roads and other public facilities as the local population among whom they physically lived. Operating among people to whom it was normal to exact revenge for wrongs — people who would ambush an ambulance or harass, kidnap and even kill a commanding officer without any reservations or qualms — I could not afford such major risks simply for the sake of keeping the pistol or Kalashnikov that had belonged to the PLO, the DFF or any other armed element. The fact that subsequent Force Commanders of UNIFIL, Lt.-Gen. Bill Callaghan and Maj.-Gen. Gustav Hägglund, continued with this practice would appear to vindicate its wisdom.

Establishment of Force Mobile Reserve (FMR). UNIFIL, with its inadequate strength, could not afford to have a standby battalion as a reserve unit; a unit of reinforced company strength had to suffice. Paradoxically, it was our experience that the internationalisation of FMR had a heightened political impact in major armed crises. Its

---

* 'Armed Elements' (shortened to 'AEs') was the term we were obliged to use to refer to all armed groups, except the South Lebanese Christian militias (the 'De Facto Forces' or 'DFF').

deployment in the At-Tiri episode in 1979 was a classic example. Indeed this was when the FMR concept was evolved.

Establishment of a Special Security Detachment for the exclusive security of UNIFIL HQ, Naqoura. After the deployment of the French defence platoon for the security of Naqoura in September 1980, such mishaps as we had suffered there during the previous year ceased. The French presence always provided UNIFIL with a viable deterrent.

Establishment of Observer Group Lebanon (OGL) teams. UN Military Observers were officers with high professional experience, combat exposure and maturity. Since UNMOs served much longer than UNIFIL troops, who rotated every six months, the use of OGL as teams to assist UNIFIL units provided the necessary continuity and expertise.

Returning captured armed elements to parent organisations. The IDF would have been only too gratified if all captured armed elements had been handed over to them. But for obvious reasons this was completely out of the question. A captured PLO fighter would happily stay as a detainee in a UNIFIL guardroom rather than be sent back to Rashadiya camp in Tyre. As far as I know, this has been the practice with all other UN peacekeeping operations.

Battalion activities in the Area of Operations

To execute our mandate under our terms of reference, we had to engage in the following operational activities.

Manning checkpoints. The main objective of checkpoints was to stop attempts by the IDF, DFF, PLO and other armed elements to encroach on the area of operations, and to infiltrate arms and ammunition. All vehicles entering the area of operations had to be fully searched for arms and ammunition; individuals entering were not permitted to carry these items or to wear military uniforms. In other words, no armed elements were permitted to enter.

Manning checkpoints was one of UNIFIL's most hazardous tasks. It brought troops into frequent clashes with armed elements, which resulted in fatal casualties to both sides. The Lebanese-PLO Cairo Agreement of 1969, which the PLO fighters always invoked to justify their presence and operational activities in South Lebanon, created severe difficulties for UNIFIL activities, particularly at the checkpoints.

Manning observation posts. These were for detection of violations of the ceasefire on the ground or in the air. If shooting broke out, an observation post was to determine who had fired first, the types of weapons used and the number of rounds expended; and it was to observe the activities of all armed groups in the area of operations and enclaves, and violations by the IDF and DFF of the rules governing entry to the area of operations. Observation posts were manned by UNTSO observers on the Armistice Demarcation Line, and their operational reports were incorporated into UNIFIL situation reports.

Patrols. There was intensive day and night armed patrolling, both on foot and in vehicles. This had various objectives, of which an overriding one was to fill in the gaps between checkpoints and observation posts to check infiltration attempts, especially of armed elements in the area; for observation of activities in the area of operations; and to show a presence in villages, since UNIFIL did not have sufficient troops to be permanently present in all villages. We were in most of them as well as in the towns.

Special equipment. In an effort to increase the effectiveness of our operations we made use of searchlights to aid our OPs and checkpoints at night; night-vision binoculars for OPs and patrols to detect infiltration; body-scanner-type metal detectors to search for weapons at checkpoints; and, in some battalions, dogs at checkpoints to sniff for explosives and on patrols to detect infiltration. We incorporated radar into our observation scheme. (A few units had radar as part of their equipment; it was provided for use in other units by UNIFIL itself.)

Buffer zone

UNIFIL could not operate in the true sense of a buffer zone, as in UNEF, or in an area of separation, as in UNDOF. The obvious fact that its area of operation was heavily populated made this concept impracticable. However, an attempt was made to identify the area close to our boundary with the Christian enclave as UNIFIL's buffer zone.

The main objective here was to prevent contact between the two groups. It was the desire of the armed elements to move or infiltrate southwards to fight the DFF, and of the DFF to move northwards to fight the armed elements. Also, it was the desire of the armed elements to pass through our lines for operational activities against Israel and the DFF, and the IDF and DFF wanted to move into villages in our area of operation to establish their presence and fight the armed elements. Patrolling in this zone was intensive, and for a long time the system worked quite satisfactorily.

Contact with the parties

UNIFIL found itself in a strange position. By its mandate and terms of reference, we had to prevent the infiltration of armed elements into the area by controlling movements. This meant, in practical terms, that we could not allow the PLO, the Arab Lebanese Army (ALA), Murabetoun, the Progressive Socialist Party (PSP), the Lebanese National Movement (LNM), the Rejectionists, the Lebanese Communists, and so on, to be in the area.* The PLO claimed the right to be there by virtue of the Cairo Agreement. The ALA and PSP factions of the Lebanese National Movement claimed that they were entitled as Lebanese citizens to be there. Consequently it is through these conflicting positions that clashes have usually occurred between these factions and UNIFIL.

The concept of peacekeeping is to talk and negotiate and not to fight, if one can avoid it. Hence the UNMOs of Observer Group Lebanon (OGL) provided two-man continuous liaison teams in Tyre ('Team Tyre') to talk with the PLO, the LNM and other armed elements to resolve clashes. In the area, 'Team Zulu' was mobile, acting as a special liaison team for the Force Commander and the Chief Operations Officer. Local commanders at the platoon and company levels also talked to their own level of local commanders of the PLO on the ground. A new team, 'Team Romeo', was established to assist in communications between the local *mukhtars* (village leaders) and UNIFIL. In serious cases, such as those concerning major ceasefire and other violations involving the PLO, UNIFIL headquarters instructed Chairman ILMAC, Beirut, to take the matter up with Arafat's office. In the most serious cases and over delicate matters, I saw Arafat personally. On issues involving Lebanese armed elements, we spoke to their leaders in Beirut and their local commanders in the villages.

Similar arrangements existed with the IDF/DFF. 'Team X-Ray' was highly mobile, running around the enclave and in constant contact with Major Haddad. 'Team Metulla' was in Metulla and co-located with the IDF liaison officer (IDFLO); it acted as a link between UNIFIL and Major Haddad. When we had to get a message to the Major, and 'Team X-Ray' could not locate him, as frequently happened when there was a serious crisis, 'Team Metulla' passed the

* The ALA were an armed militia commanded by Lieut. Khatib; the Murabetoun were a predominantly Sunni Muslim armed militia favoured by the Sunni community; the PSP were the Druze militia formed by the assassinated Druze chieftain Kamal Jumblatt and now commanded by his son Walid; the LNM were a co-ordinating body for various armed factions established in the late 1970s to coordinate the activities of some militias, including the PLO.

UNIFIL LIAISON: CONTACT WITH THE PARTIES

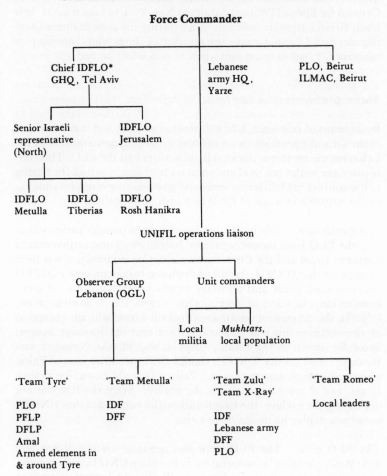

Force Commander

Chief IDFLO*
GHQ, Tel Aviv

Lebanese
army HQ,
Yarze

PLO, Beirut
ILMAC, Beirut

Senior Israeli
representative
(North)

IDFLO
Jerusalem

IDFLO
Metulla

IDFLO
Tiberias

IDFLO
Rosh Hanikra

UNIFIL operations liaison

Observer Group
Lebanon (OGL)

Unit commanders

Local
militia

Mukhtars,
local population

'Team Tyre'

PLO
PFLP
DFLP
Amal
Armed elements in
& around Tyre

'Team Metulla'

IDF
DFF

'Team Zulu'
'Team X-Ray'

IDF
Lebanese army
DFF
PLO

'Team Romeo'

Local leaders

* Israel Defence Force Liaison Officer.

message through the IDFLO, who had a direct line to Major Haddad's headquarters in Marjayoun. At least, the IDFLO invariably knew where Saad Haddad was.

Serious cases were taken up with the senior IDFLO in Jerusalem, the senior Israeli representative in Tiberias and other senior officials such as Officer Commanding Northern Command, the IDF's Chief of Staff and the Defence Minister. In extremely dangerous situations, where

lives were at stake, we requested the Office of the Under-Secretary
General for Special Political Affairs in New York to take it up at their
level. Brian Urquhart held this office during my time as Force Commander and I cannot count the number of times when, needing his
assistance, I had to rouse him when he was asleep in bed.

Major problems with our terms of reference

By its terms of reference, UNIFIL was to establish and maintain itself
in an area of operation to be defined through negotiations with the
Lebanese government, the Israeli authorities and the PLO. This constituted the major political and military problem, since all the parties
to the conflict held different views and gave varying interpretations as
to the nature and scope of UNIFIL's area of operation.

The Israeli view.   Obviously, the Israelis' main preoccupation was to
stop the PLO from mounting armed hostilities against settlements in
northern Israel and the Christian enclave. Consequently, it was their
contention that UNIFIL should be deployed to control potential PLO
concentration areas and its main supply routes and lines of communication. In tactical terms, they urged the following. First,
UNIFIL should control the area south of the Litani with the exception
of the enclave; this was to include Tyre and the Kasmiya bridge.
Secondly, north of the Litani, UNIFIL should take Nabatiya and
Hasbaya. And thirdly, UNIFIL should clear the entire area of Palestinians; it should ensure that the Palestinians did not strike against
Israel, and it should not occupy the enclave. Since the IDF was not
occupying the enclave, the Israeli authorities contended that UNIFIL
could not deploy its troops there either.

The PLO view.   The PLO were also negative towards Resolution
425. While pledging its cooperation to facilitate UNIFIL's operations,
Chairman Arafat maintained that the PLO had a legitimate right to
be in South Lebanon by virtue of the Cairo Agreement between the
PLO and the Lebanese authorities.

The PLO had reservations on four points. First, it felt that Resolution 425 served the interests of Israel; secondly, it called for the immediate and unconditional withdrawal of Israeli troops — as early as
April 1978, Arafat expressed the fear that the Israelis would not withdraw completely, and on 13 June he was to be proved right; thirdly, it
felt that UNIFIL should not oppose Palestinian resistance; and,
fourthly, it maintained the right of the Palestinian resistance to move
and keep their men in the UNIFIL area, especially Tyre, Kasmiya and

sixteen other PLO bases. Consequently, it opposed UNIFIL deployment in Tyre and its control of the Kasmiya bridge.

The position of the *Lebanese* authorities was simple and straightforward: as far as they were concerned, UNIFIL could go anywhere in Lebanon.

After discussions with Israeli and Lebanese authorities and the PLO, the UN Secretariat agreed that the UNIFIL area of operations should consist of all areas that the IDF physically used or held: this meant the whole area south of the Litani, excluding only the port of Tyre and the Kasmiya bridge. The Christian enclave should be taken over by UNIFIL.

UNIFIL operating without an agreement

'When a peacekeeping operation is firmly based on a detailed agreement between the parties in conflict and they are prepared to abide by that agreement, it is relatively easy to maintain. This has been the case, for example, with UNEF 2 and UNDOF. When, however, an operation is mounted in an emergency with ambiguous or controversial objectives and terms of reference, and on assumptions which are not wholly realistic, it is likely to present far greater difficulties. This is undoubtedly the case with UNIFIL.' These words of the Secretary-General, Dr Waldheim, in his 1979 report on the work of the Organisation sum up the truth that lack of an agreement between the parties has been the basic cause of UNIFIL's difficulty in fulfilling its mandate.

Why was it vital to have UNIFIL without an agreement between the parties to the conflict? I can only speculate that UNIFIL was a necessary instrument for the stabilisation of South Lebanon, in that it would get the IDF out of the country with dignity, establish an international presence to promote Arab credibility and dignity in the world, and demonstrate the concern of the United States for Lebanon and for its influence and credibility in Middle East politics in the eyes of the Arab countries (this was aimed at sustaining the Camp David Accord and the prospective peace treaty between Egypt and Israel). A reduction of the Israeli presence and of armed activities in South Lebanon made it less difficult for Sadat to proceed with the peace process, especially at the initial stages. The IDF invasion of 6 June 1982 resulted in the immediate withdrawal of Egypt's ambassador to Israel and the cooling of the peace process till September 1986 when, after the IDF had pulled back sufficiently, full diplomatic relations were restored. This underscores the strong impact of the Camp David Accord on the establishment of UNIFIL.

These are my personal assumptions and, if correct, they would explain a number of things. First, no serious efforts were made to have even a tacit agreement between Israel and the PLO, such as had existed between 24 July 1981 and 9 May 1982 before the Israeli invasion. The lack of such an agreement meant a lack of commitment by the parties to UNIFIL's presence and operations. The negative attitudes to Secco Res 425 and subsequent Security Council Resolutions, the difficulties and obstacles deliberately placed in the way of the troops, the irresponsible firing upon them, and the indignities of every kind to which UNIFIL's officers and men and even visiting VIPs were subjected were evidence of this lack of commitment.

Secondly, they would explain why there was little expectation that UNIFIL would survive beyond its initial mandate of six months. For example, France was only prepared, after frantic negotiations, to agree a four-month extension for the mission's first mandate. I was present with the Secretary-General when he personally spoke by telephone with President Giscard d'Estaing on the question of extending UNIFIL's first mandate. Four months was the compromise between the Secretary-General's recommendation of six months and the French willingness to accept three. UNIFIL's second mandate was from 19 September 1978 till 18 January 1979. Then the second mandate was extended for five months during which, in March 1979, the French pulled out their infantry unit. The Secretary-General's recommendation of a six-month extension for a mandate has been normal for UNIFIL and other UN peacekeeping missions.

They could explain too why the Security Council failed to give full commitment to UNIFIL, as seen in its voting patterns in the force's formative period. Voting for UNIFIL's mandates was never unanimous. Finally, Mr Begin, on his first visit to Washington in 1977 as Prime Minister of Israel, discussed with President Jimmy Carter the need for a UN peacekeeping force in South Lebanon. Was this part of an overall strategy that eventually got UNIFIL into South Lebanon *without an agreement* but made Camp David possible? These are questions to which I do not have answers, but which are vital since they affected the birth of the force and its nurture from the first day of its existence.

An agreement for a peacekeeping mission lays down rules for the mission's operations which should be discussed fully and in detail and then agreed and signed by the parties to the conflict. An agreement between Israel, Lebanon and the PLO would have conclusively defined UNIFIL's area of operations, thereby forestalling the problem of 13 June 1978 which has been the major political difficulty facing UNIFIL in the fulfilment of its mandate. Hence UNIFIL's major difficulty has been a political one: it has been brought about not by the inability of the force to fulfil its mandate, but by the machinery used in setting it up. The necessary follow-up — i.e. an agreement, such as existed in the cases of UNEF 2 and UNDOF — was missing.

Having finally defined the area of operations resulting from discussions held with the parties, we needed to decide who could enter it. We had the responsibility of preventing an outbreak of hostilities. This required control of the movement of arms and armed personnel as articulated in our terms of reference. In practical terms, it meant that no arms were to be taken into area, nor were any uniformed personnel to enter it. Then there were other questions which arose automatically. How were we to separate local Lebanese citizens from infiltrators? Were we to take weapons away from local citizens? And how did we handle Palestinians in civilian clothes travelling through the area unarmed? We finally decided that all unarmed and un-uniformed people in possession of Lebanese identity cards would be allowed to enter the area. Anyone else would be denied entry.

6

DIFFICULTIES FACING THE FORCE

The problems and difficulties facing UNIFIL can be divided into political, operational, administrative and logistics.

Political difficulties

The Christian enclaves.   Contrary to UN expectations but in fulfilment of Israeli intentions (this is where I ran into my first trouble with UN HQ — see Chapter 7), the IDF withdrew on 13 June 1978 from its final foothold, the so-called Christian enclave, and handed it over to the DFF, in the persons of its leaders Major Saad Haddad and Major Sami Chidiak, in a formal ceremony at Meiss El Jebel. Hence UNIFIL had to negotiate with Haddad over this stretch of land, which formed about 30 per cent of the total area in which it was expected to operate. The handing of this sector over to the DFF and not to UNIFIL, following previous custom, turned the whole issue into a delicate political struggle which continues to shackle UNIFIL's progress to this day. Why did Israel do that?

The Israelis' main objective in 'Operation Litani', I felt, was to secure the enclave. They pushed to the Litani to clear the area of an armed PLO presence — also to use their withdrawal to the enclave as a bargaining position, thereby legitimising their presence and tightening their hold on the enclave. This was a security guarantee for northern Israel, and it was advantageous to promote that security through the DFF under Haddad and Chidiak by fully equipping, supporting, financing and resupplying them. They could not do that with UN troops. Also they needed to have control of the gates through the Armistice Demarcation Line — more than fifteen of them – for subsequent military incursions into Lebanon. The massive invasion in June 1982 clarified this strategic move.

Restoration of Lebanese authority.   This partly implied the effective presence of Lebanese army units in the south of the country. But moving the troops there met with serious difficulties. First, the Lebanese government did not fully control the roads giving access from Beirut to the south. These were filled with armed elements — the PLO, Rejectionists, the Lebanese National Movement, the Arab Lebanese Army and others. There was also the real possibility of being fired on, if they decided to go by air, by the armed

40

elements or the DFF — occurrences which would affect the credibility of Lebanese authority. Further, there was UNIFIL's inability to help in transportation, either by land or air. We lifted twenty-four liaison officers for the battalions in January 1979, and rotated them by air every two to four weeks, but with our meagre resources we could not do much more. There was also the factor that arriving by road would give Lebanese authority a stronger impact and this would also help establish lines of communications with Beirut for subsequent resupplies and rotations. Finally, by April 1979, we had one Lebanese battalion operating in our area of operations under command. Dutchbatt, Fiji-batt, Irishbatt, Nibatt and Senbatt each had two platoons (totalling sixty men) of the battalion attached to it. The battalion HQ was at Arzun. The pairs of platoons were engaged in the same type of operations as the units to which they were attached.

The deployment of the Lebanese army in July–August 1978 and in April 1979 and its subsequent problems are dealt with in some detail later.

Imbalance in political and military strength of the parties. UNEF in Sinai and UNDOF on the Golan did not face the kind of difficulties as UNIFIL was confronted with in South Lebanon. Quite apart from the fact that there were agreements that had been hammered out and signed in Geneva between Egypt, Syria and Israel on the UNEF and UNDOF operations, Egypt and Syria were strong governments with strong and credible armies. UNIFIL, on the other hand, was a Lebanese mission, operating under a weak Lebanese government and army against a strong Israeli government, with strong and credible armed forces. Furthermore, the strong and unwavering political backing given to the Israelis was a major morale-booster for the IDF on the ground. Soviet political support for the PLO and Lebanon could not be well determined or very much felt on the ground. These imbalances resulted in all parties, but especially the IDF/DFF and the PLO, disturbing the *status quo* with impunity. The effect on UNIFIL was devastating.

Operational difficulties

Insecurity of UNIFIL headquarters in Naqoura. Naqoura was, in tactical terms, the worst possible site in which to locate UNIFIL HQ, as was made clear by the shelling incidents of April 1979 and April 1980, fully recounted later. However, we had no other suitable option. The UNTSO observers of ILMAC, for their part, were fully established and had operated from there for years; what was important in

Naqoura was that communications, particularly with UNTSO HQ in Jerusalem, were available in some form.

We did have the option to use the barracks in Tyre as the Force HQ, but the bitter experience of May 1978 showed how vulnerable Tyre would be. On that occasion Colonel Jean Salvan, CO Frenchbatt, was ambushed and shot (happily he survived in spite of having fourteen AK-47 bullets in his body), a French and a Senegalese soldier were killed, an armoured car was burnt out and some soldiers were wounded. Again, as a city-port accommodating the Palestinian refugee camp of Rashadiya, Tyre had been the major target in South Lebanon for Israeli retaliatory air and ground bombardments. A UNIFIL HQ in Tyre would have presented an easy target for PLO retaliatory attacks, and we were surely right not to have chosen Tyre.

Zahrani, south of Saida, might have been suitable, but we could not get it from the Syrians, even with the Secretary-General's intervention. A Syrian intelligence detachment of twenty-two men was based there and President Assad was not disposed to move it out.

The fact that Naqoura is in the Christian enclave, over which UNIFIL still has no control, meant that we had all sorts of difficulties in operating the HQ from there. On 6 October 1978, there was a menacing demonstration by the DFF, which could have resulted in serious bloodshed had we not used maximum restraint, when a Lebanese army helicopter which had flown in the Lebanese liaison officer was burnt on the tarmac at the Norwegian helicopter wing. There were other incidents involving firing and threats. On 29 March 1979, there were serious firing incidents resulting in the killing of one French soldier and the wounding of two others. The IDF failed to intervene because the demand by Haddad and his militias to have unimpeded access through our HQ with their tanks and armoured personnel carriers served their interest.

But despite all those difficulties, it was right and proper for UNIFIL HQ to be based at Naqoura in the Christian enclave, flying the Lebanese national flag side by side with the UN flag, and thereby legitimising Lebanese authority and sovereignity in Israeli-occupied South Lebanon. This is a major political benefit which balances the military disadvantages. The price, nonetheless, was high.

Mines and unexploded bombs and shells and knowledge of terrain. The most serious engineering problem consisted in the hundreds of thousands of unmarked mines, unexploded shells and bombs, especially cluster bomb units, spread out in the entire area of operations. This hazardous phenomenon is characteristic of any area where there has been serious fighting. UNEF in Sinai and UNDOF on the Golan were no exceptions. Our first casualty, in the Swedish contingent, was from a mine, and on the day after the arrival of Senbatt, one of its jeeps went over a mine, which killed three soldiers and wounded one. Lack of knowledge of the terrain in the area of operations was particularly harmful to new arrivals. Among the local people, children were also killed playing with cluster bombs, and there were considerable civilian casualties from mine incidents on farms. In the first six months of UNIFIL's presence, the French engineer company dealt with 1,972 mines and 1,336 unexploded bombs, shells and mine-clearing bombs, and they continued to handle between fifty and one hundred of these cases each week for some months. Such engineer services were not limited to the battalion operational areas. We also cleared farms of mines to enable the local farmers to work the land and pursue their normal occupations. We did this daily over several months.

Presence of armed elements, arms and ammunition in the area of operations.   The fact that we were operating in a quasi-demilitarised zone, that we lived among civilians, that civilians with the appropriate documents could enter our area of operations, and that we could not tell who was a genuine civilian and who belonged to the PLO, contributed overall to the build-up of armed elements in the area of operations. If one were to dress a PLO fighter, an IDF soldier and a Lebanese soldier all alike, it would be extremely difficult to identify their affiliations. Dealing with so many armed groups with varied allegiances and without well-identified and effective leadership presented us with serious difficulties.

Again, South Lebanon, like the rest of Lebanon, had become 'a jungle of weapons and arms', as Chairman Arafat put it to me. In a country like Lebanon, where the government is not strong enough to control the proliferation of arms and ammunitions, and where the army had disintegrated into confessional factional communities, compounded by the presence of the heavily-armed PLO, UNIFIL was in for a rough time, and this certainly was what we had.

Firing / shelling / kidnapping / murdering / ambushing / hijacking.   With the conflicting interests that divided the armed element and the DFF, there was constant firing and shelling between them, and because we were edployed in close promixity to their positions, we got our fair share of fall-out from these hostile activities. Even though these were mostly not directed at us, our troops and their living accommodation, the medical facilities and some mortars and vehicles received direct hits. Some indirect shellfire fell as close as 15, 10 and even 5 metres from our troops' positions. Firing on UN troops or close to our positions was a serious concern not only for all of us in

UNIFIL but also of course for contributing countries and for the Secretary-General and his secretariat at UN HQ.

There had also been periodic firing on populated civilian villages. The excuse had always been that the villagers were harbouring or protecting armed elements. We assumed responsibility, a moral obligation, for the villagers' security and protection, and consequently firing on and shelling of villages posed a major concern to us. Helicopters were fired on many times, and we were lucky to have survived all these attacks.

Occasionally troops got kidnapped, ambushed and hijacked in retaliation for actions we might have taken against certain factions. We tried as best we could not to risk serious confrontation and escalation, but because armed escorts were not always possible due to our manpower problems, and we constantly moved among these armed elements and used the same roads as they did, the danger was always present. UNIFIL troops are *not* well protected and are totally exposed to all sorts of dangers and hazards.

The cold-blooded murder of my two Irish soldiers at Bent Jbail on 18 April 1979 in the course of the At Tiri crisis is covered later. Three Senegalese soldiers were killed in Barish in circumstances that bordered on cold-blooded murder. However, exhaustive investigations failed to reveal the exact cause of their deaths.

PLO infiltration and IDF/DFF encroachment attempts. While armed PLO fighters were set to infiltrate and use our area of operations for their lines of communication to move into northern Israeli townships for hostile activities, the IDF and DFF were equally determined to use our area of operations in their fight against the PLO. Also, the IDF/DFF on several occasions tried to expand their enclave by encroaching into our area. UNIFIL had no choice but to stop the PLO and IDF/DFF in all these attempts, by whatever means lay within the limits of our standing operating procedures. Secco Res 425 had to be defended.

Operating outside buffer zone/populated areas. UNIFIL operated in densely populated areas (the civilian population of UNIFIL's area of operations is over 150,000) and outside a buffer zone. It had no well-identified and exclusive corridors of its own. Operating in heavily populated areas and using the same houses, water, roads and air space as the opposing armed groups was a serious handicap, limiting our scope of action for fear of retaliation. UNIFIL's practice of handing captured weapons back to the armed elements after a period of time for fear of serious retaliation is a good example of such limitations. Operating outside the buffer zone has led to over-exposure of the troops with all the attendant hazards.

Retaliation as retribution exacted by the local population for actions taken by UNIFIL troops served as a serious restraining factor on our military actions. This was peculiar to operations in South Lebanon. We had several cases of *sulha* and other forms of compensation exacted from us for carrying out our mandate through the standing operating procedures. If compensation was not paid (mostly it was demanded in monetary terms as *sulha*) there was brutal retaliation. Typical examples were the killing of three Fijians in an ambush as retaliation for the shooting of a Lebanese National Movement leader at a checkpoint; a money payment to the 'mother' of a militiaman shot dead by a UN soldier; and the murder of two Irish soldiers, already referred to, in retaliation for the death of a DFF militiaman in the At-Tiri episode.

Restriction on freedom of movement. As punishment for certain statements made either by the Security Council or by the Secretary-General in New York or for certain actions taken by UNIFIL in defence of its mandate, restrictions were periodically imposed on our movements. The IDF always accused us of being spies, and thus these restrictions were aimed at limiting our 'spying' activities and capabilities. From time to time roadblocks were set up to restrict our movements, mostly by the DFF. At one point, we were only free to move in the enclave on Mondays, Wednesdays and Fridays. This disrupted administrative and logistical support for UNTSO OPs, UNIFIL positions and resupplies to Nepbatt and Norbatt in the north-eastern sector of our area. Also, it was only on these days that we could fly into the enclave for medical evacuation. Periodic roadblocks were, in principle, not acceptable, but we had to live with them.

Knowledge of the indigenous population. Under more normal circumstances, arriving troops would have been given sufficient information about the indigenous people living in the area. Some knowledge of local people's culture, customs, habits and characteristics and of their religions and confessional communities, and *respect* for them, have always been helpful in peacekeeping. Early arrivals lacked this advantage, which contributed to sections of the indigenous local population viewing UNIFIL as an occupying force.

PLO caches. The PLO had a few arms caches in the area. Because they were thus able to enter as civilians and then quickly change into uniform and pick up these arms, control of the movement of armed personnel into the UNIFIL area of operation was difficult. The IDF have always maintained that by the time they withdrew on 30 April 1978, none of the PLO arms caches were left in the area, but UNIFIL has always challenged this claim. UNIFIL destroyed five PLO arms caches immediately after it had taken over the area from the IDF. Chairman Arafat never forgave UNIFIL for this act, which he considered hostile.

Troops withdrawal and redeployment. Minor redeployments to improve unit positions from the operational viewpoint are an activity that goes on continuously. However, with the withdrawal of Iranbatt and Frenchbatt, offset partly by the arrival of Dutchbatt and an increase in the strength of Nibatt (the Nigerian battalion) and Fijibatt by one company each, we had to execute a major redeployment. Having less troops to fill the area was a problem; if we had been too thin on the ground, this would have facilitated infiltration by the armed elements and encroachment by the IDF/DFF, and hence this danger had to be guarded against at all costs.

Impact of national political bias on troops. The Middle East is an area where most countries in the world have their own economic interests and political biases. This can strongly influence their troops, and it is therefore important to get the minds of troops properly conditioned for UN duties on the principles of objectivity and impartiality. Troops should arrive in the mission area as UN troops under UN command and nothing else.

Dealing with various factions which lacked well-identified leadership, notably the armed elements and the non-Fatah PLO, was a major problem for us. Difficulties with the DFF in this particular respect were considerably less since Major Haddad was its undisputed commander, and the IDF indisputably supported the DFF.

Administration and logistics

Administrative and logistical support for troops in the field is one of the most important and difficult aspects of any military field operation, including peacekeeping. In UNIFIL we realised that even though the troops had come from so many different parts of the world, with varying degrees of military experience, they had no difficulty in adapting themselves to operational duties. What was a major problem was sustaining them logistically while they were on the ground.

For technical reasons, we had been made to understand that the UN system did not permit the holding of stockpiles in ordnance depots, with heavy reserves of logistical items. Until this concept is reviewed, future UN peacekeeping missions will go through the same bitter and difficult experiences as UNEF 2, UNDOF and later UNIFIL. (The problems of non-availability of stockpiles of equipment in UNIFIL were greatly eased due to my excellent relations with the Force Commander, Maj.-Gen. Rais Abin of Indonesia, who made available to me tentage for accommodation, vehicles to ease transport difficulties, communications equipment, generators and other logistical assistance needed for the support of UNIFIL in its initial difficult period.) However, it is being gradually reviewed by the UN procurement facility for logistical equipment at Pisa in Italy. Exactly what items are in stock in Pisa I am unable to say, apart from a number of transportation vehicles, which in themselves mark significant progress.

My view is that serious efforts should be made to stockpile at Pisa — ready for immediate use when a UN peacekeeping mission is required — a quantity of the following items: tentage, vehicles (those with good cross-country performance for operations and heavy trucks for second-, third- and fourth-line support*), communications equipment, generators, refrigeration, cooling and storage facilities and clothing. Experience has shown that some contingents arrive in the mission area fully equipped while others come with little or nothing. All should be taken care of to the same degree.

Future UN peacekeping commanders, especially those who find themselves starting a new mission from scratch, will do well to remember that moving troops into an operational area is only the beginning of peacekeeping. It is essential to sustain them logistically so that they can effectively and efficiently discharge their operational task.

Initial administrative and logistical difficulties

First among these is the *non-standardisation of equipment*. Because the UN expects all contingents arriving in a mission area to bring in certain national equipment such as 'A' and 'B' echelon vehicles, weapons, radios and generators, the problem of non-standardisation is bound to arise. Repair and maintenance then pose a serious difficulty. UNIFIL in the early stages of its operation was saddled with more than sixty different types of vehicles. The maintenance company of Norway, a NATO country, had to be engaged in the repair and maintenance of equipment from Warsaw Pact countries.

In addition, there are always varying standards among the participating battalions. These are manifested in repair/maintenance

---

* 1st, 2nd, 3rd and 4th line is military terminology defining the level of administrative support. 1st-line support is provided by the unit itself, while the others are provided by the unit's superior HQ and other higher levels.

capability — first- and second-line. Also home (national) support, as an ongoing process, varies greatly, and is often inadequate. There are differences in the level of equipment provided at home before the battalions are sent to the area of operations. Some units are well equipped, others not. (The UN's aide-memoire on this subject is a useful guide.) Third- and fourth-line maintenance support was also inadequate at the initial stages, which gravely affected field operations. For logistical support to work with maximum efficiency, one needs a ratio of 4 to 1 (combat soldiers to administrative/logistics staff). In UNIFIL it initially stood at 8 to 1 — compared to UNEF's ratio of almost 2.5 to 1.

As regards other aspects, *accommodation* presented continuing problems. Many of the houses in which troops had to live had been damaged by the shelling and aerial bombing over the years, and many man-hours had to be put in to make them habitable. With time, troops were made quite comfortable in prefabricated buildings. Most *roads* in our area of operations were extremely bad, and the considerable wear and tear on vehicles that resulted became an additional headache for the Norwegian maintenance company. *Water* in the area was barely suitable for human consumption without further purification. We did not have purification facilities for the whole force, as UNEF had with the Polish logistics contingent, and most units did not have them either. This could explain why there was a major outbreak of hepatitis among Frenchbatt in the Tyre Pocket in the early stages of our operations. *Local staff* might have helped to provide maintenance and logistical support in the Force, but tradesmen were so few as to be almost completely unavailable. Most locals, being so used to the gun, were at first unfriendly and could generate no feelings of loyalty towards us.

We have already alluded to the matter of *shortened mandates*. UNIFIL's first mandate was extended only for four months and the second for five months. Subsequent mandates were extended for the normal six-month period, as always requested by the Secretary-General in his report to the Security Council. Shortened mandates therefore meant cuts in our already inadequate budgets, which had a serious effect on projects which needed long-term planning and procurement actions. This partly explains why UNIFIL's prefabricated houses and transportation programmes were behind schedule for much of the time during the formative months.

Finance

Financing peacekeeping operations has always presented serious difficulties to the Secretary-General. Peacekeeping is not inexpensive, but it is much less costly than war. UNIFIL, with a force level of 6,000 of all ranks and about 400 civilian supporting staff, cost the organisation nearly US$11,000,000 per month for its maintainance and administration in the early stages of its operation.

Some countries had declared their unwillingness to pay their assessed contributions, and others that had declared their willingness to pay fell grossly into arrears with their payments. The result of this unhealthy financial state has been, first, that reimbursements to troop-contributing countries have been extremely late. The established practice is that troops on peacekeeping duties receive their UN allowances *in situ*. Consequently, the inability of the UN to meet its financial obligations towards the smaller contributing countries, most of which are short of foreign exchange, creates enormous difficulties for those contributing governments. It is an important achievement that no contributing country has withdrawn its troops on financial grounds. This reflects an admirable consistency of purpose.

Also, inadequate funding creates immense difficulties for the provision of appropriate administrative and logistical support for the mission. A system where procurement action routinely takes from six to nine months automatically impedes planning and therefore can seriously affect the operational functioning of the mission.

7

THE ISRAELI WITHDRAWAL IN JUNE 1978 AND FORMATION OF THE DE FACTO FORCES

Unlike the previous three withdrawals by the Israel Defence Force on 11, 14 and 30 April, when the evacuated areas were formally handed over to UNIFIL and I personally took them over, the intention for the final pull-back on 13 June 1978 was that the remaining areas, which were largely conterminous with those under the control of Major Haddad and Major Chidiak, would be handed over to the Christian militias already operating there, in the so-called Christian enclave. Major Chidiak was in command of the western sector and Major Haddad of the eastern sector, with his headquarters in Marjayoun. The attitude of the IDF had been implied during previous meetings between Major-General Yanush Ben Gal, the officer commanding the powerful and élite Northern Command with responsibility for Lebanon and the Golan, and myself. This was that negotiations in regard to UNIFIL entering those areas after June 13 must be discussed directly with Haddad and Chidiak. The big question was what was to be the capacity in which these two gentlemen would negotiate with us — and of course, *vice versa*. Clarification from the Lebanese government as to their status was most important and had to be sought, of necessity before June 13.

As early as the middle of May 1978, I had started to have the uneasy feeling that the IDF had different plans for the final areas to be evacuated. Right under my nose, at an IDF position 100 metres from my office and on the road to Naqoura village, IDF bulldozers were actively preparing a tank position; when it was completed, it was jointly manned by the IDF and the DFF. Reports from UNMOs on patrol and observation post duties in the enclave brought in similar reports, thus reinforcing my apprehensions. The Israeli intentions began to unfold rather clearly when on May 13 Mr Weizman, the Defence Minister, confirmed that Major Haddad was in command of the Christian militias as the legitimate representative of the Lebanese government in South Lebanon, and that the deployment of UNIFIL in areas under his control must be negotiated directly with him.

Differences in perception on Haddad's status by the Lebanese religious groups is a true reflection of the basic confessional difficulties facing Lebanon. While Mr Weizman accorded him a high status,

Selim el Hoss, Lebanon's Sunni Prime Minister, took the position that Haddad should be given no negotiating status at all by UNIFIL since he had been defying the authorities in Beirut. The Foreign Minister Fuad Butros and the army commander Brig.-Gen. Victor Khoury, both Christians (Catholic Orthodox and Maronite respectively), contended ambiguously that Haddad had been recognised by the government as the *de facto* commander of the estranged army troops and the militia operating in the south, irrespective of whether he was accepted as a legitimate officer of the Lebanese army or not. Mr Butros and General Khoury, at a crucial meeting on 9 June at the Foreign Ministry in West Beirut, asserted that the Lebanese army command accepted the presence of Haddad and his men in the south, and entrusted them with the task of co-operating with and facilitating UNIFIL's operations. (It was following Mr Butros' declaration on 9 June, that UNIFIL officially referred to Haddad's Lebanese troops and the militias operating under his command as the 'De Facto Forces' or DFF.)

What Mr Butros had declared as Foreign Minister was conveyed by the UN Secretary-General to the Security Council. Naturally, his perception of Haddad was shared by President Elias Sarkis, a Maronite Christian, but definitely not by Selim el Hoss, the Prime Minister. Worse still, it appeared that Mr Butros had not cleared his position with the Prime Minister before conveying this important and sensitive message to the UN. The Secretary-General, after reporting the Lebanese government's position to the Security Council, was attacked in the Lebanese media as being biased, and his report as not representing the official position of the Lebanese government. As far as UNIFIL was concerned, Haddad's position was clear. We could deal with him, though not in the capacity he claimed as the representative of Lebanese authority in the south.

Up till 7 June, when I had my penultimate meeting with General Ben Gal in his Northern Command HQ at Nazareth before the fateful 13 June, I felt that my colleagues at UN HQ were still unconvinced that the areas to be finally evacuated would not be given to UNIFIL, but handed over to Haddad, Chidiak and their militias already operating in the area. Our reports had reflected our apprehensions and concerns, but I am sure that the Secretary-General and his eminent staff at OUSGSPA (the Office of the Under Secretary-General for Special Political Affairs — responsible for peacekeeping) were utterly convinced that I and my staff in Naqoura were wrong. My apprehension and concern had been underscored by Mr Weizman's confirmation on 31 May that UNIFIL had to deal with Haddad on the question of deployment into the enclave. My colleagues at UN HQ had still not been moved to action.

The main objective of this meeting was to discuss the nodalities and the timing of the final withdrawal by the IDF. The meeting was inconclusive in view of the substantial differences in principle between UNIFIL's own deployment plan and that envisaged by the IDF, by which the UNIFIL presence was to be limited to only a small part of the areas to be evacuated by the IDF. What was even more difficult for us to accept was that we had to negotiate with Haddad to establish the UNIFIL presence in these areas, if we could get into them. The IDF was determined to ensure that UNIFIL formally recognised Haddad and the DFF as officially representing Yarze, headquarters of the Lebanese army, in the south.

During the discussions, General Ben Gal produced the grid references bordering the prospective Christian enclave. I realised that UNIFIL HQ was included in the enclave, and vehemently objected. General Ben Gal, without any hesitation but with all the authority given to him and to Northern Command over South Lebanon, took his marking pencil and removed UNIFIL HQ, Naqoura, out of the enclave. He viewed this as a kind gesture and a major concession to UNIFIL, but I was incensed; I just could not reconcile myself with the idea of this general from the sovereign state of Israel treating another sovereign state unjustly and disrespectfully, and getting away with it. I felt that the Lebanese government was too helpless, with the head of the Israeli Northern Command exercising all control and authority over its land.

On 8 June, the *Jerusalem Post*, the only Israeli newspaper published in English, published two articles headed 'No conditions to Israel pull-back' and 'Lebanon Christians hit new plans', both of which gave indications of positions already stated by Mr Weizman, General Ben Gal and other IDF officials. At this stage, I felt I should take matters into my own hands whatever the consequences. If UN HQ would not do it, I would. I would go to the press and tell the world of Israel's intentions.

On 10 June I invited Allen Ben-Ami, a military correspondent for the *Jerusalem Post*, to Naqoura, and in my humble caravan we had a wide-ranging discussion on the general situation in South Lebanon. I later narrowed the conversation down to my apprehension and concern at the IDF's intention to hand over the last areas in its occupation to the Christian militias and not to UNIFIL, as had been the format on past occasions. Furthermore, UNIFIL was to negotiate its deployment or presence in those areas with the Christians after 13 June. I argued that Israel just wanted to wash its hands of the matter, and asked in what capacity UNIFIL should negotiate with Haddad and his men. I finally gave the warning that should UNIFIL be unable to succeed in executing its mandate, Israel would be held responsible.

This statement became hot news internationally. Kol Israel (Israel Radio) began its afternoon broadcast with it, and the BBC and Reuter also picked it up and broadcast it in all their bulletins throughout the day. It hit home and achieved the main objective I wanted: to expose Israel's intentions and to internationalise the issue. Since the strength of the UN largely lies in world public opinion and sympathy, I needed the world body to help Lebanon and UNIFIL's cause.

Unfortunately, but as I had expected, UN HQ in New York did not see things my way and were angry over my charges against Israel and my statement to the press. I had prepared myself for a severe reprimand from the Secretary-General, which I duly received. Dr Waldheim was indeed angry, and charged that the comments I had made in the interview were unhelpful and that in such important and delicate situations I should refrain from vague judgements, comments and hypothetical speculations. It was a good blasting, which I deserved, and a few others were to follow in the course of my three difficult years at Naqoura. At least my objective had been achieved.

My final meeting with General Ben Gal on 12 June, the eve of the controversial withdrawal, was frustrating. The IDF had definitely planned to pull out and hand over the areas to the Christians. There was little of substance to discuss, not even the means by which they would pull out, except that the IDF were leaving the areas and we could verify their withdrawal as demanded by our mandate. On 13 June, in the Christian town of Meiss el Jebel, there was a ceremonial parade for the handing over by the IDF and the taking over of the evacuated areas by Major Haddad and his DFF. The Star of David was lowered and the Cedar of Lebanon raised, fluttering in the winds of 'Free Lebanon'.

My plan for 13 June was to use UNMO teams to verify the IDF's withdrawal. The force did indeed withdraw, as I cabled to the Secretary-General. For some time afterwards, I asked myself whether I had been right to confirm this withdrawal without having taken physical control of the evacuated areas as was done on 11, 14 and 30 April. I will return to this argument in the concluding paragraphs.

The so-called Christian enclave, which in all practicalities is a security belt (*cordon sanitaire*) between Israel and Lebanon, continued to be controlled by the IDF through the DFF — defined by Chairman Arafat as occupation by proxy. Most operational activities against the PLO in South Lebanon have been launched from the enclave in which gun emplacements are manned and operated either jointly by the IDF and the DFF or by the two forces separately. I believe that the securing of such a security belt was the prime objective of the Litani operation, and that this was something we should have known.

Two major lessons emerge from this episode to which I venture to draw the attention of future commanders of UN peacekeeping missions. First, field commanders should be aware that from time to time their perception of issues on the ground will differ from that of the authorities at UN HQ in New York. The latter is compelled to look at things more in a political perspective, but the field commander on the ground is likely to see them differently, and he should always persist in making his position known unambiguously. Where he has serious misgivings, he should say so, and he should stick to his position because if things subsequently go wrong, and especially if lives are lost unjustifiably, he as the commander will be held responsible by both the Security Council and the Secretary-General. The At-Tiri episode is a classic example of this. I was naturally upset when I received the Secretary-General's rebuke, dissociating his entire secretariat from me. But within me there was a feeling of achievement, that I had brought to world attention something which was to become the main impediment to UNIFIL's ability to fulfill its mandate. It continues even today to be the major issue preoccupying the Security Council, the Secretary-General, the Lebanese authorities, the countries that contribute to UNIFIL and all the governments in any way concerned with, or sympathetic to, UNIFIL's cause in South Lebanon.

The second lesson from this episode may be rather academic and technical. Should I have confirmed Israel's withdrawal on 13 June 1978 when the areas vacated by the IDF had not been physically handed over to me, unlike Rachaya el Foukher on 11 April, Abbasiya on 14 April and Ett Taibe on 30 April, which were physically handed over to me by the IDF? Events following the Israelis' invasion in June 1982 and their further withdrawal in 1985 would appear to indicate that I acted correctly. Once my confirmation of the IDF's withdrawal on 13 June had been published as a document of the Security Council, UNIFIL had the unquestioned mandate to stop any IDF/DFF movements into its area of operations. The few attempted encroachments by the IDF and DFF were resisted with as much force as necessary. UNIFIL's image and credibility were thus reasonably satisfactory, even in the eyes of those two forces.

Unfortunately this was not the case when the IDF vacated UNIFIL's area of operations after abandoning the Awali river and withdrawing into its expanded security zone in June 1985. Since a formula could not be devised to confirm its withdrawal, which would have committed it to keeping out of the UNIFIL area of operations, the IDF with the DFF continued to move freely in and out of it. This not only caused great frustration to the Force Commander and his commanders, senior staff and troops, but also disappointed the governments contributing troops to UNIFIL, the Lebanese authorities and the very people of South Lebanon whose protection was our responsibility. These frustrations were also expressed by the Secretary-General and his immediate principal staff.

Until UNIFIL is able, through the peacemaking process of negotiations, to deploy fully to the Armistice Demarcation Line of 1949, in other words the Lebanese-Israeli border, the mission's mandate will remain unfulfilled. In subsequent parts of this book, we consider why the *status quo* is likely to continue for some time. The establishment of a security belt, as a base to protect and defend their northern settlement, has been an old dream of Israeli strategists. This is not one of those dreams that will be easily or quickly forgotten.

8

FIRST ATTEMPTS TO DEPLOY LEBANESE ARMY TROOPS IN SOUTH LEBANON

If we were to assist the Lebanese government to re-establish its authority in all parts of South Lebanon as enshrined in Security Council Resolution 425, this meant deploying Lebanese army troops, gendarmerie and civilian government officials into the area to exercise normal government functions, including the maintenance of law and order. Hence the presence of regular Lebanese troops in the south was mandatory and conformed with our mandate. Several meetings on the deployment of the Lebanese army in South Lebanon were held between Lt.-Gen. Ensio Siilasvuo (then UN Chief Coordinator, based in Jerusalem), John Saunders (Director of UNDP in Lebanon) and myself, on the one side, and Selim el Hoss the Lebanese Prime Minister, Fuad Butros the Foreign Minister and General Victor Khoury the army commander, on the other. Meetings were also held with the Israeli authorities, since the cooperation of the IDF and the DFF was of vital importance for such deployment exercises.

At a meeting between President Elias Sarkis and Selim el Hoss on 24 July 1978, a decision was taken to despatch the Lebanese army to the south, and we were requested to advise the UN Secretary-General accordingly. The planning and execution, of course, had to be worked out by General Khoury, but with UNIFIL assisting in every way possible. The Secretary-General viewed the deployment as essential if UNIFIL was to have any continued basis for its existence and operations. So already on 19 June 1978 he had instructed General Siilasvuo and myself to meet the Israeli authorities and convey to them the Lebanese government's decision. We were further to solicit the Israeli government's support and cooperation to ensure the successful execution of this exercise. General Siilasvuo and I met General Rafael Eitan, the IDF Chief of Staff, at his headquarters in Tel Aviv soon after receiving the Secretary-General's instructions, and General Eitan restated his government's position on the subject. He said that Israel favoured efforts by the Lebanese government to restore its authority in the south, and would not interfere with such a move. However, he personally had misgivings about General Khoury's ability to execute this mission and questioned the wisdom of the decision to send the troops in view of the hostilities going on in Greater Beirut at that time.

In line with the Secretary-General's directive, UNIFIL's working staff met their Lebanese army counterparts at their HQ on 27 July to discuss in detail the movement plan and the part UNIFIL was expected to play. The task force moving south was to be of battalion strength, of 700 all ranks, consisting of a brigade HQ detachment, three rifle companies, a detachment of armoured cars and a battery of 122mm. mortars. The task force, named 'Forces of the South Front' (FSF), was to be commanded by Lt.-Col. Abdid Saad. The move was to begin at 0500 on 31 July and the final objective was to be the southern commercial capital Tibnin, which was also Irishbatt's HQ. FSF was to join up with UNIFIL and military observers of Observer Group Lebanon (OGL), who would serve as guides, in Kaukaba at 1000. The route selected by FSF was via the Bekaa valley, Kaukaba, Marjayoun, El Aadeisse, Ett Taibe and Tayr Zibna, reaching Tibnin in the late afternoon. The mission of the FSF, as directed by General Khoury, was to maintain peace and stability, and restore Lebanese sovereignty in the south; to control and prevent any armed movement into its area of responsibility, as assigned by UNIFIL; and to coordinate with UNIFIL in the fulfilment of its mission. The FSF would report direct to Lebanese army HQ in Yarze. A UNIFIL military observer team would be assigned to FSF HQ for coordination, and the FSF was to be represented for the same purpose at UNIFIL HQ by its own liaison officer. Resupply of FSF was to be through the Bekaa, but if this should ever prove difficult, UNIFIL was to assist.

To assert its own authority, the Lebanese government asked for a meeting through the Israeli-Lebanese Mixed Armistice Commission of 1949 (ILMAC) to afford it the opportunity to inform the Israelis directly of its planned army deployment. However, Israel has invoked the fact that the Lebanese government declared its intention of participating in the June 1967 war to claim that ILMAC thereby became invalidated. To enforce this claim, it has considered ILMAC meetings with Lebanon as meetings between two countries, though with UN assistance, and has always requested that the chairman of ILMAC should not be present at such meetings. Consequently, Lt.-Col. Jean Espinassy, as chairman, was asked to leave the room in which the meeting was being held at Naqoura on 30 July. At the meeting Israeli delegates, Colonel Shlomo and Lt.-Col. Gary Gal, asked for details of the FSF's strength and composition and of the route and timing of its move south. The Lebanese delegation, comprising Colonel Younes, Lt.-Col. Tannir and Captain Wehbe, provided the desired information.

At UNIFIL HQ, we knew all too well that the IDF was unhappy with a Lebanese army presence anywhere in the south, even though officially the Israeli government's position was positive. The presence of the FSF in the south was not so much a military threat; it was seen more as a challenge to the image and authority of Major Haddad in the area. This was the main cause of the IDF's objection to the move. Haddad was totally against it and was determined to do all in his power to frustrate the Lebanese government's decision and Yarze's plans. This negative feeling was sensed at a meeting with General Eitan on 26 July, and was also being expressed at the ILMAC meeting. The DFF's subsequent actions to frustrate the Lebanese army plans confirm this view.

The Israeli delegation expressed its concern about the route selected by the FSF, which would pass through Marjayoun and Aadeisse: these places were under DFF control. They felt that if the FSF used that route, there would be a risk of confrontation with their surrogates, the DFF. Asked by the Lebanese what their attitude would be in such a situation of armed confrontation, the Israelis said that they viewed the exercise as a purely internal Lebanese affair, and would therefore not intervene. The Israeli delegation added that the fact that they had raised potential problems was only intended to be advisory and not a warning. The meeting was adjourned at 1215. At 1420, Colonel Gal spoke from his office in Rosh Hanikra to Colonel Younes in Naqoura, reiterating the Israeli position — that they would not intervene should any trouble occur. But what was even more important and interesting was that Colonel Gal went further and advised that the exercise scheduled for the following day, 31 July, should be postponed because of possible problems, as mentioned by his delegation at the meeting. Obviously, he was under instructions from his superior authorities in Tel Aviv or Nazareth, the Northern Command HQ.

But despite the reservations raised by the Israeli delegation, the Lebanese government was determined to push ahead with its programme, and the Secretary-General too was fully disposed to see it through. At 0800 on 31 July, the FSF left the Bekaa valley, heading south. At 1040 Colonel Gal, as Senior Israeli Representative (North), called the UNIFIL operations room to advise that a tense situation was developing in the area of operations and that UNIFIL should advise the Lebanese army HQ at Yarze to stop the move. However, the Lebanese government could not afford to lose face, so the IDF could not have its way. Consequently, I refused to heed the IDF's advice, which we in UNIFIL viewed as a threat, and allowed the exercise to proceed as planned. At 1300 the FSF arrived at Lower Kaukaba. Just before the troops reached the outskirts of the rendezvous, shells fired from Marjayoun, Haddad's HQ and the DFF's main stronghold, started to fall on Kaukaba. To avoid serious casualties, the convoy halted and radioed Yarze for further instructions. At 1450 hours, the DFF 'informed' UNIFIL to advise Yarze to withdraw the FSF from the area, failing which the troops would be shelled. Again we refused to yield to the DFF's demands.

At 1620 firing started and continued until 1740. Twenty-seven mortar rounds were fired. One soldier was wounded in the stomach, and medically evacuated by a FSF ambulance to the north. For fear of possible escalation, which could have created utter confusion, the FSF did not return fire. Already before shooting started, I had made strong protests to the IDF liaison HQ in Jerusalem. For the time being, the FSF fanned out, deploying in both Lower and Upper Kaukaba. I went up there to inspect them and found them in high spirits. I seized the opportunity of my visit to brief the commanding officer, Lt.-Col. Abdid Saad, that diplomatic efforts were being made by the Secretary-General and various governments to resolve the present impasse. I reassured him of UNIFIL's continued assistance and cooperation for the accomplishment of his difficult mission. He and his officers looked confident and relaxed, and morale was generally satisfactory.

Haddad started accusing UNIFIL of facilitating the FSF move and threatened to punish us. All day on 1 August, the Norwegian HQ in Ebel Es Saqi and the Nepalese HQ in Blate were shelled and machine-gunned. The FSF also continued to be fired on at Kaukaba.

Meanwhile, diplomatic efforts at the international level had been set in motion to ensure the successful execution of the Lebanese army objectives. On 1 August the Secretary-General sent a letter to the Israeli Prime Minister, Menachem Begin, explaining the importance of the move and soliciting Israeli cooperation to make it successful. The US and British ambassadors in Beirut were also in touch with their home governments to put pressure on Israel to cooperate with President Sarkis' government. On 3 August, Mr Begin replied to the Secretary-General, and followed the usual Israeli line by referring to the Syrian occupation of Lebanon. He wrote that Israel did not dictate to Major Haddad, but that his government would use its good offices to persuade the DFF to stop the shelling.

However, the shelling continued. The Lebanese had accused the IDF of doing the firing, but UNIFIL could not confirm this indictment. According to information available to Naqoura, the shots were being fired by the DFF, surrogates of the Israelis, but of course it was possible that the DFF were acting under the influence of the IDF, which was our experience most of the time in South Lebanon. To support and justify their actions, the DFF told Yarze that the FSF was composed of Syrians and pro-Syrian elements and that the troops were not Lebanese. This accusation was to be used against Yarze when attempts were made subsequently to deploy more Lebanese troops from the north to the south.

As a follow-up to the meeting held earlier with General Eitan on 26 July, it was agreed that I and General Ben Gal, the officer in charge of the IDF Northern Command, should meet at the earliest opportunity. On 1 August, we spoke by telephone (we were on friendly terms and called each other by our first names) to discuss a few issues and to confirm this appointment for 1600. Later the same evening, he telephoned to cancel it unilaterally, without giving any reasons. This is only a hint of the humiliation that one has to accommodate as commander of an international peacekeeping force, especially in a confused situation and an environment like that in Lebanon. But doesn't history repeat itself? The IDF command was to be subjected to the same kind of humiliation four years later in Beirut, but by the Multinational Force and at the hands of a colonel.

Despite the somewhat reassuring exchange of letters between UN HQ in New York and Israel, and the strenuous efforts made by the US government and the UN, firing on the FSF and UNIFIL positions continued unabated. Mortar, artillery and tank fire, directed from Marjayoun, El Qlea and El Khraibe, was a regular occurrence. August 7 was an especially bad day for the FSF in Kaukaba. At 2110 the DFF fired twelve mortar rounds into Kaukaba, killing one soldier and wounding six others. One vehicle was burnt out. At the same time, eleven mortar shells were fired at the Nepalese position and one scored a direct hit on a mortar position.

My deputy, Brigadier-General Jean Cuq (France),* paid a visit to the FSF in Kaukaba and found Colonel Abdid Saad and his officers and men in excellent condition and their morale high. Not only did the troops need such an exposure to make them feel like national soldiers defending a good Lebanese national cause, but they also viewed the entire exercise as a good form of military training. General Cuq had participated fully in the deployment exercise from the time when it was being prepared, and felt satisfaction at seeing the FSF in Kaukaba. General Cuq's professional competence contributed greatly to the establishment of UNIFIL, and he gave invaluable and selfless service to the UN cause.

Why Lebanese army HQ (hereafter referred to as 'Yarze') planned the FSF's route to Tibnin through Marjayoun and the strongholds of the rebellious Christian militias remains a mystery. It was obvious that

---

* Born at Aveyron, France, in 1927, he attended the French Military Academy, Saint-Cyr, and was commissioned in 1947 in the Field Artillery. He served in Indochina as a lieutenant and as a captain in Algeria, during the wars in those countries, and went on to attend the French Staff College (*Diplome d'Etat Major*) and the War College (*Brevet de l'Ecole Supérieure de Guerre*). He commanded the 35th Field Artillery Paratroop Regiment in 1973 – 5, and assumed command of the 1st Paratroop Brigade in 1977. He holds many decorations. He left UNIFIL in 1979 to command a French division in West Germany.

there was no way in which the FSF could move through these hostile areas without serious confrontation, nor was there any way it could be expected to win such a fight, since the IDF's full cooperation and support were sure to be with the Christians. Such an armed confrontation with the DFF would have put UNIFIL in a most difficult and embarrassing situation, since it would most likely have resisted physical participation in the fight. On the other hand, non-participation would have gravely affected UNIFIL's credibility, and its continued operation might have been brought into question by the Lebanese population, considering that it is a Lebanese mission and the deployment of Lebanese troops in the south is in fulfilment of its mandate. This was UNIFIL HQ's main apprehension throughout the entire exercise. My principal staff in Naqoura and I remained haunted by this fear as long as Yarze remained adamant about using this route.

In principle the Israeli authorities did not object to the presence of the Lebanese army in the south, but in practice they objected strongly, principally because they feared that the so-called 'good fence' defining the 1949 Armistice Demarcation Line between Israel and Lebanon and all the fifteen gates through it operated by the IDF would be closed by the Lebanese government by means of the FSF. Israeli politicians and military commanders dreaded this eventuality since it would mean the loss of physical contact with the Lebanese Christian population and therefore loss of full control over the security belt for offensive action against the PLO. Ezer Weizmann, Israel's Defence Minister, had repeatedly requested meetings with his Lebanese counterpart to discuss the 'open bridges' concept, similar to that applied at the Allenby Bridge linking Jordan to Israel, but the Lebanese authorities never agreed.

Sustaining the DFF was in the best political and military interests of the Israelis, and thus every effort had to be made to frustrate the FSF plan. Accusations that Yarze had sent Syrians and pro-Syrian elements in the guise of Lebanese troops were on the lips of both the local population in the enclave and the Lebanese from other parts living there — who were all under strong Israeli influence. At a meeting with me on 9 August, Generals Eitan and Ben Gal strongly criticised Yarze for sending a force which was predominantly Muslim. They claimed that the presence of such a unit was highly provocative to the Christians, and described the atmosphere in the enclave as a holy war between Christians and Muslims, the leftist Lebanese National Movement groups being predominantly Muslim and deeply sympathetic to the Palestinian cause and the PLO.

On 8 August, we noticed a reduction in the strengh of the Lebanese army troops in Kaukaba: the FSF had been reduced from its initial strength of 700 to about 200 of all ranks. They had been pulled back 7–10 km. northwards near to where Syrian army contingents were located.

Further deployment of the Lebanese army into South Lebanon and the first shelling of UNIFIL HQ

As explained earlier, the deployment of Lebanese army troops in South Lebanon had always been viewed as a challenge to Major Saad Haddad's authority and an erosion of his image — which the IDF, for obvious reasons, had to protect and defend at all costs. At the same time, an effective presence of Lebanese security forces and civilian administrative staff in the south was in conformity with Security Council Resolution 425 and subsequent resolutions extending UNIFIL's mandate. Despite the previous shelling of Kaukaba, we had no choice but to move ahead towards the total implementation of that Resolution.

On 17 January 1979, a Lebanese army liaison team of one officer and one soldier was attached to each UNIFIL operational battalion: Frenchbatt, Fijibatt, Senbatt, Nibatt, Iranbatt and Irishbatt. The stranded battalion in Kaukaba was considered adequate to service Norbatt and Nepbatt on liaison matters.

During one of my routine visits to General Victor Khoury, the Lebanese army commander, at Yarze in March 1979, the issue of further deployment of Lebanese troops into UNIFIL's area of operation came up for discussion. General Khoury intended to send a battalion of 500 all ranks, accompanied by appropriate heavy and medium guns, light arms, transport and communication equipment. A Lebanese army/UNIFIL working group, which had been set up previously, was commissioned to plan the exercise in detail.

In the early days of April 1979, contacts were made with the IDF to apprise them of the planned move. Their objection to it and their total opposition to any semblance of Lebanese authority in the area, were a foregone conclusion. Major Haddad was officially informed, and his war council immediately went into session and on 14 April issued the following statement:

UNIFIL   14/4/1979   Lebanese Headquarters
Nakura   Lebanese Forces
TELEGRAM   Marj-Ayoun
                                    War Council of the Militias in the South
                                    The Tigers of the Cannons

In our meeting today the following decisions were taken:

1. Lebanese Army Unit operated by Syria, PLO, UNIFIL and the National Front will not be allowed to enter areas close to our lines.
2. If necessary we will use force and even fight to the end with the above-mentioned forces.
3. Every position of those forces will be considered enemy position and will be dealt with as such.
4. If UNIFIL will support this move or host units of this nature, we shall start shelling UNIFIL positions and attack all UNIFIL positions or observation points in the south.
5. All the roads used by UNIFIL will be closed and blocked starting 15/4/79 6 lt.
6. Maj. Mounir Melly will be executed immediately without trial the minute he will be caught by our forces.
7. Israel has nothing to do with the above-mentioned decisions.
8. We have decided that after having spent our last shell and bullet we shall send all our non-fighting population into Israel and we shall start guerrilla warfare against the above-mentioned forces.
9. One of our targets will be the liquidation of traitors for the Lebanese army cause.
10. We call on Gen. Erskine to return immediately from his hide-out in the jungles of Africa and to take his responsibility due to his promise that no army will arrive without our approval.
11. UNIFIL should understand that a game with fire can cause a fire-storm.

Long live Free Lebanon
Long live the South
Long live the Lebanese Front
In the name of all the inhabitants of the south we sign and swear.

As soon as we received it, the full text was immediately retransmitted to New York for the Secretary-General's personal attention. Our experience at Kaukaba had been such that threats from the militias, underscored by the IDF's negative posture, could not be treated as bluff. Tension in the area, both in UNIFIL's area of operation and in the enclave, was exceptionally high. On 15 April Dr Waldheim was compelled to address a message to Israeli Prime Minister Begin drawing his attention to Haddad's threat and the necessity to move the Lebanese army troops down to the south, and requesting Israel's co-operation in the exercise. If Mr Begin bothered to reply, I did not know or see what he said. Meanwhile, plans for the exercise were completed, and after I had expressed my agreement with them, General Khoury sought Lebanese government approval and got it. Prime Minister Selim el Hoss was fully supportive of the move, if only to crush the rebel Haddad who was perceived as an Israeli puppet, sitting as king in Marjayoun.

D-Day was Tuesday, 17 April. On the morning of 15 April, the day on which the Secretary-General sent his appeal to Begin, the entire Christian enclave and the coastal road north from UNIFIL HQ were closed to UNIFIL traffic. This meant that the HQ was cut off from its field units, and consequently supplies from it to the units had to be routed through Israel — an option which, under the circumstances, was politically unacceptable. Local Lebanese workers at the HQ failed to turn up for work in the morning — such absenteeism always signalled a bad time ahead for UNIFIL. It was also observed that Christian militia 9mm. gun positions along the northern edge of the enclave had been strengthened with heavy 122mm. guns and tanks. Tanks and heavy mortars, normally located at the DFF coastal check-point, had been moved further north to the area of the Al Bayyadah hills, which dominate Rashadiya camp and Tyre town and the pocket. The DFF presence on high ground east of UNIFIL HQ became highly visible. What did IDF and DFF have in their minds? Action to defuse tension and so facilitate Lebanese army task force deployment went on concurrently both at UN HQ in New York and at Naqoura.

In the spirit of the UN philosophy of negotiation as against confrontation, 'Team Zulu', the OGL observer trouble-shooters responsible for the enclave, were tasked by my deputy Brigadier Martin Vadset,* then Acting Force Commander, to arrange a meeting with Haddad. But Haddad sent a message to Brigadier Vadset that morning saying that he was not interested in meeting him, and that if UNIFIL allowed the Lebanese armed forces battalion to move into its area of operation, 'it means war between UNIFIL and DFF', to quote his own words.

On 16 April, the Secretary-General received a request from Israeli Defence Minister Ezer Weizman to postpone the exercise for twenty-four hours to allow time for Haddad to be pacified. Could this be Begin's reaction to the Secretary-General's appeal? In the event, the exercise was rescheduled by Yarze for the 18th. Whatever the Israeli authorities may have considered to ease the execution of the exercise was not known; what was known was that little or nothing was done. At 0830 on 17 April, shells started falling in all our areas — Irishbatt,

* Martin was my colleague at the Staff College, Camberley, England, in 1968 and we respected eachother's professionalism. He left UNIFIL to become Chief of Staff of the Norwegian Army and later commander of Norway's Northern NATO Command, Bodö. Visiting Oslo with my wife in July 1986 to participate in a seminar on UNIFIL, organised by the Norwegian Institute for Strategic Studies, we had the singular honour of visiting him at Bodö, which also afforded me the rare opportunity of meeting again some of my old commanders, staff and soldiers who had served in both UNIFIL and UNTSO. In 1988 he was tasked by UN Secretary-General Perez de Cuellar to mount the UN's peacekeeping operation following the ceasefire between Iran and Iraq.

Dutchbatt, Nibatt, Fijibatt, Norbatt, Nepbatt and Senbatt. Tyre town and the pocket also took their full share. Over 300 mortar, artillery and tank shells were fired, mainly from the enclave. At 1620, Haddad addressed the following message to Norbatt: 'Is UNIFIL satisfied with what is going on? All responsibilities lie on UNIFIL. It will be more hard if Lebanese army comes in.' Firing continued intermittently until late in the evening. With the Lebanese army deployment impending, the outlook seemed gloomier than ever.

At 0740 on 18 April, an advance party of 150 all ranks with seven vehicles and light weapons arrived in the area of operations. Its HQ was located at Azoun. At 0800, DFF shelling and firing began again. Irishbatt area took 139 shells, mainly in Tibnin, Brashit and Jabal Salim; two children were reported killed. Fijibatt received twelve shells. A total of 167 shells fell in the Palestinian refugee camp of Burj Shamali and Tyre town proper, and the PLO fired back twenty-eight shells towards the enclave. Dutchbatt AO received eight shells, Norbatt ten, Senbatt five and Nibatt fifty-six, mainly in Srifa and Dayr Kifa. *At 1045 our helicopter returning from Beirut was fired on as it was about to land at Naqoura. The UNIFIL defence platoon from Ghanbatt returned fire, killing one DFF soldier. This man's death had fateful consequences.

At 2235, the major attack on the HQ started, and hell broke loose. Fourteen mortar shells were fired from the vicinity of Naqoura village. Fire at this time was not returned and there was a lull. Exactly at midnight, heavy firing started again with mortars, artillery, tanks and heavy machine-guns. The UNIFIL HQ defence platoon fought back fiercely, supported by the French logistics battalion, but damage to UNIFIL equipment was heavy. Three of the four helicopters were hit, one with damage to the body, tail and main rotor blades. Some prefabricated buildings, tents and Norair houses were also damaged. Six Irish soldiers were wounded, one seriously, and two Dutch officers received light injuries. We could not determine DFF casualties over the Naqoura hills, but we could see one man fall close to the Heliwing fence.

The death of this man resulted in a demand for compensation. Major Haddad, encouraged and supported by General Ben Gal as commander of the IDF's Northern Command, demanded LL25,000 (about US$8,000) as *sulha* for the DFF member whom UNIFIL was alleged to have deliberately killed. A meeting was held at the IDF office in Rosh Kanikra on 19 April to resolve the question of this

---

* The exactness with which these numbers are known is explained by the fact that counting heavy shells fired is one of the major functions of troops and observers on observation post duties. This work forms part of the mission's situation report submitted to the UN Security Council, and accuracy is therefore essential.

compensation. Representing the DFF were General Ben Gal, Lt.-Col. Gary Gal, Lt.-Col. Yoram Hamizirahi, Captain Moshe, Major Haddad and Abu Farah.* UNIFIL was represented by Brigadier Vadset, accompanied by Colonel Tjassens, the chief operations officer, Lt.-Col. Neale and Major Potin, both operations staff.

General Ben Gal, speaking in Hebrew with Colonel Yoram as interpreter, accused UNIFIL of shooting the DFF man, who had been laying a telephone cable, at short range and in cold blood, adding that the killing had provoked strong emotions among the DFF and the victim's relations, friends and fellow-villagers. He said that the Muslims in the area were calling for blood revenge, as was their tradition. He was afraid that even though the family had buried him without any rancour, he, Yanush Ben Gal, was apprehensive of the friends of the deceased doing something which even Haddad himself might not be able to control. He concluded by urging UNIFIL to fulfil the local customs of *sulha* or compensation for the dead man. He would continue to offer his good offices and co-operation to resolve the problem.

Brigadier Vadset argued that there was no question of UNIFIL paying compensation, because the DFF soldier had not been shot at close range and therefore not in cold blood, but killed during an exchange of fire. After a prolonged argument, the meeting was adjourned.

In early April, I had left the mission area for Nigeria to take part in a seminar on peacekeeping organised by the International Peace Academy. This was why my deputy Brigadier Vadset was in charge of UNIFIL at the time of the Lebanese army deployment and the fighting at Naqoura. From Lagos, I had flown to Accra to see my family and take a short rest before returning to South Lebanon. While there I decided not to listen to the BBC or watch television. I just wanted to rest my body and soul, but the devil always has his own ways. On the morning of 21 April, the third day after the shelling of the HQ, Lieutenant-General Joshua Hamidu, Ghana's Chief of Defence Staff and an intimate friend and colleague of mine, stopped by my house on the way to his office. He wondered why I was sitting in Accra while my HQ was on fire. That was the end of my leave, and the next day I was on a Swissair plane flying back to Naqoura. The fighting had ceased, but tension was high and tempers had not cooled. There was a special welcome waiting for me: the demand by Haddad and his men for *sulha* for the militiaman killed on the 18th.

---

* Lt. Col. Hamizirahi and Capt. Moshe were IDF officers who worked closely with Haddad; Abu Farah was a DFF liaison officer with UNIFIL.

The most serious humiliation in my life

Compensation exacted by the South Lebanese from UNIFIL for vehicle accidents and other occurrences involving death or injury became part of our way of co-existence with our hosts in South Lebanon. Huge demands of money by Major Haddad and the DFF for any of their men killed or wounded by UNIFIL troops greatly hampered our operations. If *sulha* were not paid the blood feud had to continue, and since UNIFIL troops, operating without any exclusive corridors, were extremely exposed and thus susceptible to ambushes with exorbitant cost in human life, we had little choice but to accede to some form of compensation.

I arrived back at Naqoura from Accra on the evening of 24 April, and the next day resumed my duties. The demand for *sulha*, failing which there would be blood revenge, was actively pending. We were trying to figure out how to defuse tension when in the morning of 9 May, unknown to us, three Dutchbatt soldiers manning UNTSO observation post 'Hin' were abducted and detained in a house by the DFF. In view of the ongoing blood feud and emotional situation, I resolved to get them released as soon as I possibly could, preferably the same day. Issues involving the lives of my men always took top priority. As I had done before from time to time over similar issues, I tried to enlist the help of national ambassadors accredited to Israel to intercede with the Israeli authorities. Sometimes such intercessions worked, and in any case there was never any harm in trying.

I therefore went to Jerusalem to see the Dutch ambassador, and he readily agreed to see Israeli Foreign Ministry officials immediately. Having seen him, I decided to return to my Naqoura HQ to monitor developments. While in the vicinity of Herzliya I had a call on my motorola to proceed to Metulla; Major Haddad urgently wanted a meeting with me. My staff in Naqoura, in view of the delicate situation, had agreed to the meeting and 'Team Zulu' was proceeding towards Metulla at that moment. In the circumstances, I agreed to meet Haddad and decided to go directly to Metulla, about two-and-a-half hours' drive from Herzliya. The radio message also suggested that I should stop on the way at the office of the IDF liaison officer, Lt.-Col. Gary Gal, for a short meeting. I did see him, and he confirmed the message I had received on the radio. Metulla was the HQ for IDF liaison officers attached to Haddad; hardly anyone ever met Haddad formally without one of these Israeli liaison officers being present.

'Team Zulu' were nervously waiting for me in the hotel immediately opposite the IDF liaison office; they were nervous because of the impression they had received on arriving at Metulla that this meeting was not going to be of the normal kind to which we had become accustomed. There was an angry crowd in and around the place where our meeting was to take place. I had to do a quick mental appreciation. Should I go ahead, or should I turn back to Naqoura, bearing in mind the plight of my Dutch soldiers? There was no way they could kill me on Israeli soil in the presence of Israeli personnel, so the risk was worth taking. I decided to go ahead. As I entered the room, which was crowded with South Lebanese, both men and women, I was immediately attacked. Hands came at me from all sides and hit me on the face, back, shoulders, everywhere. Haddad was present and ostensibly tried to stop them, but that would appear to have been only for the record. The IDF personnel who were there made sure they kept themselves out of sight. 'Team Zulu' tried to rescue me, and they suffered some blows for their pains. Eventually, phase one of the meeting was over.

Naturally, my men and I were badly shaken, but I tried to put on a smile, albeit a dry one. Again, for the sake of my Dutch prisoners, I pondered whether or not I should leave. But again I decided to go through with it because — as I reasoned to myself — it was possible that the worst part of the organised show was over. My Turkish driver FSO Necati Sertoglu, hearing the commotion, had dashed into the room and retrieved my missing gorgets, badges of rank and beret. I could see on his face the sympathy he felt for his poor general. He had been my driver since my command of UNTSO and had become a friend, so his reaction was quite natural.

At this stage, I wanted to stay in the room for as short a time as possible. Haddad gave me a seat and sat next to me. I looked straight into his eyes but he could not reciprocate. He appeared full of guilt. He tried to apologise for what had happened, putting the blame on my men for killing his man in cold blood. He asked me to understand the highly charged emotion of the villagers. At this stage, he tried to introduce a woman from among the mob as the mother of the dead man. I ignored her but realised it was she who had attacked me first as I had entered the room. Haddad pleaded with me to have the LL25,000 compensation paid to end the blood feud. This was the crux of the matter.

I first inquired about my three Dutch hostages and demanded their immediate release. Haddad said he would release them only if I would arrange the payment of the requested *sulha*. I agreed and again demanded the immediate release of the Dutch soldiers. He also agreed. I took leave, charging 'Team Zulu' to discuss the release arrangements with him.

I jumped into my car with a deep sigh of relief. At least I was alive. What I had feared during the five minutes I was on my 'cross' was that some fanatic would pull a trigger, as there had been a few AK47s in the room. Also, I would have the hostages back that night, thus enhancing my credibility in the eyes of my 6,000 UNIFIL troops in South Lebanon, the Dutch government and people, and the UN Secretary-General and his Secretariat, even if at considerable personal cost. And, in addition, the Israeli authorities, by condoning what had taken place, could not escape responsibility: this gave me a card that I could play at a later stage in my command. However, I never did play it.

I arrived at Naqoura at about 2000 and was met in my office by Martin Vadset. He had been the first person apart from 'Team Zulu' and my driver to know of my ordeal, and he was clearly moved to see me. My first task was to call Brian Urquhart: I gave a brief summary of what had happened in Metulla, and told him that I had acceded to the payment of *sulha* and would be receiving my three Dutch hostages back within the next few hours; I asked for his agreement to what I had done. Brian expressed profound regret for what had happened; he said he approved of the agreement and promised to bring the entire ordeal to the immediate attention of Dr Waldheim. He encouraged me to continue as I had been doing.

Whenever soldiers' lives are at stake in peacekeeping duties, contributing countries understandably become anxious, and this was particularly so in the case of Lebanon. In the present situation where three Dutch soldiers had been abducted, it was normal for the authorities in The Hague, through their permanent representative to the UN in New York, to pressurise the Secretary-General and Brian Urquhart to do all they could to procure the safety of their men: if they should come to any harm, the national political repercussions could be unfavourable both for the Secretary-General and for UNIFIL's operations. I was well aware of this political pressure.

For the record I confirmed my telephone conversation with Brian in a cable, but in the concluding words I appealed to Dr Waldheim not to take up my humiliating ordeal with any government; also I did not want any press release issued in the subject. I told him that this was the high and painful price that had to be paid for being Force Commander of peacekeeping troops in a volatile area like Lebanon. The Secretary-General and Brian respected my feelings. I did not mention my humiliation at the time to anyone, not even my wife.

My Dutch hostages were released a couple of hours after I got back to Naqoura. They came to see me in my office and, together with Martin Vadset, my senior political adviser James Holger,*

---

* James Holger, a citizen of Chile, joined us as an international civil servant of great political expertise and maturity. He had served in the Chilean foreign service for many years, including five with his country's permanent mission to the UN in New York. He joined the UN in 1977. After leaving UNIFIL in 1980, he served as the Secretary-General's Special Representative in Cyprus.

'Team Zulu' and their own commanding officer, we all had a few beers. On 11 May my chief administrative officer Erik Anderson arranged payment of the *sulha*, LL25,000, through 'Team Zulu', thereby closing the episode.

A year later I had the consolation of hearing Brian Urquhart tell of his own similar experience in the Congo during one of his peace-making shuttles. His theme was that it is 'better to be beaten than eaten'. He was right.

9

UNIFIL SHOWS ITS TEETH IN AT-TIRI, APRIL 1980

The month of April in both 1979 and 1980 seemed to spell doom for UNIFIL's efforts to assist the Lebanese government to restore its authority to all parts of the south. In 1980, at just about the same time as in the previous year, problems started brewing up for UNIFIL. This time, it was not the Lebanese army coming south but UNIFIL showing its teeth in defence of its mandate and itself.

On 6 April tension began building up when at 1555 a DFF tank and two jeeps arrived at the main road intersection controlling movements into and out of At-Tiri village. This was an Irishbatt position, known as 6-15A. The tank shoved the Irishbatt armoured personnel carrier aside to clear the way for the accompanying jeeps to enter the village. The Irishbatt troops at 6-15A immediately surrounded the DFF men and began negotiations to effect their eviction from the UNIFIL area of operations. The DFF men said that they intended to set up a permanent checkpoint in At-Tiri village and to patrol the area as they wished. Irishbatt refused these requests.

This was the beginning of the At-Tiri confrontations which eventually resulted in the tragic cold-blooded murder of my two Irish soldiers, Privates John Barrett and Derek Smallhorne, and which provoked the emergency meeting of all the eleven countries contributing to UNIFIL in Dublin in May 1980.

I despatched 'Team Zulu', our trouble-shooters, to go and investigate what was happening in Irishbatt's area of responsibility and to give the commanding officer of Irishbatt whatever assistance he needed. At the CO's request, and following serious discussions with 'Team Zulu', the Force Mobile Reserve (FMR) was mobilised. UNIFIL was at war.

The deployment of the FMR was as follows. The Senegalese detachment on Hill 880; the Dutch battalion detachment on the track between Hill 880 and position 6-15A; the Fiji battalion detachment between positions 6-15 and 6-15A, as immediate reinforcement for the Irishbatt troops in the immediate vicinity of At-Tiri; and the Nigeria battalion detachment at 6-15 in the area of Bayt Yahun. The Ghana battalion detachment was in reserve at Tibnin, Irishbatt HQ.

On 7 April at 0830, a heavy exchange of small arms fire began, initiated by the DFF, to which we responded. Private John Griffin from Ireland was wounded in the head and evacuated by our helicopter wing, Italair (Italy had taken over the helicopter wing from Norway in July 1979). He was flown to Rambam hospital in Haifa, Israel, where he later died. The bullet had lodged in his brain and surgery was considered impossible. During the fighting, nine Irishbatt soldiers were captured and taken as prisoners to the village of Safal Hawa.

At-Tiri is a small village, and since the beginning of our operations it had been controlled by Irishbatt. Strategically it was of significance to both UNIFIL and the DFF. Irishbatt had lost the important village of Bayt Yahun to the DFF in the early stages of the mission, and the loss of At-Tiri in addition would immediately have had a grave effect on the credibility of UNIFIL operations. From Bayt Yahun, harrassing fire had frequently been aimed from there towards the nearby villages of Brashit and Haddatha, each of which was about 3 km. away. This was because the DFF had always suspected these two villages, which were under Irishbatt control, of harbouring PLO and other armed elements hostile to them. However, between Bayt Yahun and Haddatha was 'Hill 880', a commanding feature dominating the entire area which includes Ayta Zutt, Haris (Dutchbatt HQ), Tibnin (Irishbatt HQ), Brashit, Shaqra and Haddatha. The roads in the area, which constituted the main supply routes for Irishbatt, were also dominated by Hill 880. Hence, in our view, the main objective of the DFF in their attempt to take At-Tiri was to use this village as the springboard to capture Hill 880, the loss of which would have jeopardised our operations in the whole Irishbatt area of operations. However, the commanding officer of Irishbatt, Lt.-Col. Jack Kissane, a 'Kerry man', had already grasped the significance of the hill, and discussed its occupation with me seven weeks earlier, and I had agreed that he should go ahead and establish an observation post on it. Thus when Haddad and his men started to execute their plans for At-Tiri, we were ready to give fire cover from the hill to the platoon defending the village.

As a peacekeeping force, UNIFIL would always choose negotiation rather than confrontation. At 1545, my Deputy Force Commander Brigadier Ole Nielsen (Norway) met Major Haddad with the objective of finding ways and means of defusing the tension in At-Tiri. Haddad reiterated his desire to set up a command post in At-Tiri and patrol the general area. Brigadier Nielsen told him that his request was totally unacceptable to UNIFIL, and in response to this Haddad threatened to execute the nine captured Irish soldiers held at Safal Hawa, one at a time, if UNIFIL troops were not withdrawn from At-Tiri. Brigadier Nielsen made it clear to him that UNIFIL would not give an inch on this issue and demanded the unconditional release of our nine Irish prisoners. He also warned Haddad that if the DFF had not withdrawn by 1100 the following day, 8 April, UNIFIL would seal off the entire area of At-Tiri and thereby prevent any supplies getting through to his men. If armed confrontation resulted from this action, we would respond with full force. Security Council Resolution 425 had to be defended whatever happened, and in any case the loss of At-Tiri would have meant a serious encroachment which, on top of the encroachments we had already suffered, would harm the credibility of UNIFIL operations. Our stand on At-Tiri was non-negotiable.

It is of vital importance for the commander of a peacekeeping mission always to keep the Secretary-General (through OUSGSPA) informed of all activities and actions — those taken and, if possible, those planned or anticipated. This enables the Secretary-General in turn to do a number of things. He can keep the Security Council informed as and when that becomes necessary; direct appropriate issues to the right parties to the conflict for the defusing of tension and resolution of the problem; make the right approaches in seeking the support and cooperation from appropriate individual Council members in helping to resolve issues; give correct briefing to contributing countries which might be anxious to know what is going on and what they can do to assist him; and, finally, give the appropriate directives to the commander in the field. In situations of armed confrontation, where men's lives may be lost, home governments naturally become anxious and it is vital that they are kept informed through their permanent representatives at the UN.

Hence I was in constant touch with Brian Urquhart, Chief Executive of OUSGSPA, on the At-Tiri situation. In the most urgent situations, I had to call him by telephone which, as already mentioned, usually meant getting him out of bed because of the seven hours' time difference between Naqoura and New York. Brian and his wife Sidney fully understood the difficult and delicate situation we had on our hands in South Lebanon and were always ready to receive my calls. We were dealing with matters of life and death.

Brian fully supported our stand on At-Tiri, expressing his admiration and commending us for our firm handling of the crisis. This gave our morale a vital boost: UNIFIL was motivated and encouraged. He further informed us that the Secretary-General was planning to meet the contributing countries as soon as possible to brief them and secure their full support for the stand UNIFIL was taking — and to enlist their support in dealing with the Israelis. The peacemaking process had been put into high gear.

The Secretary-General sent an urgent request to the Israeli mission to the UN to take all possible action to reverse the dangerous situation in At-Tiri. The US mission was also informed, and the Secretary-General requested it to give strong support to the démarches being undertaken by UNIFIL on the ground, by the Chief of Staff of UNTSO in Jerusalem (Major-General Erkki Rainer Kaira of Finland), and by the OUSGSPA in New York.

At 0730 on 8 April, three of the nine Irish soldiers captured the previous day were released — an indication that the peacemaking process both at UN HQ and on the ground in the UNIFIL area was working. The three men confirmed that they had been held in Safal Hawa. They were medically examined by the medical officer of Irish-batt and found to be in good shape. UNIFIL HQ requested the IDF's assistance to enable Observer Group Lebanon ('Team Zulu') to visit the remaining six still being held. But the situation in At-Tiri was getting steadily worse. At 1320, small arms fire impacted on an Irish armoured personnel carrier. Nine minutes later, twelve heavy machine-gun rounds struck position 6-15, and at 1412 two similar rounds hit an Irish vehicle. At 1423, while position 6-15 was under fire, additional sniper fire was directed at other Irish positions, and one Irish soldier received a leg wound. At 1445 the Irish battalion commander, Jack Kissane, ordered his men to return any fire from the DFF, with controlled fire. At 1457, the Irish company commander in charge of the detachment in the area of At-Tiri also ordered his men to open controlled fire on the DFF. A local ceasefire was subsequently arranged, negotiated between the Irish company commander and the local DFF leader, but at 1738 tension started to rise again. The DFF had tried to bring ammunition into the southern end of At-Tiri, and on being stopped by the Irish, threatened to throw hand-grenades at them if they were not allowed to pass through. This threat was ignored.

While fighting was taking place on the ground, the peacemaking process continued. Later that day, Brigadier Nielsen sent a letter to the IDF liaison officer, Lt.-Col. Gary Gal, expressing our deep concern at the At-Tiri situation and regretting the IDF's inability to help reduce tension and get the situation back to normal, which it could do by advising Major Haddad to withdraw his men from the area. The letter further said that UNIFIL troops had full authority to return all DFF fire immediately. Finally it expressed apprehension that failure by the DFF to withdraw from the At-Tiri area could precipitate a major confrontation between us, which we should try our utmost to avoid.

The peacemaking process at the higher level to complement our efforts on the ground was being conducted simultaneously at UN HQ in New York. The US mission to the UN in New York informed Brian Urquhart that the US ambassador to Israel, Samuel Lewis, had had talks with Prime Minister Begin and the Defence Minister Ezer

Weizman, and been told that Israel would send instructions to Haddad to release all Irish prisoners, stop his threats and withdraw his men from At-Tiri. During the Secretary-General's emergency briefing of the contributing countries on the serious situation in At-Tiri, the Irish ambassador said that his government had protested strongly to the Israeli mission in New York regarding Haddad's activities and would do so in Jerusalem also. Other contributing countries also assured the Secretary-General of their démarches with Israel in support of his efforts in New York on UNIFIL's stand in At-Tiri. Mr Lewis's efforts were clearly bearing fruit, because at 1822 the six remaining captured Irish soldiers were handed over to us in Bayt Yahun. Meanwhile the other aspects of the confrontation continued unabated.

The next day, 9 April was relatively peaceful for UNIFIL. There were heavy movements in other sectors in South Lebanon, but these were not connected with the At-Tiri confrontation. On the evening of 6 April, some hours after the first hostilities in At-Tiri, PLO fighters had attacked the northern Israeli settlement of Misgav Am and the IDF was reacting to it. The IDF's standing operating procedures demanded massive retaliation for such attacks, and this was the pattern for the whole period that I spent in the mission area. No Israeli government can afford to appear weak in the eyes of its own public and therefore has to react with full force against all such hostile actions directed against Israel and Israelis. For us in UNIFIL it was interesting that the IDF's preoccupation with the raid on Misgav Am and its operational reactions to it eased tension in At-Tiri; the IDF had always claimed to have no influence over DFF activities.

When UNIFIL's confrontation with the DFF started on 6 April, I arranged for an emergency meeting with the IDF Chief of Staff, General Rafael Eitan, in Tel Aviv. One of the points on which I addressed him was the futility, from his point of view, of getting UNIFIL over-preoccupied with hostilities that were being provoked by the DFF, since such confrontations compelled UNIFIL to direct its operational resources southwards, thus obviously preventing it from directing those resources in the appropriate directions, particularly the north and west, to stop infiltration attempts by the PLO and other armed elements. I made General Eitan understand that the ongoing confrontation in At-Tiri was unproductive for Israel, and that Major Haddad and the DFF should be got out of At-Tiri as soon as possible. For this I needed his support and cooperation. I have always felt that if the DFF had not provoked UNIFIL into the At-Tiri confrontation, the Misgav Am tragedy might possibly not have occurred.

The IDF, in hot pursuit of the outrage perpetrators of Misgav Am, moved a large quantity of troops and equipment into South Lebanon,* supplementing the mortars, artillery pieces and tanks already located at the IDF's permanent camps along the 1949 Armistice Demarcation Line. For the Lebanese authorities and for the UN this constituted a serious incursion. Its extent had to be investigated on the ground, and a first-hand report submitted to UN HQ, since the Secretary-General had to report to the Security Council on the IDF presence and activities on Lebanese territory.

It was while my much respected and liked Chief Operations Officer, Colonel Benjamin van Genuchten (the Netherlands), was investigating the extent of the IDF incursion that his Cherokee vehicle ran over a mine about 3 km. north-east of Shaqra. He received a large soft-tissue injury in the thigh and some facial injuries, while his driver was badly shaken and received a few facial bruises. Considering the damage done to the vehicle, which was a total wreck, it was miraculous that the two were not killed outright. Ben was in great pain when I saw him at Norwegian Medical Company just after his heli-evacuation to our base hospital in Naqoura. Brian Urquhart sent a cable expressing his distress and his best wishes for a speedy recovery, and this was consoling and heart-warming for Ben and his driver.

Concurrent with UNIFIL's operational efforts to verify the IDF incursion, UN HQ had also set in motion the peacemaking process to get the IDF to withdraw. The Secretary-General sent a letter to Prime Minister Begin, expressing concern at the grave situation in At-Tiri and the continuing harrassment of UN personnel, both UNIFIL and UNTSO observers. While deploring the PLO attack on Misgav Am, the Secretary-General expressed his deep concern at the Israeli incursion and appealed to the Prime Minister for his government to make efforts to withdraw IDF troops, ease the tension and hostilities in At-Tiri, and cease the harrassment of UN troops. But whatever Begin's reaction may have been, it was not felt on the ground. On 10 April at 1430 sixteen armed men attempted an incursion into the Irish area of operations, and the DFF were confronted and driven back by the Irish and Nigerian elements of the Force Mobile Reserve. An hour later, Major Haddad personally tried to

---

* The exact dispositions were as follows:
In the Irishbatt vicinity: 9 M113s (US-made armoured personnel carriers), about 140 troops, all in the general area of Safal Hawa and Kunin, 3 half-tracks, and 5 heavy troop-carrying vehicles.
In the enclave bordering Ghanbatt: 9 M113s, about 40 troops, 2 M151 jeeps, and 1 bulldozer.
In the Nibatt vicinity: 3 tanks inside Nibatt area of operations at Dier Seriane, 5 tanks at Tallusa in the enclave; 12 M113s, about 200 troops, a fleet of TCVs, 1 ambulance, and 2 bulldozers.

enter At-Tiri village. When he was stopped, this precipitated another serious situation. Tension had started building up again in At-Tiri, with UNIFIL's attention being redirected away from the IDF incursion.

On 11 April, I asked Brigadier Ole Nielsen, my deputy, to visit the troops in the area of confrontation. He was accompanied by the senior political adviser James Holger, the chief press and information officer Timur Göksel and the chief logistics officer Colonel Jean Apied. The team was led by the commander of the Irish battalion, Lt.-Col. Kissane. Unfortunately for the DFF, a *Newsweek* reporter joined the party. The main object of the visit was for the senior headquarters staff to become acquainted at first hand with the situation on the ground, and, no less important, to convey to all ranks deployed in the area the appreciation of the Secretary-General, his staff in New York and UNIFIL HQ itself for their courage and excellent performance. Another most important object was to impress on them the necessity for UNIFIL to continue standing firm. The morale of the troops was reported to be high, as is always the case when operations are going well.

On approaching the immediate area of At-Tiri, the visiting team came under a burst of heavy machine-gun fire from the DFF. Thanks to the *Newsweek* reporter, this incident was widely publicised in the world media — thus helping to win the sympathy and support of the international public for the peacekeepers. The Irish and Senegalese troops returned fire and silenced the DFF, thereby enabling the visit to proceed as planned.

Exchanges of small arms and machine-gun fire continued through most of the day. The DFF went further by inciting women and young children in the area to throw stones at UNIFIL troops and to burn tyres. Ghanbatt had one of its armoured personnel carriers set on fire and burnt out. In the course of the fighting, Private Seveti Sovonaivalu (Fiji) was shot and wounded in the head. He died the following day.

This provoked the Dutch to bring their TOW anti-tank missile into action for the first time since they had relieved the French in March 1979, and as the result a DFF half-track in the At-Tiri area was totally destroyed. We did not know what happened to the troops around it but if there had been any in the immediate vicinity they could hardly have survived. I would not have been surprised if, when the TOW went into action, the DFF troops manning positions around At-Tiri had abandoned their posts and headed with full speed towards Marjayoun, their HQ in the enclave. By 1625 UNIFIL was in full control of At-Tiri. The remaining DFF troops who were slow to move out were rounded up by the Irish and Fijians in their mopping up operations in the village. Later, at an exchange of prisoners, two DFF prisoners and a dead body found there were handed over to Abu Iskander, one of the DFF Lebanese leaders who handled liaison matters for Major Haddad.

All Lebanese who heard of the DFF's defeat on 11 April at the hands of UNIFIL in At-Tiri were jubilant, and for most of the day messages of congratulation poured into our HQ. But we knew all too well that Major Haddad was in no way going to accept what he saw as humiliation, and had no choice but to counter-attack. UNIFIL troops were accordingly regrouped to face it from whichever direction it might come within the area of the continuing confrontation. Additional reinforcements from Senbatt, Ghanbatt and Nibatt were brought in to strengthen the positions of our Force Mobile Reserve in the At-Tiri area and at Bayt Yahun.

At 1800, when the DFF had regrouped, At-Tiri came under intense small arms, heavy machine-gun and tank fire. UNTSO's 'Ras' observation post in the enclave also came under fire. At 1820, the Dutch opened up with their TOW anti-tank missiles against the DFF tanks that were firing on our positions. By 2025, all was reported quiet in and around At-Tiri. Haddad later called UNIFIL HQ for an exchange of prisoners, to which we agreed. We swapped his two DFF men for our five Irish soldiers, who had earlier been captured at their isolated position 6-24 in the enclave. The Irish soldiers at positions 6-25 and 6-26, also in the enclave, had managed to reach Irishbatt HQ, Tibnin, with all their weapons and equipment. However, the worst was yet to come for UNIFIL.

The At-Tiri operations from 6 to 11 April 1980 brought out some important principles relevant to peacekeeping.

First, the determination of UNIFIL to hold on to At-Tiri village amply demonstrates the principle of firmness. Its stand was no doubt facilitated by the fact that the village's importance — both strategically and for ensuring that UNIFIL's credibility did not suffer — was fully understood by Irishbatt and by the contingents constituting the Force Mobile Reserve.

The unswerving support of the Secretary-General, OUSGSPA and UNIFIL's contributing countries was also essential. Only by constant contact between UNIFIL HQ and OUSGSPA could actions undertaken in the theatre of operations and at the superior HQ be coordinated. More important, it ensured that actions on the ground were consonant with those taken by the Secretary-General and OUSGSPA. Any conflict over the conduct of these actions could have undermined the entire operation.

Also, successful coordination of actions is only possible where there is an integrated or unified command. It is hard to imagine that the US-sponsored Multinational Force which operated in Beirut in 1982 could have handled At-Tiri as a unified and integrated operation. The way it was constituted, politically directed and commanded would have made it all but impossible.

The political support given to the Secretary-General by some individual members of the Security Council and by countries contributing troops to UNIFIL underscores the concept that the strength of a peacekeeping mission depends, to some extent, on the support it receives from the member-states of the UN and by contributing countries. Also démarches made by the United States — whose political clout with Israel makes it an important player in the Middle East crisis and a party to the conflict in Lebanon — and by some of the contributing countries complemented the efforts of the Secretary-General and OUSGSPA and were extremely helpful.

Concurrently with UNIFIL's active engagement in its operational tasks in the area of confrontation, the peacemaking process went on at UN HQ in New York. In situations such as we went through in At-Tiri — and there were other instances — such parallel working of the UN peacemaking machinery at HQ proved effective. Its adoption has to be strongly recommended to any peacekeeping sponsors.

Finally, a UN peacekeeping force is able to fight in defence of its mandate and of its troops and equipment whenever that becomes absolutely necessary. When the case is right, the full support of the Secretary-General, the Security Council and the contributing countries can be assured.

The role of Colonel Jack Kissane

The check to the DFF achieved in At-Tiri was a major source of encouragement for both Lebanon and UNIFIL. If the Lebanese army could not face its adversaries in Beirut, UNIFIL could do that for them in At-Tiri in the south of the country. The local Lebanese population felt equally encouraged: at least it was clear that UNIFIL could give them some protection when it became absolutely imperative. As for UNIFIL itself, we felt more united than ever. And finally, the fighting in At-Tiri presented a practical demonstration, as well as a definition, of the use of force in self-defence in UN peacekeeping operations.

UNIFIL was fully prepared to defend At-Tiri principally because the commanding officer, Lt.-Col. Jack Kissane, had earlier sensed the potential danger of that village and the neighbouring ones and had consequently occupied the only dominating ground in the area, Hill

880. Hence, an essential role in procuring UNIFIL's victory — and all the important benefits and lessons that flowed from it — was played by Colonel Kissane. He showed initiative before hostilities broke out, and when they did break out, he acted with great courage. In sum, he was a leader by example. Although, when the fighting was over, I thanked Jack for preparing UNIFIL for the situation and leading us to victory, a better opportunity to pay tribute to him in the presence of his superior authorities presented itself later. In March 1986, when I was winding up to leave the Mission area, I received an invitation to pay an official visit to Ireland, which I accepted with profound pleasure. In June, a month after completing my tour of duty with UNTSO, my wife Rose and I were the guests of Lieutenant-General Tade O'Neill, General Hogan's successor as Chief of Staff of the Irish armed forces, and his wife. General O'Neill, as a colonel, had served in UNIFIL as Military Adviser to General Callaghan, and we had first met then. We stayed in the officers' mess in McKee Barracks, with General O'Neill paying personal attention to us; Commandant Noel Kelly, my former ADC in UNTSO, seizing this opportunity to exercise himself once again in his former capacity; a young subaltern, Lieutenant Una Maher, following in Noel Kelly's footsteps by taking care of Rose; and Commandant Dermot Murphy as the President of the Mess Committee. It was thus not surprising that our visit was as relaxing as it was enlightening. Rose and I loved the Irish scenery, but most of all we felt at home because of the natural warmth of our hosts.

On 20 June General O'Neill was our host at dinner in the mess, and it was moving for me to see so many of my former colleagues and friends from UNTSO and UNIFIL present: Brigadier-General Vini Savino; Colonels Steve Murphy, Jack Kissane, Des Swan, Ned Doyle, Ted Sheehy and Tom Ryan; Lt.-Col. Gerry McMahon and Commandant Harry Smith, my former UNTSO news editor. Also present were former Chiefs of Staff and Ministers of Defence, with whom I had collaborated over a long period: Lieutenant-Generals Carl O'Sullivan, G. O'Sullivan and Louis Hogan, former Chiefs of Staff; Pat Cooney and Jim Tully, former Ministers of Defence; Major-General J.J. Barry, Quartermaster-General; Commodore L. Moloney, Assistant Chief of Staff; Commodore Brett, Naval Flag Officer; and Dr Somers, Secretary at the Department of Defence. They were the cream of the Irish defence organisation.

Here, as already mentioned, was the opportunity to pay a public tribute to Colonel Kissane. In response to the toast proposed by the Chief of Staff, I paid Jack a glowing tribute, saying that without his foresight in occupying Hill 880 and without his courage and steadfastness once fighting had begun, UNIFIL would have lost At-Tiri and, with it, our image and credibility as a UN peacekeeping force. He had exhibited the rare qualities of a good leader by example, and his actions did immense credit to himself, the Irish people and his government. I was extremely proud of Jack and, I concluded, everyone present at the dinner should be also. When I flew out of Dublin a few days later I felt satisfaction at having been able to say these things.

Shelling of Naqoura, 12 April 1980

UNIFIL HQ is located at the coastal entry into the small village of Naqoura which is populated by about 800 Shiite Muslims. It lies on the coastal plain, about 500 metres north of the Armistice Demarcation Line of 1949, and is separated from the Israeli military manned border of Rosh Hanikra by a no-man's-land 3 km. in depth. The premises occupied by UNIFIL HQ used to serve as the Lebanese customs and imigration post for all movements between Israel and Lebanon. From here the coastal road runs north through the port of Tyre, over the Kasmiya bridge to the oil refinery port of Zahrani, and through Sidon, also a port, to Beirut. UNIFIL HQ is bounded to the east – and dominated – by a ridge which runs almost parallel to the Mediterranean. Naqoura village lies immediately east of the HQ, and the Christian village of Alma Achaab is about 3 km. east from Naqoura. It was from the eastern ridge that the DFF fired their mortars, artillery, tanks, heavy machine-guns and small arms at UNIFIL HQ on Saturday, 12 April 1980.

There was a story that former Lebanese President Suleiman Franjieh blamed former Lebanese President-elect Bachir Gemayel for killing his son Tony Franjieh on 13 June 1978 in his northern hometown of Edhen and would not forgive him, even after Bachir was assassinated in a bomb attack at his operational headquarters on 14 September 1982. Suleiman Franjieh allegedly maintained that because it was not he who had killed Bachir, then there had been no revenge. If this was the attitude of the Lebanese élite, then what Major Saad Haddad and his DFF had in mind for UNIFIL HQ on 12 April 1980 should be no surprise to a Lebanese. Haddad and his DFF had been humiliated at At-Tiri and had to wreak his revenge on UNIFIL HQ, where the orders had been issued that led to their defeat the previous day. It was an easy target.

The Naqoura shelling has been described as the most atrocious and inhuman attack on UNIFIL since it was established. There was a similar attack a week later, on the 19th, but it was less vicious. For more than four-and-a-half hours, the HQ and most of the adjacent supporting elements were subjected to continuous and indiscriminate firing. For two-and-a-half hours of that time, UNIFIL HQ itself was hit eighty-five times by artillery, mortar and tank shells.

The firing and shelling were concentrated on the main compound area accommodating the operations room, the communications and administration blocks, the Force Commander's building (my office, bedroom, kitchen and w.c. were badly damaged), the living areas, the mess and OGL offices. However, much else was hit: one need only mention the Contingent guard area, the French engineer platoon area, 'Tara' Camp (accommodating the HQ defence platoon supplied by Ghanbatt and the Irish administrative staff of Camp Command), the Heliwing (comprising the workshop hangar, the landing pads and the Italair offices), and the field hospital. The last-named consisted of the operating theatre, treatment rooms, admission wards, offices, kitchen, dining room and the living blocks of the Norwegian medical company. At 1550 all outgoing telephone lines were cut, and thus telephone contact with UN HQ in New York and UNTSO HQ in Jerusalem was impossible. UNIFIL's telephone link to the outside world was through Haifa in Israel. We could however communicate with both HQs on our HF radio communication system, and additionally with UNTSO HQ on the VHF from the operations room.

At 1600, small arms fire started to impact on the operations room building. Almost immediately the commander of Italair, Major I. Bonvicini, made an attempt to move our four helicopters out to the area of the French engineer company in Hannaniya, but as the crew were preparing to mount them, they came under small arms fire and consequently had to abandon the helicopters on the helipads. Earlier attempt to get clearance from the IDF to fly them out from the heliwing, as part of our standing operating procedures, failed because there were no telephones and Lt.-Col. Gary Gal could not be contacted on the VHF that linked him to Observer Group Lebanon. Whenever an emergency arose from hostile situations between UNIFIL and the DFF, it was the IDF liaison officers' particular standing operating procedure to be absent from their office and out of contact. By the end of the day, all the four helicopters had been hit and were badly damaged. One was a complete write-off and had to be replaced.

UNIFIL fought back fiercely. The Ghanbatt defence platoon and the French logistic battalion in support threw in all they had at their disposal. An attempt to call in the 120mm. mortars from Dutchbatt was abandoned because of the fear that some of the mortar shells might fall wide and kill innocent civilians in Naqoura and Alma Achaab. The firing and shelling, which had begun at 1600, ceased at 2040.

Extensive damage had been done to UNIFIL HQ and to both UN

property and contingent-owned equipment. With the destruction of the helicopters, UNIFIL had lost its medical evacuation capability, and in view of the bad roads in the area, this obviously had serious consequences. Fifteen prefabricated buildings were completely destroyed, and a further ten were damaged — this resulted in twenty officers and men losing all their personal effects. Ten vehicles, including a fire-fighting truck, were destroyed. The HF long-range communication equipment was damaged, and the main despatching board was completely destroyed. Of Italair's spare parts and tools kept in the hangar, 80 per cent were destroyed by mortar shells. The camp's plumbing was damaged, and the entire electrical system was destroyed. Donald Bridge, UNIFIL's chief communication officer, and his team of electricians worked tirelessly throughout the night and most of the following day, a Sunday, to restore power to the HQ. Three concrete buildings were badly hit, and of these, as already mentioned, one contained my own quarters: its ceiling was destroyed, and the entire floor where I lived and worked was flooded when the water-tank was struck by machine-gun fire. My bedroom also received a good number of machine-gun rounds.

With pools of water all over my apartment and only candles to light it, at least for the first few hours, I may have looked miserable, but I was not depressed: a commander cannot afford to give up hope at any time of serious military confrontation. The subordinate commanders, staff and troops will look to their commander for leadership and he must be mentally disposed to give it to them. In fact, the morale of all the officers and men in Naqoura was satisfactory, considering the ordeal. They felt strengthened by this atrocity which they considered as nothing short of attempted murder.

Major Haddad and his DFF had been cowardly to turn their operational attention from At-Tiri, where we had combat troops to face them, to Naqoura where all we had was a small defence platoon for local protection. It was a particular shame that they shelled the heli-wing, because these helicopters had always been used to evacuate local people needing emergency medical help. And it was a shame too that the Norwegian medical company, which had always, day by day, admitted and cared for these local people as well as civilians from the enclave, should have been so contemptuously attacked. Even DFF families had used the Norwegian medical company and continued to use it after this attack for delivery of their babies. I can only express my admiration for our Norwegian doctors, nurses and staff who had to move their patients into shelters where, during the shelling, they continued to perform surgical operations on soldiers who had been wounded in the At-Tiri confrontation.

We took great consolation from the fact that with the one exception of Lt.-Col. A. de la Forge (French), who was slightly wounded in the chin by a sniper bullet, we suffered no other casualty, killed or wounded. God was definitely with us, a belief I always cherished especially at moments when our lives were in extreme danger.

Establishment of a special French UNIFIL HQ defence unit

Even though it was almost impossible to defend UNIFIL HQ militarily, it made good sense politically to have it at Naqoura. As explained earlier, there was no suitable alternative location. But if UNIFIL, for this reason, had to continue operating from Naqoura, then the defence of the HQ needed a review so that what we went through in April 1979 and April 1980 would not be repeated. This we had, thanks to F.T. Liu, one of Brian Urquhart's directors in OUSGSPA.

A few weeks after our disaster, Mr Liu paid us a visit in Naqoura, accompanied by Major-General Timothy Dibuama (Ghana), the Secretary-General's Military Adviser, and George Lansky, the pioneer director of the UN's indispensable Field Service Operations branch. The defence of UNIFIL HQ was naturally Mr Liu's top priority, and in the course of our discussions he suggested the possibility of having a French detachment specially tailored for the purpose. My principal staff and I found the suggestion practical and gave it an immediate welcome. He tasked us to prepare a military paper on it for him to submit to Brian Urquhart for consideration. This was done, in haste but expertly, by the operations staff. When I visited New York in July 1980 for consultations with the Secretary-General and Brian, we had the opportunity to discuss the subject further.

The French defence detachment became operational at UNIFIL HQ in September 1980. We located it on the crest of the high ground immediately east of the French logistic battalion. The presence of this élite combat detachment, perched on the hill and constantly observing the movements of the IDF/DFF, achieved the element of deterrence that we had lacked since our command functions had begun to be exercised from Naqoura in March 1978. Indeed, from September 1980 till the time of writing, there has been no more shelling of UNIFIL.

At-Tiri remained in UNIFIL's hands and the DFF remained in its vicinity. We lost two men, and the DFF must have lost a few as well. After all, in such operations you cannot avoid suffering casualties, and we accepted this in a proper military professional spirit, but for the Arab Christian militia the matter did not end there. One of their armed militiamen aged nineteen years was killed in the fighting.

UNIFIL was accused of his murder, and they vowed to avenge his death. I was a worried force commander — after all, I too am human.

The murder of Privates John Barrett and Derek Smallhorn

As we have already seen, blood revenge is the traditional Arab way of resolving conflicts where deaths have occurred. This was all too evident, not only as between the armed Lebanese factions in Beirut, Tripoli and South Lebanon but also as between them and the PLO throughout the length and breadth of the beleaguered country. Pulling the trigger was the involuntary reaction, a phenomenon that worried the peacemakers and peacekeepers who had come from peaceful countries all over the world. For, say, a Norwegian coming straight from beautiful and orderly Oslo into the ruins of Ebel Es Saqi, this characteristic was as alien as it was confounding. Peaceful conciliation could only begin after blood revenge — or a *sulha* money payment — had been exacted.

On the morning of 18 April, I went to At-Tiri on a command visit to see the troops who had fought so hard for UNIFIL and the UN. In a situation such as we had had in the previous week, a commander should be seen by his officers and men. It is an expression of concern for the troops and of interest in what is going on. Most important, such a visit also identifies the commander with the troops and the unit commander's actions and activities. My deputy, Brigadier Nielsen, with a few senior staff officers had paid a similar visit to the men in At-Tiri a few days earlier. The troops were happy to see me and *vice versa*. I talked to them, thanked them for their selfless and invaluable contribution to world peace efforts, and wished them luck. Their morale was high when I went and higher when I left.

From At-Tiri I went to Irishbatt HQ at Tibnin, and on my arrival there I picked up a 'medevac' (medical evacuation) situation report on my motorola. An Irish soldier had been shot in the stomach at Bent Jbeil by the DFF. I went straight to Irishbatt operations room with the CO, Lt.-Col. Kissane, for a further report on the incident. The reports coming in were ominous. An Irish convoy heading to the 'Ras' observation post to help evacuate the Irish soldiers on duty there had been seized and contact with two of the kidnapped soldiers had been lost. All of us in Tibnin became extremely worried and anxious for the safe return of the two soldiers. I flew to Naqoura and went straight to the Norwegian medical company to visit the wounded soldier flown in earlier. He was on the operating table and I could not see him. My Deputy Force Commander and the senior operations officer had tried to get in touch with the senior Israeli liaison officer, Lt.-Col. Gary Gal, for his assistance in getting our two men back, but as always in such periods of crisis, he was 'not in'. I continued carefully monitoring the situation from my office.

In Naqoura we lived and operated like a family. With no staff-college or other textbook solutions for the sort of operational difficulties that confronted us from day to day, the best solution was to put all heads together to ponder over problems and find solutions to them. Since 1600, some of my principal staff had assembled in my office. Among them were the Deputy Force Commander and the chief logistics officer, Colonel Jean Apied (French), and Colonel Eamon Quigley, Deputy Chief of Staff (Irish). Though in charge of logistics, Colonel Apied was an infantryman and I always respected his view on operational matters. At 1700, I received a telephone call from Gary Gal. My two men were safe and I should despatch an officer immediately to Bayt Yahun, where he would be met by an IDF/DFF escort to bring them back. I was overjoyed and so were the officers with me. I immediately summoned Lt.-Col. Nick Vey (USA), chief of Observer Group Lebanon (to remind the reader: a detachment of UNTSO observers under UNIFIL's operational control). I briefed him, put him on a helicopter, and by 1720 he was off to Tibnin on his way to the rendezvous at Bayt Yahun. I took a glass of cold beer and offered dinner to the staff still in my office.

Nick Vey got to Bayt Yahun but there was no IDF/DFF escort waiting. I called Gal back and he suggested that Vey should proceed to Safal Rawa, where a party was waiting for him. At 1945 Gal called back and said that he regretted to inform me that the two soldiers had been killed. For a moment I went blank and speechless, but I soon recovered. Followed by Nielsen, Apied and Quigley, who were all confused and dumbfounded, I dashed straight to the operations room. I tried to call Mr Weizman, the Defence Minister, but he was not available. I spoke to Major-General Ben Gal, chief of IDF Northern Command, and also called Ambassador Brown, deputy to US Ambassador Sam Lewis in Tel Aviv, to report this outrageous murder. I asked Mr Brown to inform Mr Weizman. In the meantime I had telephoned Brian Urquhart in New York. Finally I called Jack Kissane and advised him to inform Dublin immediately. By 2110, the bodies had been brought to the Norwegian medical company by Observer Group Lebanon, and Colonel Quigley went to see them at the hospital. Thomas Barrett and Derek Smallhorn had been murdered in cold blood.

Dublin Summit, May 1980

The summit meeting of ministers and government representatives from the eleven contributing countries following the murder of Privates Barrett and Smallhorn was unprecedented in UN peace-keeping history, at least in the Middle East. Representatives from Fiji, France, Ghana, Ireland, Italy, Nepal, the Netherlands, Nigeria, Norway, Senegal and Sweden met in Dublin — not at UN HQ in New York under the Secretary-General's chairmanship, as in previous times. The Secretary-General was represented at the meeting by the USG, Brian Urquhart. They had met to express their disgust, abhorrence and outrage at the murder of two defenceless peacekeepers of the international force, and to find ways of strengthening and giving better protection to the force in South Lebanon. The meeting was a psychological show of force and a morale-booster for UNIFIL including its 400 civilian staff. The Lebansese authorities must have been equally strengthened by the Summit, which of course also discussed the Lebanese crisis in its entirety. Israel felt uneasy at the gathering of these contributing countries, some of which were its allies and friends. The DFF had been accused of murder and an unreasonable and unjustifiable act of blood revenge, and there was no way Israel could escape responsibility. Major Haddad may have been taken to task by General Eitan, the Chief of Staff, and General Ben Gal because for a long time after the Dublin Summit, he suffered a loss of influence and this was heavily felt in the enclave. The IDF took direct charge.

What UNIFIL needed to help it fulfill its mission was political support and cooperation from all parties. The Dublin summit made that point. However, it was not enough to change the attitude of Israel towards UNIFIL and Security Council Resolution 425.

10

HUMANITARIAN ACTIVITIES —
WINNING HEARTS AND MINDS

The rendering of humanitarian assistance and services to the indigenous Shiite population of South Lebanon became a part of UNIFIL's function from the beginning, and by the end of the first mandate in September 1978 it had become an activity of major importance. Regrettably, it was an activity little known to the outside world.

South Lebanon, especially south of the Litani river, is the poorest part of the whole country, and it is an area that has been totally ignored by Beirut for many years. Anyone travelling south from Beirut along the coastal road cannot escape noticing the vast disparities in economic and social facilities. From Beirut to Saida, there is everything that goes to make life worth living, but the Zahrani oil refinery near Saida marks the end of civilisation and the beginning of poverty and hardship: this is South Lebanon, home of the majority of Lebanese Shiites. From South Zahrani to Naqoura and from Naqoura to Chebaa in the eastern mountains, there is no evidence of economic life apart from the rearing of sheep, cattle and goats and some tobacco farming.

The 1975 – 6 war and the continued attrition between the PLO and the IDF had exacerbated the already difficult living conditions of the people there. Houses and schools had been destroyed, the continuous air raids had damaged electric cables and the poles supporting them, water pipes had been damaged, and roads destroyed. The scars of war were everywhere, even on the farms where hundreds of thousands of cluster-bomb units ('CBUs') and hand-grenades lay unexploded, preventing farmers from working. The few doctors and skilled workers who could find remunerative work elsewhere had fled in fear for their lives.

When UNIFIL arrived in March 1978, South Lebanon was in a sorry state indeed. The villages were virtually empty, and the only areas with any semblance of life were those under IDF control, which were to become the Christian enclave or Israel's security belt. Some villages, like Khiam, Kaukaba, Ebel Es Saqi, Rshaf and Marhawin, had been completely abandoned. Rshaf in the Irishbatt area of operations had been particularly badly damaged, and Khiam in the Norbatt area had been turned by the IDF into a training ground for 'house-to-house fighting in urban areas'. One of the immediate tasks of the Iranian company detailed from UNDOF and the Swedish company from

UNEF was to assist the remaining families to recover the remains of their dead, buried under the debris of destroyed houses, for reburial with dignity. In this particularly difficult task, the outstanding performance by the Iranians in the villages of Ghandaruya and Bourj Qallawyah will always be remembered by the bereaved families and the other indigenous villagers. Strewn in the public thoroughfares and among the streets, farms and houses were the bloated corpses of goats, cattle, donkeys and horses. The Iranians helped to bury as many as they could to prevent the outbreak of disease.

The arrival of the French combat and logistics battalions marked the beginning of the major rehabilitation programme, involving engineering works. Minefields were cleared, and unexploded artillery and mortar shells were collected and blown up. For a long time, village *mukhtars* and mayors requested our assistance in clearing their farms of cluster-bomb units, hand-grenades and mines. The French engineers worked with the highest professional efficiency, and seemed tireless despite the hazardous conditions. Early on, UNIFIL suffered major casualties from mine accidents: Swedish Master Warrant Officer Karl Oskar Johansson on 29 March, French Master Corporal Alain Godiris on 23 April, and Senegalese Corporal Victor Sina, Sergeant Roussa Fall and Sergeant Bocar Dealle, all on 1 May within twenty-four hours of arriving in UNIFIL's area of operations from Damascus — from which it becomes apparent what difficulties both UNIFIL troops and South Lebanese civilians had to face from mines.

Not only was it an absolute necessity to engage ourselves deeply in these humanitarian services if we ourselves were to survive and discharge our moral obligation to the unfortunate and helpless population, but I also felt that the only way to bring back the hundreds of thousands of South Lebanese who had fled their homes and become refugees in Saida, Beirut and other parts of the country was to make South Lebanon once again a safe place in which to live and work. Furthermore, I felt that getting the villages intensively repopulated might restrain Israel from making indiscriminate air bombardments, and thereby help UNIFIL to maintain peace and quiet, which was the task given us by Security Council Resolution 425. Getting the people back again to their homes and villages was the first step, and once they were back we had to get them to stay there. A feeling of stability was essential if the Lebanese government were to exercise real authority, even in a small way.

The IDF had established a good image in the area of Marjayoun where free medical services were being administered in the enclave to Lebanese who wanted them. If the hearts and minds of the South Lebanese were drawn to Israel, that was in no way going to help UNIFIL's cause and the fulfilment of its mission. It was my ambition to do all we could to turn Lebanese hearts and minds towards Beirut, that is northwards and not southwards. The facts of life in South Lebanon and for the people who lived there had unconsciously added a public relations dimension to UNIFIL's humanitarian services. We had no choice but to intensify our services to beat the IDF's public relations.

Dr Waldheim, the UN Secretary-General, visited Damascus in the middle of 1979, and when I was updating him on UNIFIL's activities and the situation in my area of operations, I emphasised the urgent need to increase the emphasis on humanitarian programmes. We could only bring back life and normality in South Lebanon, having encouraged those who had fled the area to return, if we made available to them medical facilities, work, an environment of peace and quiet and all the basic amenities which go to enhance normal living. This, the poorest part of Lebanon, needed all the help the international community could give it. With the Secretary-General's blessing, the humanitarian activities which UNIFIL was undertaking already were intensified, with the full support and collaboration of the Lebanese government, UNICEF, UNDP, the Red Cross and the Save the Children Fund.

Ever since the beginning of my involvement in Lebanon, I had felt an immense pity for the young boys who had nothing to do except carry around AK47s. I realised that most of them were carrying the guns less because of any enthusiasm for a cause than as a means of livelihood. Hence if we could provide them with alternative sources of livelihood, making them more responsible citizens and giving them something to make life more meaningful to them, they could put their weapons away. I approached the United States ambassador in Beirut, Mr Dean, and he was most enthusiastic and forthcoming. Like the UN, Washington wanted peace and stability in Lebanon. Indeed, perhaps Ambassador Dean needed stability in Lebanon more than we did, for Camp David and the Israel-Egypt peace treaty had to succeed. We agreed that to organise training workshops in some of the villages in areas controlled by UNIFIL was the best answer. Funds were provided, and among the trade skills taught were stonemasonry, carpentry and plumbing — this in a few selected villages including Qana, Marakah, Haris and Kafr Dunin. Ghassan Sayyah, executive director of Lebanese YMCA, was appointed by Ambassador Dean to supervise these trade-training workshops.

The Lebanese government undertook the rehabilitation of roads, water pipes and electric cables and poles. The Council for Reconstruction and Development, presided over by Dr Mohammed Attalah with his office in Baabda, the seat of the Presidency, was the Lebanese government organ charged with this programme. Destroyed water systems, particularly in Ras-el-ain, Ett Taibe and Siddiqine, received much of our attention. Electricité du Liban also contributed to the rehabilitation of broken electric cables and poles and installing booster pumps in Brashit, Shaqra and Markabe. Electrical rehabilitation works in the area of Nabatiya were always dangerous because of the regular shootouts between the PLO positions in that area, particularly Beaufort Castle, and Major Haddad's DFF based in Marjayoun. Whenever work had to be done in Nabatiyya, the DFF would be informed that UNIFIL's working party was in the town: we had little difficulty in securing Haddad's support for this exercise since Marjayoun depended on Nabatiyya for its electricity supply.

UNIFIL provided Lebanese government technicians and workers with transport from Beirut and, once they were on the job sites, with protection and security. And with its own resources UNIFIL provided water and reconstructed school buildings and houses. The Fiji battalion went as far as to assist in rehabilitating the cemetery in Qana, where their HQ was located. The clearing of mines and destruction of unexploded bombs to make farming and normal living conditions possible was undertaken exclusively by the French engineer company: watching them at their work in the heavily mine-infested village of Bourj Qallawayah, I doubted if I could ever have qualified as a sapper. Unavoidably, there were some accidents. As for medical assistance, all battalions ran special clinics for the local population in their respective regimental aid posts. Norway provided the field hospital in Naqoura for serious cases up till September 1980, when Sweden took over.

The following story may appear absurd and unbelievable but it did happen — at Tibnin, which has served as the Irishbatt HQ since it joined UNIFIL in May 1978. When the Irish arrived there in this large commercial town, it was virtually empty, but their presence, like that of all the UNIFIL battalions, served as a strong inducement to inhabitants who had fled to come back to their homes. The Irish opened a clinic in one of the abandoned homes, and a nice one too, to care for the locals. As was mentioned earlier, medical services, like everything else, had broken down following the Israeli invasion. After a year's absence, a private medical doctor who had served the people of Tibnin before the invasion returned to the town, and seriously accused UNIFIL of putting him out of work because Irishbatt had been dispensing medicine to the villagers during the year he had been away. He demanded compensation from Irishbatt for the period that the unit had been looking after his patients. That is Lebanon. Obviously, UNIFIL refused to agree to the doctor's demand for compensation, which even his own people of Tibnin considered ridiculous.

I was proud that we were able to help the South Lebanese to return to their homes and stay in them, and that we gave medical assistance. By our standard operating procedures, helicopters could not fly after sunset because this invariably attracted fire from the few armed elements who had encroached into our area of operations; nonetheless, we flew our helicopters into the area to pick up serious cases, irrespective of how late it was. More serious cases which could not be handled at the Naqoura field hospital were transferred to Rambam hospital in Haifa. Israel has no choice but to maintain an efficient medical system to service her continuing state of war with the neighbouring Arab states, and one could only be profoundly impressed by the professionalism, dedication and cheerfulness with which UNIFIL patients, whether troops or Lebanese civilians, were accepted and looked after by the Israeli doctors, nurses, para-medics and the entire administrative staff. We sent special cases to Tel Hashomer near Tel Aviv, Hadassah Mount Scopus in East Jerusalem and Hadassah Ein Kerem in West Jerusalem. In all these hospitals my men received excellent care, as well as warmth and friendliness. UNTSO observers and the international civilian staff and all their families mainly received their medical care at both Hadassahs. I take this opportunity of paying tribute to the Israeli medical staff, and thanking them for saving the lives of my men and of a small but significant number of Lebanese civilians.

Dutchbatt provided an orphanage in Tibnin from funds donated by philanthropic organisations at home in the Netherlands, and Norbatt, with similar financial support from Norway, rehabilitated roads, houses and public amenities in Rachaya el Foukhar, where the inhabitants were mostly old people. UNIFIL humanitarian support also extended to education. Because of the fighting in Beirut and the resulting difficulty of travelling by road from there to Naqoura, we flew in Ministry of Education supervisors and sealed boxes containing examination papers to facilitate the writing of *baccalauréat* examinations by the South Lebanese, which they did at UNIFIL HQ, under UNIFIL invigilation and with strict security. Organising public examinations in Lebanon is difficult, as the administrative and teaching staff at the American University of Beirut can testify.

I am glad that the international community joined UNIFIL in helping the poor villagers of South Lebanon. And it was a joy to me when subsequent Security Council Resolutions made the provision of humanitarian services UNIFIL's principal task when its mandate was renewed after the Israeli invasion in 1982.

11

THE PAINS OF TRAGEDY

Checkpoint duties became the most difficult of all UNIFIL's operational tasks, principally because of the dangers they involved. They were contained in our standing operating procedures, evolved from the UNIFIL concept of operations as mandated by our terms of reference, which in turn had been determined by the Secretary-General and approved by the Security Council. In all his reports submitted to the Security Council for the extensions of the force's mandate, the Secretary-General noted the dangers that confronted the troops and paid tribute to their courage, selfless dedication and the professional execution of their tasks.

UNIFIL personnel suffered serious casualties from mines, either when they drove or walked over them or when clearing them from the farms. Some casualties came about in the course of combat actions. What caused the deaths of three Senegalese soldiers in Barish could not be determined, and there were the murders of my two Irish soldiers. Some of these deaths were of course particularly difficult to take because of the circumstances. Occasionally, weapons were discharged accidentally, and of course there were deaths from natural causes.

One of the worst days ever experienced by UNIFIL was 3 February 1979, when four officers, a NCO and a private soldier were killed and four private soldiers were wounded. In a declared war such casualties can readily be accepted, but not on a peacekeeping mission. The only consolation was that the six Fijians became casualties while defending UNIFIL's mandate as prescribed by Security Council Resolution 425, and the four Norwegian officers were killed while attempting to evacuate the Fijians by helicopter.

The casualty statistics for UNIFIL operations during the period of my command clearly showed that the Fiji battalions suffered more killed and wounded than any other unit in the force. I attribute this sad situation to two causes. First, the Fijians came to UNIFIL to do business — to execute its standing operating procedures to the letter. There was no compromise. Their steadfastness meant that the PLO could not have easy access with their arms and ammunition into UNIFIL's area of operations. This infuriated the PLO, who had hitherto been the masters of South Lebanon, able to move about freely. The controls and restrictions now imposed on them dented their credibility in the eyes of the local Shiite Lebanese, who had effectively been their subjects up till UNIFIL's arrival. The PLO claimed their right to be in South Lebanon by virtue of the Cairo Agreement of 1969, and would not readily accept any restrictions from foreign troops whom they viewed as forces of occupation. Their power was now suffering at the hands of UNIFIL, notably the Fijians. Secondly, the Fiji area of responsibility covered some of the major infiltration and supply routes for the PLO and other armed elements. Their checkpoint in Al Bazuriyah was one of the most dangerous in UNIFIL's entire area. This factor, coupled with the professional disposition of the Fijians at checkpoints, made armed clashes more frequent than with other battalions. A high casualty rate was thus a natural outcome.

In the early afternoon of 3 February, five armed elements were denied entry at the Fijibatt checkpoint west of Ayn Ebel. There was no shooting then, but approximately at 1550, from a Mercedes car, four or five PLO fighters opened fire at the Fijibatt checkpoint close to the entrance into Qana. Fire was returned by the Fijians and the Lebanese gendarmes. One Fijian soldier was wounded and later died in Naqoura hospital, and a PLO fighter was also killed. A few minutes later Fijibatt HQ in Qana came under rocket and heavy machine-gun fire. This caused no casualties. At about the same time, about thirty-five armed elements surrounded the Fijian checkpoint about 2 km. east of Qana. The Force Mobile Reserve, spearheaded by the French, had by this time reached Qana and was able to contain the situation in and around the Fijians' HQ.

The PLO fighters were spreading out and putting pressure on the Fijians in their entire area of operations. Fighting broke out in the vicinity of Hananiya, Al Bazuriya and Ayn B'al. We were strongly convinced that these PLO activities were deliberate and had been coordinated by their HQ in Tyre. Their plan was to encircle the Fiji area of responsibility and punish the Fijians so that they would submit to their wishes. The PLO wanted free access to the Fijian area for their supplies of arms and ammunition, but Fijibatt would not allow it, and this led to the fighting. Fiji was left with Lance-Corporal Sagar and Private I. Qaranivalu killed and Privates I. Tuidravu, E. Sivua, N. Nabobo and S. Deo wounded. PLO casualties must have been still higher to have provoked them into the even more furious action that followed. It was thanks to Frenchbatt and the Force Mobile Reserve that our casualties were not higher. The Fijians stood their ground, but worse was yet to come.

At 1630, the evacuation of the Fijian casualties was ordered, and at 1645 the helicopter crashed as it attempted to land near Siddiqine. Its rotor blades had hit the overhead electric cables, and the entire rescue team were killed: Major Egil Kjoldaas, the doctor, and Lieutenant

Jostein Berg, a nurse, from the Norwegian medical company, and Second-Lieutenant Per-Frode Eriksen, the pilot, and Lieut. Kjell Edgar Ruud, the mechanic, both from the Norwegian helicopter wing.

With the death of my four Norwegian officers, compounding the already miserable situation caused by the six Fijian dead and wounded, I was profoundly upset. The morale of UNIFIL at that moment was understandably low. This was peacekeeping and not war. I was also worried about the possible political repercussions in Suva and Oslo.

In July, five months later, Norway reduced its participation with UNIFIL by handing over the helicopter wing to Italy. Whether or not this decision was influenced by what happened on 3 February is difficult to tell, but it is important to note that up till July 1979 Norway was fully stretched in its contribution to UNIFIL operations. Its contingent had been the second after the French to arrive, and it had a full combat unit manning our north-eastern sector; it also handled the maintenance company at Tibnin and the field hospital and the heliwing, both at Naqoura. This was an unparalleled contribution for a single country, and I do not believe that by giving up the helicopter services Norway was expressing dissatisfaction with UNIFIL. In September 1980 the field hospital at Naqoura was handed over to Sweden.

The UN Military Observers (UNMOs) suffered fewer serious casualties than UNIFIL troops. The worst UNTSO disaster during my entire seven years in command of the Observers happened suddenly on 25 September 1982 when in a single mine explosion I lost four officers — three majors and a captain. It happened in the only possible place, Greater Beirut.

The biggest single tragedy in UNTSO's annals

My wife Rose and our children always spent the three-month summer school vacation with me in the mission area, and on the morning of 24 September 1982, I saw them off on their journey home at Ben Gurion airport in Tel Aviv. I then immediately headed straight for Beirut. The drive afforded me the opportunity to stop and chat with my UNMOs operating on the Golan Heights and to pay a courtesy call on the UNDOF force commander in Damascus.

I arrived at Beirut in the early evening, and before checking in at my hotel paid a brief visit to Observer Group Beirut (OGB) HQ, which at this time shared accommodation with Lebanese army HQ in Yarze. The following morning, I went there again and received a full briefing from the head of OGB, Lt.-Col. Pierre Letourneur, and his staff. Briefings normally covered the political and military situation in as much detail as possible.

It was my usual practice, whenever I was on visit to Beirut, to get as many of the UNMOs and the civilian staff as possible together for a dinner, and we had one scheduled for that evening of 25 September. At lunchtime, Commandant Paul O'Donnell, my Irish ADC, briefed me on the plans for it. As always, after lunch, if I had time, I took a brief nap, finding it good for my health.

At about 1715, I received a phone call from Lt.-Col. Letourneur informing me that four of our military observers, while on mobile patrol, had hit a mine on the road in the vicinity of Zandukhan, about 10 km. east of Beirut. I could not believe my ears, but it had to be true. I quickly got out of bed, cleaned up and drove straight to Yarze, where the mournful faces of the Lebanese guards by the main entrance confirmed the story. Apparently news of the accident had been relayed to OGB through Lebanese army channels, and furthermore Lebanon Broadcasting had been quick to broadcast the story on the national radio.

As could have been expected, there was pandemonium in OGB. Information on the accident was scanty, UNMOs were not familiar with the area of the accident, and worse still it was getting dark. The immediate task was to recover the four bodies. The general situation of uncertainty prevailing in Lebanon demanded that an officer with special courage should drive to the scene to recover his four colleagues, who were now identified as Commandant Michael Nester (Ireland), Major Randall Carlson (United States), Captain Karl Lasonen (Finland) and Major Harley Warren (United States). That quality, fortunately, was found in Commandant Michael Lynch, of Ireland, who drove at that late hour into hostile and dangerous territory.*

Losing men in peacekeeping is always extremely unpleasant, but losing four in one incident was too much to bear. All of us in UNTSO and UNIFIL were profoundly saddened. Strangely, all the four had their residences in Nahariya, having been posted to OGB from OGL, and thus the UNIFIL personnel knew them well. The Lebanese army commander, General Victor Khoury, and his staff were all very upset.

The following day, 26 September, I felt I should go to Nahariya to see the families and convey my condolences to them personally. This was one of the most difficult tasks I had to face in the ten years of my command. General Callaghan, Force Commander UNIFIL, kindly

---

* Subsequently, on my recommendation made through UN HQ, Commandant Lynch was decorated with one of the highest honours in his own country.

offered to go with me, a gesture I greatly appreciated. He knew how upset I was, and his words to me were extremely comforting.

Talking to Mrs Nester brought tears to my eyes. Only a month before, her husband had been my host at lunch at Khiam observation post, and for the half-hour I was able to spend with her, my mind was on Michael and OP Khiam. In those difficult moments I consoled myself that I had been in Beirut and not sitting at my HQ in Jerusalem when the tragedy happened.

12

SUCCESS OR FAILURE?

The United Nations Organisation has frequently been made the scapegoat for the failings of its member-governments. UNIFIL too has been blamed by various governments, organisations and individuals and by the press for its inability to carry out its mandate, under Security Council Resolution 425 of 19 March 1978, to assist the Lebanese government to extend its authority from Beirut to all parts of South Lebanon. The fulfilment of this task implies the full deployment of UNIFIL to the internationally recognised border (the Armistice Demarcation Line of 1949) to exercise full control of the area. The notion of assisting the Lebanese government further implies bringing the Lebanese army, gendarmerie and civilian administration to exercise their normal governmental functions effectively in South Lebanon. This has always been, and remains, UNIFIL's ultimate objective.

UNIFIL has been assisted since its inception by observers from the UN Truce and Supervision Organisation (UNTSO), which provided seasoned and dedicated commissioned officers from Argentina, Australia, Austria, Belgium, Canada, Chile, Denmark, Finland, France, Ireland, Italy, the Netherlands, New Zealand, Norway, Sweden and the United States. Soviet observers have been excluded from participation in Lebanon, and this has had the understanding of Moscow.

Most often, UNIFIL's critics point to the mission's weakness and ineffectiveness in dealing with hostilities and violations in its area of operations. We have been criticised by both the Israeli authorities and the PLO. The Israelis would have wished to see UNIFIL deal with the PLO in the same way as the IDF would do. General Ben Gal and General Eitan could never forgive us, having apprehended PLO fighters attempting to infiltrate through our lines either into the Christian enclave or into Israel, for then releasing them back to their HQ in Tyre. The PLO prisoners would have been only too glad to stay in our guardrooms and enjoy good food and uninterrupted sleep, away from anti-Israeli guerrilla operational duties.

The IDF could not understand why UNIFIL checkpoints would not allow IDF/DFF patrols to pass through them to clear up locations of the PLO/LNM (Lebanese National Movement), together with villagers who sympathised with them, in UNIFIL's area of operations. Joint patrols with Major Haddad's DFF were suggested many times;

Above: Soon after the establishment of UNIFIL, Senegalese soldiers arrive to take over positions from the withdrawing Israeli forces. *Below*: Refugees returning to their homes in Southern Lebanon after UNIFIL had been set.

Above: Destruction resulting from the Israeli invasion of Southern Lebanon from March 1978. *Below*: The deserted town of Khiam, Southern Lebanon.

Above: UNIFIL troops conducting a routine check for arms and explosives at a checkpoint. *Below*: Dutch troops on patrol in their area of responsibility.

Above: One of the UNTSO observation posts on the Lebanese-Israeli border.
Below: Norwegian medical team bringing a wounded civilian from the UNIFIL area of operations for treatment at the Base Hospital in Naqoura.

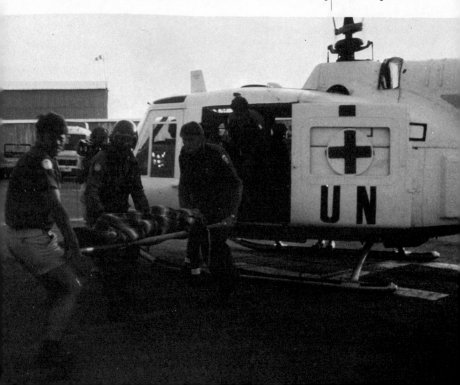

Above: French engineers preparing a position for the construction of shelters for troops. *Below*: Troops' quarters in Naqoura destroyed by shelling from Major Haddad's De Facto Forces, April 1980.

Above: The author as UNIFIL force commander with his deputy Brigadier-General Jean Cuq of France with (*right*) Major-General Ben-Gal, Israel Defence Force commander, Northern Command, and an IDF section commander (*far left*) at the taking over of the Abbassiya sector from the IDF on 14 April 1978. *Below*: Meeting on 28 March 1978 between UN representatives and the PLO. *From left*: Mr Farouk Kadoumi (PLO), the author, Chairman Yasir Arafat, Dr James Jonah (UN Secretary-General's office), Lt.-Col. J. Espinassy of France, chairman of the Israel-Lebanon Mixed Armistice Commission (ILMAC).

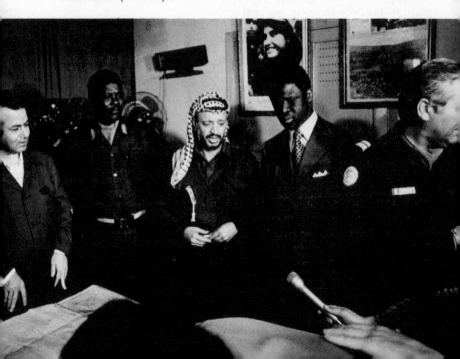

Above: The author, as UNIFIL force commander, inspecting the Nigeria contingent (Nibatt 3) during their medal parade at Nibatt HQ in Tayr Zibua, on 7 September 1979 (on left, the parade commander, Lt.-Col. Tuji Olurin).
Below: The author, as Chief of Staff, UNTSO, at a medal parade for UNTSO military observers, held at an observation post on the Lebanese-Israeli border.

Above: The author's successor as UNIFIL force commander, Lt.-Gen. William Callaghan of Ireland, presents him with a set of crystal glasses. On the right: Mr (later Sir) Brian Urquhart, Under Secretary-General of the UN responsible for peacekeeping operations. *Below*: Troops of the Fiji battalion entertaining their guests with a national dance, following their medal parade.

why could UNIFIL not accept such an offer? The PLO/LNM, on the other hand, felt we were aiding the IDF/DFF by giving them intelligence-related information concerning their dispositions, equipment and activities. They never accepted that UNIFIL's standing operating procedures forbade them to enter our area with arms, and they felt humiliated at being searched at our checkpoints; they saw themselves as the indigenous people of Lebanon and UNIFIL troops as foreign 'occupation forces'.

These negative attitudes led to scores of shooting incidents, which escalated into major hostilities causing fatal casualties. The Fijians, who were deployed along the Tyre Pocket and therefore manned and controlled the major infiltration routes into the area of operations, paid the heaviest price for such PLO/LNM-provoked confrontations. The Fijians had a no-nonsense professional attitude to their duties, which I always admired and respected.

The net result of these attitudes on the part of IDF/DFF and PLO/LNM towards UNIFIL was that each side accused us of cooperating and collaborating with the other side. The PLO accused UNIFIL of siding with the IDF and the DFF; but at the same time the Israeli authorities, the IDF and Israeli citizens criticised UNIFIL for its impotence in dealing with PLO 'terrorists' and their activities against Israel, notably the northern border townships of Nahariya, Kiryat Shemona, Metulla and Misgav Am. In fact, I thought this was a healthy equilibrium because the reverse would have eroded our credibility. Whenever, at a meeting with either the IDF/DFF or the PLO/LNM, an accusation of cooperation and collaboration was made, I refuted it and added that if that were so, UNIFIL soldiers could not have been killed in Lebanon by the IDF, the DFF, the PLO, the LNM and other armed elements. In addition, some senior Lebanese government officials, feudal warlords, community leaders and factional representatives criticised UNIFIL for its impotence in dealing with the IDF and the DFF.

Being a *Lebanese* mission and finding itself in such a complex situation, UNIFIL had no choice but to accommodate most of these criticisms. However, what I fould most difficult to live with were criticisms from prominent and influential Lebanese. The most vocal of such critics was Kamal Assad, the Shiite Speaker of the Chamber of Deputies (parliament). Mr Assad felt that UNIFIL too weak in handling the situation in the south and should be dispensed with. He would have liked to see us driving the IDF and DFF out of Lebanon once and for all. What he failed to realise was that it was due to UNIFIL's activities that Ett Taibe, his home town in the south which he had not seen since the beginning of the civil war in 1975, was now full of life and back to normal. So that he could see what UNIFIL meant to 200,000 of his disowned, impoverised Shiite population in the south, I offered him a helicopter flight from Beirut to Ett Taibe and Naqoura and back with all guarantees for his safety, but he turned the offer down. However, after I had made this gesture, he stopped his criticisms of UNIFIL.

There is little doubt that countries providing troops and observers to serve in Lebanon had their own political perceptions and biases towards the governments and organisations operating in one way or another in Lebanon. Nevertheless, UNIFIL had to operate within the concept of UN peacekeeping principles. There was no way that it could function effectively without being impartial and objective in its dealings with all parties, whatever the political biases of contributing countries might be. UNIFIL had rules and guidelines for all its operational procedures — how to act and react — and no departures from them were entertained by me as the Force Commander. As already mentioned, I found consolation in the fact that both parties accused us of collaborating and cooperating with the other side. This was sufficient proof of our impartiality and objectivity, and I would have been seriously concerned had these accusations been only one-sided. My warning to contingent and battalion commanders to stick exclusively to the Force standard operating procedures and be wary of being extolled by one side was well heeded and paid healthy dividends.

As to the operational functioning of UNIFIL, I feel some satisfaction that the Force concept of operations, evolved at the inception of the mission, has remained unchanged, since I handed over command to General Callaghan in February 1981 and Major-General Gustav Hägglund from Finland took over from him in May 1986. Not only that, but the Force standard operating procedures, developed from the Force concept, continue to be the main guide for the Force Commander, his principal staff and his contingent and unit commanders in the field. This has provided continuity of policy, and in the complex, tense and ever-changing situation in South Lebanon, continuity is an essential factor. My successors could have made any operational change they desired, but this did not happen, not so much because they were unable or reluctant to do so as because there was no need. The factor that has led to the near-perfection in developing the Force concept and standard operating procedures is a major lesson to which I would draw the attention of commanders, at all levels, of any peacekeeping operation.

Commissioned officers of all ranks have to understand and appreciate that every commander has his own personal style of command. It is difficult to determine which particular style is best, but perhaps the quality of command should be judged by the end-product or result. Consultation with my principal staff and field commanders, especially on vital issues affecting the force, has been a style organic to my personality. In my appointments back home — whether as commander of One Signal Regiment as a major, as Director of Operations and Plans and Director of Communications in the Ministry of Defence as a colonel, and as Army Commander as a brigadier — and as Deputy Force Commander and Chief of Staff in UNEF, I have always maintained my style of seeking the views of my principal staff and field unit commanders. As commander, it fell to me to initiate the thoughts and ideas which I invariably threw to the staff to work on. It is amazing what a commander can get from his staff and subordinate commanders if they know that the commander respects their ideas and comments.

In my experience with UNIFIL, I realised that the final product of a policy embodied only about 30 − 40 per cent of my inputs. The remaining 60 − 70 per cent was contributed by the staff and subordinate commanders. Hence with every major policy governing UNIFIL operations, many different brains had been cracked to produce the outcome, and it is difficult, if not impossible, to reverse procedures which are the outcome of so much free and unrestrained discussion. One important and interesting policy which provoked constant and baffled criticism from the Israelis and from some of my working colleagues and battalion commanders who arrived later in the mission area of operation was the practice of UNIFIL HQ of returning weapons captured from the PLO and other armed elements, at a specified time. They found the policy repugnant. Unfortunately, no critic has yet been able to offer any viable and practical alternative, hence the practice has continued.

There are no staff-college solutions to most problems a commander will face, in peacekeeping as in other roles, where the use of force is liable to be a political factor. The solutions will come from the mission commander, the principal staff and the contingent and unit commanders. Collectivity in policy development through consultations promotes continuity. A Force Commander should try and develop professional mutual trust, respect and acceptability with his commanders and staff, for without it he will definitely have a difficult and perhaps unsuccessful command.

As UN peacekeepers, all of us had to be friendly and fair but firm not only with the civilian population in the area of operations but also with the opposing groups among whom we operated. Our actions and activities should be aimed primarily at executing our mandate, defending the UN flag and serving the interests of the civilian population. Since these objectives often conflicted with the interests and aspirations of the opposing parties, it was inevitable that UNIFIL and Observer Group Lebanon in the honest execution of their day-to-day functions and activities would get into trouble with one party or the other – as we did.

UNIFIL's difficulties started from, the day – 19 March 1978 – in the Security Council when Resolution 425 was passed. This was underscored by the Secretary-General, Dr Kurt Waldheim, in his annual report for 1979 on the work of the Organisation. The extreme complexity of the Lebanese situation, with its political instability and uncertainty and the proliferation of uncontrolled private armies and weapons, has compounded UNIFIL's difficulties. The same difficulties that have confronted UNIFIL in its operations in South Lebanon also haunted the IDF in Greater Beirut and the Chouf and Aley mountains, and continued to haunt them after they were redeployed to the line of the Awali river in September 1983. They also confronted the US Marines, French paratroopers, and Italian and British troops of the Multinational Force in Beirut. For as long as the Lebanese crisis lasts, no peacekeeping force mounted in Lebanon, no matter how heavily armed, can escape them.

Because the problems of South Lebanon are offshoots of the entire Lebanese crisis, they cannot be resolved in isolation from the problems facing Beirut and the entire country. Thus to expect UN peacekeeping activities to resolve the entire crisis in the south is quite unrealistic and unfair to the Organisation. The day-to-day difficulties in Greater Beirut and Tripoli have their adverse repercussions in the south, and *vice versa*. For this reason I have always exhorted government officials, diplomats, parliamentarians and Chiefs of Defence Staff of contributing countries visiting their troops in UNIFIL to be more understanding, patient and sympathetic with UNIFIL, whose performance, in the environment in which it operates, is excellent.

This view was expressed by General Yitzhak Rabin before his appointment as Israeli's Minister of Defence. In an interview with the *Jerusalem Post*, published on 5 September 1983, he said: 'I have changed my mind about the value of UNIFIL after witnessing the ineffectiveness of the Multinational Force. It was my experience in Beirut that whenever they see an armed civilian, they call in the Lebanese army, not daring to disarm these men. At least, UNIFIL has tried to disarm such men.' We were therefore surprised that Rabin's perception of UNIFIL took an about-turn when he became Defence Minister a year later. Perhaps that is the reality of politics.

I fully understand the need for UNIFIL to deploy right up to the Armistice Demarcation Line of 1949 to fulfil Security Council Resolution 425, but for the time being pressure on the parties to the conflict should be focussed on the need for their political cooperation and support to facilitate UNIFIL's operational functioning. Too much pressure on UNIFIL to move to the border while it is obviously unable to do so gravely exposes the mission's major weakness which is inherent in the instruments of its establishment. This situation further frustrates the Security Council, the Secretary-General and his secretariat, and the command in the field. Politics is all well and good, but politicians must accept practical realities on the ground. I feel that the pressure Washington, Moscow and other members of the organisation direct at UNIFIL should rather be directed at helping Baabda (the presidential palace), Serail (the Prime Minister's office) and Yarze (army HQ) in Beirut to find a permanent, just and lasting solution to the Lebanese crisis. Israel's periodic criticism of UNIFIL as being unable to control the area should be seen in the light of its strategic objectives. Israel has no choice but to control the Christian enclave as its security belt. If it were to commend UNIFIL for performing well, then of course there could be no justification for the IDF's continued presence on Lebanese sovereign soil.

Again, in the armed and hostile environment that exists in South Lebanon, clashes of one kind and another are bound to occur between UNIFIL and the IDF/DFF. These often create ill-feeling among contributing countries, thereby having a negative effect on the bilateral relations between Israel and those countries. The IDF's harassment of Irish troops created difficulties for the official visit of the Israeli President, Chaim Herzog, to Ireland in mid-1985, and the kidnapping of twenty-one Finnish soldiers in late 1985 generated anger in Finland and a reaction from the Finnish government. Yet it was Finland, in the 1984 session of the UN General Assembly, which initiated a compromise formula that saved Israel from being subjected to the Credentials Committee: this was being sought by those whose ultimate aim was to have Israel expelled from the world body. Some Arab countries have always sought ways and means of achieving this end, due to the Palestine issue. The real possibility of Israel's relations with the Netherlands being affected in the same way as relations with Ireland because of IDF/DFF clashes with Dutchbatt was the principal reason why Brigadier-General Leveran, chief IDF liaison officer, raised objections to Dutchbatt being deployed in March 1979 in the area where they were to share borders with the DFF. There are strong Dutch-Israeli ties, rooted in the Dutch having saved the lives of thousands of Jews during the Second World War. It is noteworthy that after Israel's bitter experiences of peacekeeping in the Chouf mountains, its criticism of UNIFIL became considerably toned down. In one of my regular meetings with General Moshe Levy when his troops were in the Chouf, he showed a full understanding of what I was saying, and to a question he replied 'General, we are still learning.'

I have always nursed the impression that Syria would prefer Israel's presence in Lebanon in order to keep the Golan quiet, because it cannot afford to open up two military fronts against Israel; and that the two countries would prefer to mess themselves up in Lebanon rather than on their own territory. Since the October 1973 war, all confrontations between them have taken place in Lebanon; for example, the air battle of 1982, in which Syria lost almost a quarter of its air-power and presumably the same percentage of its best aircrew, was fought in Lebanese air-space. Even with the serious provocation of Israel's virtual annexation of the Golan in December 1981, Syria preferred to raise the issue at the Security Council and later at the General Assembly rather than move a single tank on to the Golan. The Israelis, on the other hand, were quick to bomb the Osira nuclear plant in Baghdad on 7 June 1981, and have bombed PLO bases in Tunisia, rather than interfere with Syria's SAM 5s, the presence of which has provoked more rhetoric than physical action.

To summarise, the problem of South Lebanon cannot be resolved permanently in isolation from the problems of the whole of Lebanon; to think otherwise is unrealistic. The operational difficulties that UNIFIL has faced are indeed a by-product of the main political problems facing Lebanon, but they are also inherent in the Security Council instruments setting up the Force. UNIFIL's humanitarian activities, on the other hand, are also in fulfilment of Security Council Resolution 425. Its presence and its international representation are the principal re-assurance for the 200,000 South Lebanese, and its functioning in all aspects should be motivated and encouraged to continue.

Peacekeeping missions do not by themselves resolve problems, but they help to reduce tension and stabilise their area of operation, thereby providing an environment conducive to a satisfactory resolution through governmental, diplomatic and political machinery. UNIFIL should therefore be encouraged to function more effectively, and more serious efforts should be made through this machinery to assist the government in Beirut to resolve the national crisis. The peacemaking efforts made by the UN Secretariat have been persistent and painstaking. Most of the time, these efforts have been fraught with serious hazards, which partly explains the high esteem in which Brian Urquhart was held by the respective authorities in Lebanon, Syria, Egypt, Jordan and Israel, as well as by all of us who worked with him in his capacity as the Secretary-General's envoy for peacemaking activities in the Middle East.

UNIFIL may not have been able to fulfill Secco Res 425, but it has helped to stabilise the south to a large extent. Its area of responsibility is the safest and most stable in all Lebanon, and has provided a safe haven for inhabitants of Beirut, Sidon, Tyre and neighbouring villages when those places have been the scene of serious fighting.

Above all, UNIFIL's presence has meant employment and better standards of living for the forgotten, ignored Shiites of South Lebanon.

Not many countries outside the region cared seriously about Lebanon before UNIFIL was established in 1978, providing an international presence made up of countries from all parts of the world. Contributing governments that send their men into South Lebanon involuntarily become more interested in what is going on not merely in the south but throughout the country, and more sympathetic towards its problems. Most government dignitaries visiting UNIFIL stopped in Beirut for formal discussions with the President, the Prime Minister, the army commander and other government officials on the country's situation. Such visitors would also stop in Israel to talk with civilian and military officials there not only about Lebanon but about the whole region. Thus UNIFIL's presence has been an incalculable asset in promoting peacemaking efforts in the region. This factor is often ignored.

Striking a balance

In order to assess the success or failure of a UN peacekeeping mission, one has to grasp the fundamental principle, mentioned above, that such a mission is designed basically to create the environment that is conducive to the peacemaking process. The point is that peacekeeping missions are not designed to solve the problems; they are not ends in themselves, but means to an end. In this context, some of the peacekeeping missions of recent times offer illustrations.

The UN Emergency Force 2 (UNEF 2), for example, did not solve the problems between Egypt and Israel in Sinai. Rather, it created a peaceful environment which enabled the two countries, with US support, to negotiate and sign a peace treaty following the Camp David Accord in 1979. It is indisputable that UNEF 2 was highly successful.

The UN Force in Cyprus (UNFICYP) has been able to maintain a peaceful situation in Cyprus, thereby permitting the Greek and Turkish Cypriot community leaders to continue their negotiations aimed at resolving the island's problems. The UN Secretary-General has a Special Representative residing in Cyprus who assists the community leaders in their talks. Many hopes for significant progress were pinned on the promixity talks held at UN headquarters in 1984 under the direct patronage of Secretary-General Perez de Cuellar, but these talks unfortunately fell through. One cannot condemn UNFICYP as a failure merely because the mission has been in operation since 1964 and the Cyprus problem still persists. Because UNFICYP has been able to exercise its primary function of keeping Cyprus peaceful and thereby allowing the Greek and Turkish Cypriots to continue their intercommunal talks, I would rate it a success.

Using the same criteria, I would again assess UN Disengagement Force (UNDOF), which separates Syrian troops from the IDF on the Golan Heights, as highly successful even though the Golan problem still remains. UNDOF's presence was sufficiently reassuring for President Hafez el Assad not to attempt a confrontation with the IDF when Israel virtually annexed the Golan Heights in December 1981. UNDOF has been in operation since June 1974, keeping the areas of separation and limitation of Syrian and Israeli forces on the Heights peaceful and quiet, presumably until the time when Syria and Israel, which view eachother as arch-enemies, can sit together and negotiate a solution to the Golan Heights issue.

UNIFIL, on the other hand, has been seen as a failure, for three principal reasons: its inability to deploy to the border, the continuing hostilities in South Lebanon, and the fact that it was unable to stop the Israeli invasion of 1982. I disagree with this assessment.

It is true that UNIFIL has not succeeded in completely fulfilling its mandate by not being able to extend to the 1949 Armistice Demarcation Line, i.e. the Israeli-Lebanese border. However, the inability to execute this important aspect of its mandate can be traced back to the instruments for setting up the Force. As has been argued above, if there had been an effort to have an agreement between the PLO and Israel, this problem would have been forestalled.

In determining whether, among its tasks, UNIFIL has been able to maintain peace and quiet in its area of responsibility, the situation of South Lebanon has to be seen within the context of the general situation in the entire country. Looking at UNIFIL and the south in isolation from that general situation gives an erroneous impression not only of UNIFIL's achievements but also of the high price it has had to pay for them. UNIFIL's area of operations, compared with other parts of Lebanon, is the safest place in the country to live. This is best appreciated when one considers the large number of refugees who flock into the area from Tyre, Sidon and Beirut when fighting breaks out in those cities. UNIFIL's presence has meant that some 200,000 indigenous people in South Lebanon can gain a livelihood; without it, I doubt if they could survive there as they do today. The Israelis, on the basis of alleged provocation by the PLO and other resistance fighters, will not permit them to live in peace. The situation in South Lebanon may not be all that peaceful, but it would be worse without UNIFIL. Perhaps the success or failure of UNIFIL can best be judged by imagining the disbandment of the force — the IDF would in all probability move in to stay, and the near-normality that exists today would vanish. So while Security Council Resolution 425 has not been fully implemented and UNIFIL cannot claim to have succeeded in that objective, yet its effective humanitarian services in keeping the 200,000 Lebanese in the area alive, and its operational activities in making its area of responsibility one of the few safe havens in Lebanon, have meant that it has not failed either.

The criticism that UNIFIL has been a failure because it could not stop the Israeli invasion of Lebanon in 1982 is misplaced, and reflects a misunderstanding of the prime objectives and capabilities of a UN peacekeeping mission. We have dealt with the objectives in some detail elsewhere, and will therefore concentrate here on the issue of a peacekeeping mission's capabilities.

On several occasions since UNIFIL's operations began in March 1978, the IDF/DFF have attempted encroachments and incursions, both minor and major, into UNIFIL's area of operations. All these attempts have been resisted, with force when necessary. For example, both the IDF and the DFF have shown an obsession over the village of Yater, which they accuse of sheltering Palestinian 'terrorists'. Many attempts were made to attack the village, but these were always resisted by Dutchbatt in whose area of responsibility it was located. The DFF succeeded in establishing a position in the vicinity of Blate after serious confrontation with Norbatt late in 1980. In the course of that confrontation, which took place in the presence of IDF personnel, Colonel Ole Roenning, Norbatt's commanding officer, was physically assaulted by personnel of the DFF. This is part of our humiliation in keeping the peace in Lebanon.

Force does not have to be used to resolve the issue in every case of confrontation. Chapter 13, 'The Use of Force in Self Defence', tells how UNIFIL was able on 9 May 1979 to stop a major attempted incursion by the IDF into its area of operation without firing a single shot. On the other hand, in the At-Tiri confrontation UNIFIL had to fight a mini-war to stop encroachment into its area by the DFF.

Resistance by UNIFIL has not been restricted to stopping incursions and encroachments by the IDF/DFF. Most of its casualties suffered at the hands of armed elements have been precipitated by actions against infiltration attempts by the PLO and other armed elements. Checkpoint duties are aimed principally at checking the movements of arms, ammunition and armed personnel into the area of operation, and it is in the execution of these tasks that UNIFIL has suffered most of its fatal casualties.

UNIFIL has also offered passive resistance in several instances to prevent the IDF from destroying property owned by the local indigenous Lebanese population. The Israeli authorities perceive the bulldozing of houses as a severe exemplary punishment to be meted out to the West Bank Palestinians and Gazans who have been considered as inimical to the security interests of the state of Israel. Consequently this harsh punishment was introduced into South Lebanon when they invaded the country in 1982. The IDF, assisted by their collaborators the General Security Service (GSS) personnel, blew up several homes owned by the local Shiite Lebanese as part of a 'scorched-earth' policy after the withdrawal of the IDF from the Awali river in 1985. However, UNIFIL troops were able to save several other houses from destruction by perching themselves on their roofs.

In all attempts at incursion, encroachment and infiltration, UNIFIL troops were able to react for the following practical reasons. First — in the case of the IDF/DFF — unusual movements of personnel, vehicles and equipment in the vicinity of a particular unit's area of operations gave the impression of possible hostile activity by them, and — according to the Force's standing operating procedures — called for an increased 'Alert' in that area. Hence, a unit with its eyes and ears well open could almost always organise itself to offer resistance to an IDF/DFF incursion. Secondly, for a good reason, the IDF mostly tried to obtain the support of the particular unit into whose area it was planning an incursion. This, of course, was good enough information for the unit to prepare to resist. Thirdly, information concerning DFF plans and intentions trickled in from the locals living in the area; DFF personnel had their families and friends living there and some of them, especially those bound by family ties, were more sympathetic to the UN cause than to the aspirations of the IDF whose cause the DFF partly served. This was because UNIFIL's humanitarian services to the local Lebanese had won the hearts and minds of the people. As for the armed elements, it was less difficult to detect their intentions since they always moved in small numbers and most often had to use UNIFIL checkpoints where they were confronted — hence the relatively high UNIFIL casualties resulting from checkpoint duties.

Thus it is clear that in situations where UNIFIL has had good enough information as an early warning, it has been able to react swiftly and effectively in defence of the mission's mandate.

Operations 'Litani 2' and 'Peace for Galilee'

In my estimation, Israel's intention to invade Lebanon again in 1982 was present as early as the few months following the March 1978 invasion. At one of my first meetings in June 1978 with the officer commanding Israel Northern Command, Major-General Ben Gal, at his headquarters in Nazareth, he was already talking of 'Operation Litani 2' ('Litani' was the code-name for the March 1978 invasion). By expressing this intention so soon after the IDF's final withdrawal on 13 June 1978, he gave me to understand that Israel would go back into Lebanon when it had a pretext. Hence operation 'Peace for Galilee' (the code-name for the June 1982 invasion) was not much of a surprise to me, except that it came four years later than anticipated.

Then an incident in September 1980 fully convinced me of Israel's determination to go back into Lebanon. On 10 September 1980, I was in my office in Naqoura when the Commander of Dutchbatt, Lt.-Col. J.M. Steenaert, came to see me. He said that he had been summoned the previous day by Lt.-Col. Gary Gal, the IDF liaison officer, to his office in Metulla, Israel, to discuss an 'urgent and important matter'. For the IDF to summon UNIFIL personnel direct without passing such requests through our HQ was an infringement of our standing operating procedures, and I was particularly sensitive to our commanding officers and senior staff officers being called in this way, for obvious reasons. Colonel Steenaert had been with Colonel Gal for barely twenty minutes when General Rafael Eitan, IDF Chief of Staff, and General Ben Gal entered the room. This could hardly have been a coincidence, and sure enough it was not. It had all been planned and possibly rehearsed.

General Eitan took charge of the meeting and spoke at length of the PLO 'terrorists' and their build-up in UNIFIL's area of operations, and the need for Israel to react to safeguard the security of its northern townships. He asked Colonel Steenaert what his battalion would do if the IDF decided to invade Lebanon, using his battalion area as one of the main axes of its advance; he added that the IDF wanted to avoid the shedding of Dutch blood if possible. It happened that Dutchbatt was deployed in the south-west of the UNIFIL area, and an IDF invasion of South Lebanon would definitely have as one of its objectives the destruction of Rashadiya refugee camp, the strongest PLO base in the area of Tyre. The quickest approach to attack the camp would be through Dutchbatt's area of operations.

As to why the IDF considered it necessary to seek the possible Dutchbatt reaction, we have already alluded to Israel's especially friendly relations with the Netherlands since the Second World War; thus Israel might have felt concerned about negative political reactions from The Hague if the planned attack resulted in casualties among the Dutch troops. The Israeli authorities had been unhappy for this same reason when the Dutch replaced the French in March 1979. Secondly, I believe that the IDF wanted to test UNIFIL's reaction to its intention to exploit the UNIFIL area of operations for a massive movement into Lebanon. General Eitan obviously knew that as commanding officer of a UN peacekeeping force, Colonel Steenaert's loyalty was first to the UN and not to any party to the conflict and that he would not keep such an informal meeting to himself. I thanked Colonel Steenaert, and immediately summoned my Senior Political Adviser, James Holger, to discuss the issue, which of course we viewed as very serious. James and I agreed that Brian Urquhart should be immediately informed. The question was how the information could be conveyed in secret and thus without provoking serious alarm not only in Lebanon but also among the international community. We agreed that James should fly immediately to UN HQ to discuss the issue personally with Brian and the Secretary-General. I then called Brian on the telephone and requested his authority for James to proceed to New York immediately. He was curious and wanted to know my reason for such a request, but I declined to discuss it on the telephone. He 'got the message' and gave his full approval for James's journey.

Naturally the Secretary-General, Kurt Waldheim, and Brian viewed the IDF's intention, as expressed by General Eitan, with the utmost concern, and the peacemaking process had to be put in motion immediately. The Israeli government was cautioned against any infringement on Lebanese sovereign territory, and Washington was requested to assist the Secretary-General's démarches to restrain Israel from carrying out its plans. Since no attack was launched, one can safely assume that the peacemaking process launched by the Secretary-General and Brian Urquhart was successful and that James Holger must have handled the issue expertly in his meetings with them.

So UNIFIL did its bit by preventing 'Operation Litani 2', threatened by General Ben Gal in June 1978 and General Eitan in September 1980. Or did it merely postpone the invasion for two years? The important lesson for us from this episode was that when there is sufficient information concerning a threatened attack, incursion or other hostile activity by a party to the conflict which could destabilise the area, UNIFIL can always react to it, either directly from its own resources in the field or indirectly through the Secretary-General and OUSGSPA. Whenever the conditions for peacekeeping or peacemaking are right, and the parties to the conflict are supportive and cooperative in helping to defuse the tension, UN efforts in the field are always fruitful. This was so in 1980, but unfortunately the launching of 'Operation Peace for Galilee' on 6 June 1982 caught General Callaghan (then Force Commander of UNIFIL), his field commanders and his senior staff completely off balance. It was a major surprise attack, and the military planners in Tel Aviv probably used this vital principle of war to minimise casualties to their own troops and

UNIFIL and to catch the PLO *in situ*. Sadat had applied the same surprise element against them in the October 1973 war in Sinai and they were only repeating it in Lebanon.

General Callaghan was in fact called to the HQ of the IDF Northern Command at Nazareth on the morning of the Israeli invasion, but only to be presented with a *fait accompli*. General Eitan and his OC Northern Command, General Driori, told him that the IDF were already on the move through UNIFIL's area of operations. It was from Driori's office that he was able to call his HQ to inform his Deputy and the operations staff of what was happening. UNIFIL was gravely embarrassed: without an effective leader — through no fault of General Callaghan — it had to end up badly in this Israeli invasion. The environment was not conducive to effective peacekeeping. Yet how much could UNIFIL have done, even if General Callaghan had been in Naqoura at the start of the invasion? One of the three main IDF axes of advance was the coast road with its entry into UNIFIL's area of operations through a checkpoint manned by a Dutchbatt detachment of about a section strength (eight men). The heaviest weapon this detachment had in support was an armoured personnel carrier with a .50mm. calibre gun: what could it do to stop an invading armoured column of Merkava (Israeli-made) tanks? The best weapon for fighting a tank is another tank, and this UNIFIL does not have, being equipped according to its mandate with light defensive weapons only. Like all other UN peacekeeping missions, it is not designed to withstand a major military assault such as that of June 1982.

The best the Dutchbatt detachment could have done, if it had had enough warning, would have been to create artificial obstacles to its approaches on the coast road. However, such obstacles would have been less effective since the IDF's Merkava tanks could have easily tracked through the orange orchards. This was what the IDF actually did when it had to fan out for its assault on Rashadiya Camp, the major target on its western front. However, the Norwegian battalion, deployed in UNIFIL's north-eastern sector, was able to block the IDF's movement on its north-eastern axis with road blocks carved out of heavy rocks; these rocks had been prepared and were in position for activation to create obstacles by cutting ropes that automatically released them to roll into position. The terrain in the north-eastern sector is rocky, with deep gorges and valleys, and this made the obstacles prepared by Norbatt very effective. The IDF had no choice but to abandon its originally planned axis and determine another route for its advance. The Dutchbatt position on the coast road was less fortunate in terms of terrain. This concept of road-blocking had been instituted by Colonel Zacharias A. Backer,* who served as CO Norbatt from March to September 1979, and was endorsed and strengthened by Colonel Ole Roenning* during his year of command of Norbatt from then till September 1980.

Perhaps UNIFIL could have offered a little more resistance, taken some casualties and made a few more 'martyrs', thus consoling some critics who have accused it of doing nothing to stop the IDF. Whether such casualties, in a show of force designed for political convenience, are justifiable is a highly debatable issue. What difference would a few more martyrs have made to UNIFIL's credibility in the eyes of its traditional critics? Did those critics raise a finger in April 1980 when UNIFIL did show its teeth and defeated Haddad and his Israeli-supported DFF forces in At-Tiri in defence of Secco Res 425? Even though UNIFIL has its operational limitations, as was made clear on 6 June 1982, it has managed on the whole to keep the IDF and DFF reasonably well separated from the PLO and other armed elements, thereby reducing the constant danger of major confrontation between the parties in conflict and thus creating an atmosphere conducive to peacemaking.

UNIFIL can only be as effective and strong as the parties want it to be. No peacekeeping mission can function effectively without the political support and cooperation necessary to enable it to carry out its mandate. Israel, as the most powerful country in the area both militarily and politically, with the help of Washington, does not support UNIFIL, and the Lebanese government has not been in any position to influence this unfavourable situation. UNIFIL is a Lebanese mission, but Lebanon is not a direct party to the conflict. Worse still, it has not been able to influence the activities of the PLO, which has tried to establish its own state within Lebanon. Had there been agreement involving Lebanon, Israel and the PLO for its functioning, it is conceivable that UNIFIL might have been strong enough to execute its mandate and handle certain day-to-day hostile actions by the parties more effectively. But, operating exclusively on Secco Res 425, which has never been respected by either the IDF or the PLO, UNIFIL has been made incapable of fully executing its mandate and terms of reference as set out in that Resolution. The Secretary-General's remarks on this in his 1979 report on the work of the UN fully support this contention. UNIFIL thus has to draw its strength from the member-nations of the UN, from the countries contributing to its operations, from the Security Council, and from all peace-loving

* Colonel Roenning returned to the Middle East in 1982 to serve as the first Chief Operations Officer of the US-sponsored peacekeeping mission, the Multinational Force and Observers (MFO), established in Sinai to monitor the Egypt-Israel peace treaty. Colonel Backer returned to UNIFIL in 1985 to serve as its Chief Operations Officer.

countries of the world community. It needs the support of countries which wish Lebanon well and are in the position to influence both Israel and the PLO to cooperate with UNIFIL and assist its peace-keeping functions. In this the eleven countries which have contributed their 6,000 officers and men have an important role to play.

Finally, like everybody and everything in this world, UNIFIL is not perfect. But we should remember that nowhere can there be a security system which is totally foolproof. If a would-be assassin could manage to wound President Reagan, and if a bomb could partly destroy the hotel in which the British Prime Minister Margaret Thatcher was staying, then we should acknowledge UNIFIL's imperfection with some pride. Despite its inability to perform in such a way as to satisfy the IDF, or to stablise the area and satisfy the Lebanese, or to keep the Israelis out of the south and satisfy the PLO — or to deploy to the Armistice Demarcation Line in fulfilment of its mandate, I cannot see any viable alternative to UNIFIL's continuing presence, at least for the time being.

The award of the 1988 Nobel Peace Prize to the United Nations for its peacekeeping efforts around the world was fitting tribute. UNIFIL surely contributes to those efforts.

13

THE USE OF FORCE IN SELF-DEFENCE

Self-defence within the context of UN peacekeeping operations has always been a difficult, sensitive and sometimes rather confusing issue, all the more so in an area like South Lebanon where lightly-armed UNIFIL troops constantly find themselves in confrontation with the heavy-armed IDF, DFF, PLO and other armed elements. By the terms of its mandate, a UN peacekeeping force is provided with weapons of a defensive character, and it may not use force except in self-defence. The latter would include resistance to attempts by force to prevent it from discharging its duties under the mandate of the Security Council.

UNIFIL operates in a semi-war zone. The IDF are armed with tanks, half-tracks, armoured personnel carriers, heavy mortars and artillery pieces. So are their surrogates, the DFF. In support of their ground troops, the IDF operates its combat aircraft — Phantoms, Kfirs and the US-made 'F' series — whenever it chooses to do so. Daily air reconnaissance over Lebanon is an IDF standing operating procedure. The PLO and other resistance fighting elements are also equipped with heavy offensive weapons. Standing between the two opposing groups is UNIFIL, whose heaviest weapons are 120mm. mortars. The Security Council only agreed to equip UNIFIL with armoured personnel carriers when the Secretary-General was able to convince the fifteen Security Council members that they were necessary for defensive actions and to protect the troops from small-arms fire and landmines. I was delighted that the Dutch, on replacing the French in March 1979, came in with their TOW anti-tank guns, which were good for UNIFIL's morale, and proved their worth in the At-Tiri confrontation in April 1980.

As commander of a peacekeeping force operating in an arms-infested territory full of nervous, untrained, trigger-happy little boys, I was reasonably sensitive to casualties. Heavy casualties were acceptable to the armed elements since blood did not mean much to some of them. It was my strong and unshakable feeling that contributing countries would be prepared to accommodate a few casualties in the cause of UNIFIL troops defending its mandate, themselves and UN/contingent property, but that casualties suffered outside this spectrum of operational activities could provoke national political difficulties and serve as a catalyst for the collapse of the mission. There

114

was no way contributing countries would be prepared to receive sealed coffins from Naqoura at their respective international airports on a daily basis. That would be a negative and disheartening standing operating procedure.

The possibility of continuous armed confrontations with the armed elements was a real threat to us. Checkpoint duties exposed the troops to hostilities most of the time since the use of force to discharge those duties effectively was frequent. The incidents in Fijibatt's area of operations between 21 and 24 August 1979 illustrate the practical interpretation and application of the use of force in self-defence by UNIFIL.

Incidents in the Fijibatt area of operations, 21 – 24 August 1979

Checkpoint 1-17 was at the western entrance of the village of Qana, Fijibatt HQ, on the main road leading from the Tyre Pocket. Its main task was to check and monitor all the considerable volume of traffic proceeding from the Tyre Pocket area towards Qana. It was manned by a section (8 – 10 men) from the Fijibatt defence platoon assisted by a Lebanese gendarme. Members of the Lebanese army section were also posted on the roof of the nearby Qana school, which gave them a clear view of the checkpoint. The purpose of deploying Lebanese army personnel and gendarmes was to promote an effective Lebanese government presence in the area, and thus fulfill UNIFIL's mandate.

In the early afternoon of 21 August 1979, a civilian vehicle approached the Qana checkpoint. It was stopped in the normal way and the driver was invited to get out to enable the customary check to be made. The driver objected to the search, but nonetheless the vehicle was searched. Nothing was found and the man was allowed to drive on, but before departing he threatened retaliation. He had possibly felt humiliated to have thus submitted to orders from foreigners.

Approximately twenty minutes later, intense automatic fire was directed at the checkpoint by a group of men from a position about 200 metres away. The Fijian sentry at the checkpoint immediately returned fire. The exchange lasted approximately three minutes. Meanwhile, Fijibatt reinforcements were being deployed, but they did not take part in the engagement because it ceased just before they arrived on the scene.

Indications were that the armed elements, who were about a section in strength, were members of the Popular Front for the Liberation of Palestine (PFLP), a splinter group of the PLO and under the command of Georges Habash, from the village of Al Kuraybah on the outskirts of Qana. Unconfirmed reports indicated that one of the armed elements was wounded in the exchange of fire. There were no injuries to Fijibatt or attached Lebanese personnel.

PFLP hostilities continue

At 0730 on 21 August, seven armed elements (AEs) approached the same checkpoint from the direction of the Tyre Pocket, and were stopped by the Fijibatt soldiers manning it and asked to allow their vehicle to be searched. It was a UNIFIL standing operating procedure that occupants of any vehicle should get out of the vehicle before search was undertaken. Five of the AEs alighted but two refused. A Fijian sentry noticed that one of the men in the vehicle had a pistol; he was ordered to surrender it but refused.

The five men who had alighted objected to the weapon being surrendered and attempted to overpower the Fijibatt soldiers at the checkpoint. One of them tried to snatch a general purpose machine-gun from a Fijian soldier, but was overcome by the supporting Fijian sentry. The struggle continued. The AE with the pistol suddenly ran forward to snatch a rifle from one of the Fijian sentries, and there was a struggle between those two. The AE was not able to seize the rifle, and then drew his pistol, cocked it and aimed it at the sentry with the apparent intention of firing. The sentry, in self-defence, fired at the AE with two rifle rounds, seriously wounding him in the chest and jaw. The other six were overpowered and detained at the checkpoint. The wounded man was evacuated to Tyre hospital. Some time later, a PLO liaison officer arrived on the scene, and after brief negotiation the six detained AEs were released into his custody.

We learned later that the wounded man had died. He was identified as Major Ibrahim al Kheisham, aged thirty and a senior commander of the Organisation of Communist Action of Lebanon (OCAL), a faction of the Lebanese National Movement (LNM). Retaliation was to be expected, but when?

At approximately 0935 the following morning, after news had got about that the commander had died, information was received at Fijibatt HQ that the AEs were preparing to attack the checkpoint from a wooded area approximately 200 metres away. Fijibatt operations staff were aware of this development, and the officer commanding 'C' Company was ordered to take command of the two platoons at the checkpoint, which had been reinforced. Concurrently, Dutch and Senegalese armoured detachments of the Force Mobile Reserve were mobilised as reinforcement and deployed into the area of confrontation.

At 1025, the AEs began firing at the checkpoint. Fire was returned and a fire-fight developed outside the checkpoint perimeter. The Dutch and Senegalese armoured vehicles opened up with their heavy machine-guns in support of the Fijibatt detachment. The firing ceased ten minutes later, but began again at 1115 and continued until it finally ended at 1155. While the number of AE casualties could not be ascertained, local information indicated that at least four of the attackers had been killed and many others seriously wounded. There were no injuries to UNIFIL troops.

At 1110, while 'C' Company were still under pressure at checkpoint 1-21, about seven AEs were sighted by the battalion HQ observation post moving around on the eastern flank of 'B' Company's checkpoint 1-16. Soon afterwards, another observation post reported sighting a further fifteen to twenty AEs moving towards the checkpoint from Dayr Amis; this is in the so-called 'Iron Triangle', a heavily fortified AE base within UNIFIL's area of operations and from which some of the attacks on UNIFIL troops had originated. Evidently an attack on the observation post was imminent, and Dutchbatt armoured personnel carriers were mobilised as a reinforcement for 'B' Company. About fifteen minutes later, the checkpoint came under semi-automatic rifle fire. Fire was returned and the exchange lasted till 1152. At 1230, three Dutch carriers arrived at battalion HQ. One was deployed with the troops who were securing the high ground in the vicinity of the reservoir behind the HQ; the aim was to deny the salient to AEs approaching from Jabal Al Kabir area and generally prevent attacks on the HQ from its flanks and the rear. The two other carriers were despatched to reinforce checkpoint 1-16.

At 1245, as the carriers were approaching the checkpoint, intensive rocket-propelled grenade and small arms fire was directed at both the checkpoint and the carriers. Fijibatt machine-guns at battalion HQ immediately engaged the AEs so that Dutchbatt could dismount, deploy and support the checkpoint personnel. On being fired upon and having suffered four casualties, seven AEs on a slope on the western side of the checkpoint scattered in confusion. They were totally vulnerable at this stage and Fijibatt machine-gun fire was directed to force them to withdraw. This was successful. But now — apparently because of their lack of success from other directions — the AEs changed their tactics and concentrated on attacking from the north on the Wadi Jilu side of the checkpoint, no doubt aware that machine-gun fire from battalion HQ could not affect them on this axis of advance. The AEs continued intensive firing with grenades and small arms at the checkpoint and at Dutchbatt troops in carriers who by this time had deployed about 200 metres northwest of the checkpoint. The AEs made repeated attempts to capture the checkpoint, but were unable to do so despite their heavy losses — it is believed that ten of their men were killed.

The UNIFIL troops also had casualties. A message was received at UNIFIL HQ at 1330 hours that three Dutchbatt soldiers, including the carrier troop commander, had been wounded, two of them seriously. An armoured ambulance evacuating the wounded was fired on twice by the AEs with grenades, but fortunately they missed. A possible grenade-launching site was strafed by Fijibatt machine-gun fire, and stopped the further firing on the ambulance. The wounded were evacuated to Qana where they were transferred to a helicopter for evacuation to the Norwegian medical company hospital in Naqoura. In the continuing fire after the medical evacuation, another solder was wounded in the thigh.

At 1420, a message was received at Fijibatt HQ from the AEs saying that they wanted to negotiate a ceasefire. This was agreed, and at 1440 the firing stopped. Shortly afterwards two AEs approached the checkpoint from the Dayr Amis side. As they entered the area, one of them suddenly drew a pistol and levelled it at the head of the checkpoint commander, Second-Lieutenant Jekoiono, who had gone forward to meet them. This took the officer and his men completely by surprise as they had accepted the offer to negotiate in good faith. There was a confrontation but no shots were fired. The PLO liaison officer in Tyre was summoned to intervene, and by 1735 all was reported quiet in the area.

The casualties suffered by the AEs were high compared to those suffered by UNIFIL, who had four men injured, two seriously. The indications were that some fifteen AEs were killed and many more wounded in what was considered the most serious clash involving UNIFIL up to that date. Considering the AEs' heavy casualties and the Arab tendency to seek vengeance, it could reasonably be assumed that they would retaliate. This they did two days later with the ambush at Wadi Jilu.

Ambush of Fijibatt motorised party near Al Bazuriah, 24 August 1979

The ambush mounted by armed elements against Fijibatt troops on 24 August 1979, which resulted in the deaths of three Fijian soldiers and the wounding of two others, was ostensibly an act of retaliation for the killing by Fijian soldiers of a prominent AE officer, reputed to be the leader of the 'Lebanese Communist Action Party' in South Lebanon. However, if considered in the light of other incidents in the period immediately before the fatal ambush, it could be construed as the final act of retribution mounted by AEs to salvage their pride and reassert their credibility in the eyes of the local population and their sympathisers in the south. Fijibatt, having been responsible for the AEs' reversals on 16 July at Raqlihy, on 21 August at Qana and on 22 August at Al Bazuriah and Ruaysaf Al Ayn, automatically became the prime target for their revenge.

At about 1630, two Fijibatt vehicles returning from Al Bazuriah were ambushed by a group of gunmen in concealed positions along a line of pine trees. Privates Seru and Tulega and Driver Nadomo were killed, Private Nabalarua was seriously wounded, and Private Raoaujau received cuts and scratches after being flung into the road when the jeep in which he was travelling collided with the leading jeep. It appeared that the group was fired on from both front and rear. Probably Driver Nadomo, who was driving the second jeep, was shot at first from the rear and died instantly from a massive head wound, causing the vehicle to go out of control and collide with the front jeep which had stopped because of the firing.

From evidence gathered at the scene, it appeared that four gunmen had fired forty-eight rounds from AK47s, and that they had been in position for about six hours before the attack, allowing other Fijibat vehicles to pass along the same route unscathed. Of the ambushed soldiers who survived, Private Nabalarua entered the drain to his left and was protected by a concrete wall beside it, but was helpless because of serious wounds he had received. Private Driti and Corporal Vulaono also went into the drain for protection, and escaped to a nearby shop for assistance. When Driver Apirato regained consciousness after his fall from the jeep, he too went to the shop. He tried to wave down passing cars to get help, but none would stop. He later went back and helped Private Nabalarua out of the drain. Shortly after the ambush, Second-Lieutenant E. Sandys of Fijibatt arrived with his platoon and the area was secured. The dead and injured were evacuated by road to Qana and airlifted by UN helicopters to Naqoura.

Fijibatt, of course, was operating within UNIFIL standing operating procedures and thus in defence of Security Council Resolution 425. All the action it took came within the scope of self-defence.

Another episode, in the Irishbatt area of operations, further illustrates UNIFIL's practical application of the use of force for defence. It was on 9 May 1979, when Lt.-Col. Vincent Savino, commanding officer of 44th Irish Battalion, was departing on the completion of his six months' tour of duty. Thus it was a 'rotation day', a time when units are thin on the ground and relatively weak. The IDF decided to invade the Irishbatt area with a full battalion, ostensibly looking for two terrorists, who had allegedly raided the Israeli village of Ramin the previous night. The IDF's mission was to punish the men on the spot — and one can easily imagine how this would have been done.

At about 0840 on 9 May, two IDF platoons and two armoured personnel carriers entered the village of Shaqra. UNTSO's 'Mar' observation post had earlier seen IDF troops moving into Lebanon through border pillar 33, about 2 km. north of the village of Ramin. The initial strength of the Israeli group was soon increased to about one company.

At 0910, the Irish battalion moved two platoons and two carriers to reinforce its unit at Shaqra. The IDF immediately increased its force to two companies, reinforced later by about twenty tanks, thirty-seven jeeps, eight carriers and three half-tracks. One company was deployed at Shaqra village and another was poised outside the village. Subsequently, most of the IDF force was located between Shaqra and Houle to the east.

On learning of the incursion, UNIFIL's observation posts lodged a strong protest with the Israeli authorities. Then, at 0933, UNIFIL HQ received a message from the IDF liaison officer at Tiberias to the effect that the Israeli force would not open fire unless the Irish battalion fired at it.

A Force Mobile Reserve composed of detachments from the Dutch, Nigerian and Senegalese battalions was mobilised, put under the command of the Irish battalion and ordered to proceed to Irishbatt HQ at Tibnin. Later it was redeployed into Brashit. This was in fact the beginning of the formation of UNIFIL's Force Mobile Reserve.

At 1012 hours, the DFF appeared on the scene. Major Haddad, accompanied by two senior IDF officers, arrived at 'C' Company HQ for talks with the Irishbatt commander. During the negotiations that followed, the IDF officers proposed that their soldiers should search some houses which the Israelis suspected were occupied by AEs. The IDF would withdraw its troops after the search. About an hour and a half later, the IDF task force under Brigadier-General Amos Baram, then deputy commander of Northern Command, wanted to know if the commander of UNIFIL had agreed to the proposed search arrangements. I emphatically refused to allow IDF soldiers to search the houses within our area of responsibility. In the event, two houses were searched by soldiers of Irishbatt, and nothing was found. The IDF did not take part in the search, but they remained only about 100 metres away from the houses. A request by the IDF to have a third house searched was refused.

Brigadier Baram's task force then moved to the Irish company in Shaqra and demanded permission for access through the company area. The company commander refused. Baram demanded to speak to me on the VHF radio and was allowed to do so. He requested to see me in Shaqra, which I refused. The appropriate person for such a meeting was my chief operations officer, the Dutch Colonel T. Tjassens. Tall and imposing, he was just the right man for the dimunitive Brigadier Baram. I gave him a full briefing and delegated authority to him to negotiate with Baram. Under no circumstances would the IDF be permitted to use our area for their battalion-size force chasing 'two terrorists'. It all sounded ridiculous, but that was the uncomfortable situation UNIFIL had to face to keep the peace in South Lebanon.

Colonel Tjassens stood firm. At one stage, in the presence of Baram, he called me on the VHF to brief me on the situation, a good move psychologically. I replied in a loud tone to make clear that we meant business and so that the IDF task force commander would hear me clearly. Brigadier Baram must have got irritated, because he asked to speak to me on the radio, to which Colonel Tjassens agreed. He threatened to use force, and I gave him the unambiguous warning that we would resist with force if he did so, and that if UNIFIL sustained any serious casualties the Israeli government would be held fully and exclusively responsible. On instructions from General Ben Gal, his own commander, Baram turned his task force about and headed towards Marjayoun, and that was the end of the affair. A show of force, depending on how one plays it, can be an effective means of self-defence.

The At-Tiri confrontation, recounted earlier, and these two episodes should help to clarify the use of force in self-defence. Commanders of ONUC (Congo) and UNFICYP (Cyprus) would be able to cite similar episodes to show that UN troops can initiate and use force under certain conditions and in certain situations. The erroneous idea that UN troops are forbidden to use force is widespread among the general public.

The only serious constraint we had in UNIFIL was the use of our only heavy offensive weapon, the 120mm. mortar, an area weapon which can cause damage on impact within a radius of 350 metres. Since the DFF, the PLO and other AEs operated from locations densely inhabited by Lebanese civilians including old men, women and children, and it was probable that our mortars would kill more of these civilians than AEs, UNIFIL just could not use them. The world press would have excitedly flashed the news of UN troops killing innocent children in South Lebanon. UNIFIL might also have been branded as being in cahoots with the IDF/DFF, which would have been damaging indeed. Being a Lebanese mission whose prime objective was for the restoration of Lebanese authority in the area, we could not afford to take any action that could have a detrimental result for the interests and concerns of Beirut.

14

THE UNITED NATIONS AS A PEACEKEEPER COMPARED WITH THE MULTINATIONAL FORCE AND THE ORGANISATION OF AFRICAN UNITY

Critics have always looked at UNIFIL in the same perspective as UNEF 2 and UNDOF. This is especially true of the Israelis, who are involved in both areas and whose criterion for assessment is understandably limited to their experiences in Sinai and the Golan. It is also true of the world press in its criticisms of UNIFIL's inability to fulfil Secco Res 425 in contrast to the successes of UN operations in Sinai and on the Golan.

Some of the world powers sitting in the Security Council did not appear to understand the complexity of the situation in Lebanon, and therefore could not fully appreciate UNIFIL's difficulties and operational limitations, especially in the earliest phases of the mission. This is strongly suggested by the Security Council's lack of consensus to support the Secretary-General's recommendations for the six-month extensions of the first and second mandates. France, for example, could not see why UNIFIL was still in operation six months after being mandated to stabilise the ground and help restore Lebanese authority in the south. Ambassador Bishara of Kuwait was unhappy with the Secretary-General's recommendation for UNIFIL's operating strength to be increased from 4,000 to 6,000; he had asked me informally why I needed 2,000 additional troops and whether this was aimed at fighting the PLO.

The Multinational Force (MNF)

Initially I thought it unfortunate that the Multinational Force (MNF), consisting of the United States, Britain, France and Italy, and not a UN-sponsored entity, should have supervised the PLO's evacuation from Beirut in August 1982. But sitting at UNTSO HQ in Jerusalem, and observing the MNF's activities and operations, I had second thoughts: it struck me that it was good for the United States and Britain to have a more intimate contact with the situation on the ground in Lebanon, because these experiences might increase their sympathy and political support for UNIFIL and the UNTSO observers, and encourage them to help us counter criticism from the world press and the Israelis.

The situation in Lebanon is complex, fluid and extremely tense, and the atmosphere of unpredictability and uncertainty this creates has a serious effect on peacekeeping activities. Widely experienced commanders at all levels were exposed to dangers of a different kind from those experienced by peacekeepers in Sinai and the Golan. Nonetheless, the peculiar difficulties experienced by UNIFIL were shared by the MNF — only the tactics employed by the two forces were different.

I have always wondered why it was necessary for the MNF to go through the same bitter experiences and difficulties as UNIFIL, at all levels of command, had suffered in Lebanon for four-and-a-half years before the MNF came to Beirut. Had the MNF authorities talked a little more with UN HQ in New York, and had there been better practical cooperation between MNF commanders and some of us UN commanders then operating in the area, might not the tragic car-bomb attacks which took over 300 American and French lives in 1983 have been avoided?

The US Defense Secretary Caspar Weinberger gave an interview on 22 January 1983 in which he protested to his Israeli counterpart at the firing at close range by IDF troops on the US Marines operating in Greater Beirut. The IDF frequently attempted to pass through the US Marines' checkpoints, to be met by US resistance. One such attempt provoked a US Marine officer, in challenging the IDF, to pull out his pistol and threaten to shoot if the IDF insisted on passing through. (The US officer was commended for his courage and style, but while I concede that he was courageous, I had reservations about his style.) Such incidents — firing at close range and attempts at infiltration and encroachment — punctuated our peacekeeping activities in Lebanon, and UNIFIL was thoroughly used to them. Asked whether the Israelis had responded to US protests, Weinberger is reported to have said 'I would hope they will very shortly', but the IDF never did. UNIFIL was used to the IDF not responding to our protests.

Major-General Amir Driori, the officer commanding the IDF Northern Command, accused the MNF of shielding the PLO and of being unable to prevent its fighters in early 1983 from ambushing the IDF in Khalde close to the MNF area of operations, and firing Katyushas 40 metres from the Beach Hotel where the troop withdrawal negotiations between Israel and Lebanon were being held. Similar accusations had been levelled against UNIFIL by everyone holding a gun in Lebanon.

Some of the frustrating experiences to which the IDF had subjected successive UNIFIL commanders now became the lot of the IDF itself. General Driori's first few attempts to meet the US Marine commander (a colonel) failed to materialise — the US commander had good reasons for turning down the General's repeated requests for a meeting. I just sat back at my HQ and giggled. General Ben Gal had done it to me, Driori had done it to General Callaghan, and now they were at the receiving end. Hence the great lesson of peacekeeping in Lebanon: i.e. who needs whom. We needed the IDF for its support and cooperation in Lebanon, and now the IDF needed the MNF for the same reasons.

There are some major observations to be made concerning the MNF operations. First, the withdrawal of MNF 1 immediately after the successful evacuation of the PLO in August 1982 was a mistake. This principle of withdrawal runs contrary to UN practice. After the IDF's withdrawals on 11, 14 and 30 April and 13 June 1978, UNIFIL remained *in situ* with its operations. If the MNF had remained in its areas of operations until effective arrangements had been made for the vacuum created by its withdrawal to be properly filled, it is possible that the September 1982 Sabra and Chatila massacres would never have happened. UNFICYP, UNDOF and UNEF are likely to continue their operations until the time comes when their withdrawal will not have a negative affect on the *status quo*.

The lack of a unified or integrated command in the MNF resulted in uncoordinated operational actions by individual contingents. No military operations can be successful if there is not an overall commander. The glaring absence of a force commander in the MNF and the corresponding absence of a force standing operating procedure resulted in each contingent responding to enemy fire according to the political wishes emanating from Rome, London, Paris or Washington. Thus the troops on the ground were in a situation of grave danger. Peacekeeping missions should be commanded on the ground by the military and not by politicians and ambassadors, as was done with the MNF.

Peacekeeping missions should not have to be involved in the internal political affairs of their host-countries. The MNF inadvertently became involved in the Lebanese conflict by taking up arms in support of the Lebanese army, which is perceived by the Muslims as a Christian army and not a national one. Consequently it became part of the Lebanese problem and lost its impartiality; thus the only option it was left with was what it actually did in February 1984, namely to return home. I have since wondered whether the MNF ever fully understood the basic ingredients of the Lebanese crisis. It is easy to see the big issues, but sometimes it pays to understand the small ones as well, as UNIFIL continues to do.

The way the MNF used fire in self-defence contrasted sharply with the UN's application of fire. Under no circumstances would the Security Council authorise the Secretary-General to introduce 16-inch guns such as those fired by the US battleship *New Jersey*, combat aircraft such as the F-14 Tomcats, or heavy artillery and mortars, into its peacekeeping orbit. The use of these heavy weapons had the unfortunate effect of provoking the armed groups in Lebanon and consequently drawing the MNF into the reprisal game. The Lebanese crisis is basically political, and only political approaches can solve it. Hence, if the Israelis and the Syrians have been unable to solve it through the barrel of the gun over a period of more than a decade, how could the MNF have done so in a few months? Peacekeeping troops should retain the right to defend their mandate, themselves and their equipment, but the commander must always bear in mind at the same time that excessive use of fire is a double-edged weapon. In a country like Lebanon, where there is already a proliferation of weapons, an influx of further weapons is unhelpful.

The way in which the MNF withdrew undermined the credibility of its mission. On 7 February 1984, the British Prime Minister Margaret Thatcher called a series of emergency Cabinet meetings, attended by the Defence Secretary Michael Heseltine, the Foreign Secretary Sir Geoffrey Howe and the Minister of State at the Foreign Office, Richard Luce. An aide of the Prime Minister announced that the status of the British contingent in the MNF was being discussed but not its unilateral withdrawal. Sir Geoffrey Howe said in a radio interview that if the moment did arrive when the government judged that British troops could no longer play a useful part, then their presence had to be discontinued. The US Marines withdrew into their ships the following day, 8 February, and the French and British almost immediately followed suit. Such a withdrawal has no parallel in UN peacekeeping annals.

But apparently on instructions from Rome, the Italian withdrawal was coordinated partly with UNTSO's outstation in Beirut, Observer Group Beirut (OGB). A few days beforehand, the Italian ambassador in Lebanon, Signor Olivieri, requested to see me in Beirut. We met at the OGB premises in Hazmieh, and he told me that he had instructions to ensure that their pull-out from the Sabra and Chatila refugee camps did not create a vacuum, and that his government's wish was that we should take over. The Italians had operated in the refugee camps as their part in the MNF operations, and undertaken humanitarian activities there, especially by providing medical services for the Palestinian refugees. Rome was thus eager to ensure that their withdrawal should not deprive the refugees of these services.

OGB already maintained a regular presence in the camps as a

standing operating procedure. Military observer teams conducted both mobile and foot patrols, talking to the refugees and giving sweets and cookies to the children. This friendliness and showing of the UN flag had endeared the UN observers to the inhabitants of the camps. Taking over from the outgoing Italians was not much of a problem, except that OGB did not have the logistics to perform the required humanitarian services. Fortunately, the UN Relief and Works Agency (UNRWA), whose mandate is to cater for the refugees, was readily available to resume its former humanitarian tasks. OGB, however, made itself available to help the UNRWA staff. This support was important, given the hostile and unpredictable situation in the area of Greater Beirut at that time. Signor Olivieri suggested that we had a second meeting, which I readily accepted, agreeing also to the presence of the Italian MNF commander, Brigadier-General Angioni. The three of us discussed the issue at length. We then formed a small committee under the chairmanship of my Chief OGB, Lt.-Col. Fourrier, with UNRWA and Italian MNF representatives as members, to work out the *modus operandi* in some detail. This was done to the full satisfaction of Signor Olivieri, Brigadier Angioni, myself and OGB, thus permitting the Italian MNF to depart from Beirut leaving behind peace in the camps, at least for a short time.

Apart from any other considerations, I am sure that Rome was all too conscious of the Sabra and Chatila massacres in September 1982 and did not want history to repeat itself. This is the kind of coordination or contact between the MNF and the UN on the ground, dealing with practical realities, that I strongly advocate. At least, we should evolve ways of shunting politics and facing realities pragmatically so that we may save a few human lives. If the US Special Envoy Philip Habib was prepared to let me know his thoughts on the Israeli invasion of Lebanon, and the US consulate in Jerusalem also found it convenient to discuss with me pertinent matters relating to the establishment of the Multinational Force and Observers (MFO), then I consider it would have been possible for the MNF to talk to us, if only on account of the practical experience of which we in UNTSO and UNIFIL had a great deal.

The peacekeeping potential of the Organisation of African Unity

As a peacemaker and peacekeeper, and as an African, I have always wished and hoped that the OAU would develop and successfully promote a peacekeeping mission to contain disputes, conflicts and tensions requiring such intervention in some of our African countries.

I therefore followed the OAU peacekeeping approach to the Chad situation with particular interest and enthusiasm.

My experience from mounting UNIFIL from its very inception in March 1978, participating in UNEF in Sinai in 1974 – 5 and contributing to the setting up of UNDOF on the Golan in June 1974 has left me in no doubt that effective logistical and administrative support is the single most important determinant of success or failure for any peacekeeping force in the field. The crucial problem for a peacekeeping force is not so much the positioning of its troops in the field as how best to sustain them in the field. Good initial planning is necessary, and material resources have to be available. I will highlight these essential requirements.

Logistical and administrative support embraces various elements — feeding, accommodation, medical services, transportation by both ground and air, engineering, communications, repairs and maintenance. A single country cannot possibly handle all of them. The OAU Secretariat could approach each OAU member-country and negotiate with it which of these essential elements it would agree to support. That country would then become exclusively responsible for ensuring the availability and readiness of its particular section of logistics, which could then be mobilised at reasonably short notice to support a peacekeeping mission immediately the OAU had decided to mount it. In UNEF (1973 – 9) logistical support was provided jointly by Canada and Poland, which provide the same services in UNDOF. In UNIFIL, transportation and supplies have been provided by France and Sweden, repairs and maintenance by Norway, medical services first by Norway and later by Sweden, engineering jointly by France (later Sweden) and Ghana, communications by the contributing countries and the UN, and finally helicopter transportation by Italy. With negotiation and willing acceptance by member-states, this could be done.

Joint military and civilian administrative support. The OAU not only requires a military and civilian administrative division to support the troops in the field once operations have begun. There is also an urgent need for such a wing to engage in contingency planning long before troops are placed in the field. This would necessitate the presence of a small military and civilian wing as a permanent section of the OAU Secretariat in Addis Ababa. Such a military and civilian supporting staff could have undertaken various important tasks before and during the 1982 Chad operations.

First, the political decision taken by the Summit to send troops to Chad could have been translated into a military operation, and this would have facilitated the work of the force commander. That this was not possible was a serious deficiency, for which I feel that the OAU Secretariat was unfair, in all respects, to the Nigerian force commander. Secondly, the OAU would have been advised to establish well in advance what overall support was required to support the troops once they were in their operational disposition; what each contributing contingent was expected to bring as nationally-owned equipment/resources; what each contingent could afford to provide, and hence what the OAU had to provide as first-line support for the contingent; and what were the availability of market resources locally. And thirdly, secondly-, third- and fourth-line support for the force and mission needed to be prepared. If such a joint military and civilian administrative wing, no matter how small, existed as a permanent division of the OAU Secretariat, its task when there is no mission in operation would be to look ahead, plan and advise the Secretariat — in other words, contingency planning. When a mission is in operation, the wing would monitor its needs and demands and ensure that they can be satisfied.

The *financing of a peacekeeping mission* is a considerable burden, because peacekeeping is, quite simply, very expensive. However, it is much less expensive than war and all the destruction of both human and material resources that it causes. If there is the political will to decide on a mission and have troops moved into an area of hostilities, the financial support has to be available to sustain them and the operation. Hearing the BBC news on the Chad operations, I had the impression that the financing was made the responsibility of the countries providing contingents, and I hope that this impression was wrong. Since it was a decision of the OAU, the finances should have been borne by all OAU member-states; the organisation would be discouraging potential participants if the financial burden were to be limited to them only. On the other hand it would be encouraging the peaceful resolution of disputes if the cost of *failure* were to be shared out among all member-states. A joint military and civilian administrative support division and a review of the financing of peacekeeping missions are not new ideas. These are systems practised by the UN, and have been proved to be effective and efficient. Thus there is every reason for the OAU to adopt them if it expects its peacekeeping missions to be more successful in the future. Truly, it has no choice in the matter.

One cardinal principle which the OAU should observe is that peacekeeping missions should not under any circumstances get themselves involved in the local internal disputes of the host-country. If this should happen, the mission would be taking sides, and thus lose its status of objectivity and impartiality. The experience of the MNF in Beirut provides that vital lesson here.

ORGANISATION OF AFRICAN UNITY:
PROPOSED ORGANISATION OF PERMANENT MILITARY AND
CIVILIAN SUPPORT DIVISION

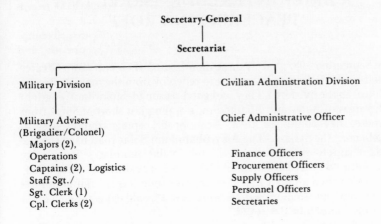

Secretary-General

Secretariat

Military Division

Military Adviser
(Brigadier/Colonel)
  Majors (2),
  Operations
  Captains (2), Logistics
  Staff Sgt./
  Sgt. Clerk (1)
  Cpl. Clerks (2)

Civilian Administration Division

Chief Administrative Officer
  Finance Officers
  Procurement Officers
  Supply Officers
  Personnel Officers
  Secretaries

15

A BRIEF INTERLUDE: ISRAEL IN A PEACEKEEPING ROLE

In September 1982, barely three months after their entry into Greater Beirut, the IDF were compelled to redeploy from the main centres of Beirut to the outskirts. They had good reason to deploy in strength in the areas of Aaley and Bhamdoun, stopping just short of Sofar from where they could see their Arab peacekeeping counterparts in Lebanon, the Syrians. The Aley-Bhamdoun-Sofar road has been the main supply route from Syria for Walid Jumblatt's Progressive Socialist Party (PSP) and Nabih Berri's Amal against IDF occupation. Blocking such a major line of communication was the minimum the IDF could do. In more serious hostilities, I would expect such a main supply route to be destroyed.

Co-existing in the Chouf mountains are the Druze and the Christians, who are in the minority. The Christians have a long-standing quarrel with the Druze, and still insist on avenging the defeat the Druze inflicted on them in 1860. We have seen in previous chapters that revenge for defeat and death is an Arab tradition, at least in Lebanon. The strong presence of the IDF in the Chouf had so reassured the Christian Lebanese Force (LF) as to encourage them to move into the Chouf on a massive scale. Reports that the IDF had encouraged the LF to do this on the eve of its departure cannot be confirmed, but the Israeli authorities should have foreseen the serious consequences much earlier and averted them. The situation was obviously explosive and the explosion was only being delayed by the IDF presence. The IDF, it seems, had also played down the profound feelings of affinity which Druze serving in its own ranks had for their brothers living in the Chouf and serving with the PSP.

Fighting soon broke out between the LF and PSP, and for the first time in its history the IDF found itself in a peacekeeping role. Throat-slitting, kidnapping, destruction of property and all forms of atrocity, mutually executed, became the order of the day. The IDF could not shoot either in support or in defence of either side; in other words, it found itself in the tricky, difficult, uncomfortable and often hazardous situation experienced by UNIFIL troops in South Lebanon ever since their arrival in 1978. It could alienate neither its old allies, the predominantly Christian Phalangists of Sheikh Pierre Gemayel, nor the Druze PSP. Hence, after a little over a year in a peacekeeping role in the Druze-controlled Chouf mountains, the IDF had to redeploy south to the Awali river, just north of the ancient port of Sidon.

The IDF General HQ in Tel Aviv gave two main reasons for leaving the Chouf area: first, to reduce its area of operations and consequently save manpower, and secondly because the government budget could not sustain such wide-ranging and open-ended operations. As always, there was the unstated reason: that peacekeeping, the conflict-control mechanism for which they had not been trained and which they had not expected, had inadvertently been imposed upon them. The IDF could not adjust itself to the UN peacekeeping principles of impartiality, objectivity, fairness, firmness, friendliness and, above all, patience. It thus had no option but to abandon the Chouf, with the expected result that major hostilities exploded between the Christian Lebanese forces and the Druze PSP.

16

REFLECTIONS ON ISRAEL'S PROBLEMS IN SOUTH LEBANON

The issue of the so-called Christian enclave, sometimes called the security belt, is not new, but the international community only became aware of it closely with the IDF's apparent withdrawal from South Lebanon on 13 June 1978, described in Chapter 7. As early as 1958 Moshe Sharett, as Foreign Minister in Ben-Gurion's administration, recorded in an Israeli Cabinet discussion, the need 'to find an officer, even a captain, saying we should win his heart or buy him, to get him to agree to declare himself the saviour of the Maronite population. Then the Israeli army would enter Lebanon, occupy the necessary territory and set up a Christian regime allied to Israel and everything would turn out just fine.'* This in fact was the dream of Moshe Dayan, and that captain eventually turned out to be Major Saad Haddad.

When I first came into the area as UNTSO Chief of Staff in January 1976, Haddad was already operating in the eastern half of the enclave with his HQ in Marjayoun, His assistant Major Sami Chidiak had charge of the western half with his HQ in the Christian town of Ayn Abil. Naqoura itself was under the control of the PLO, and with the main routes into and out of Naqoura village mined, ILMAC observers manning the five UNTSO observation posts on the 1949 Armistice Demarcation Line needed to obtain permission from the PLO, and to be escorted by them, when passing through Naqoura to reach their posts. Haddad, for his part, had blocked Marjayoun, and the only route ILMAC could use to re-supply or send relief observers to the Khiam observation post was from Beirut through the '*Arkoub*', the Fatahland, where the PLO guerrillas had most of their fighting bases.

The control of the Christian enclave by Major Haddad had to be formalised: the Israeli authorities were determined to see that through, and 13 June, the day when the IDF would finally withdraw, was set for this procedure. The ceremony at Meiss el Jebel on that day, at which the IDF handed over the border strip to Haddad and his De Facto Forces with all due pomp and circumstance and the respective lowering and raising of the Israeli and Lebanese national flags, marked the turning of Dayan's dream into reality. Haddad, as I saw him, was extremely sensitive to the security of the enclave, and his DFF

---

* See Ya'acov Sharett (*ed.*), *Moshe Sharett — Personal Diary* (Tel Aviv: Ma'ariv Publishing House, 1978).

were highly dedicated and motivated in contrast to Brigadier-General Antoine Lahad's South Lebanese Army (SLA), which was bedevilled by desertion and money problems: in 1985 its troops went on strike, for the first time in the history of its operations, because they had not received their pay from Tel Aviv. This never happened in Haddad's DFF, nor could it have happened. Why the difference in attitudes?

With the 'Black September' of 1970 having thrown out the radical elements of the PLO and Chairman Arafat from Jordan into Lebanon to continue the war against Israel particularly from the southern border area, the sensitivities of the DFF were understandable. The DFF were composed of both Christians and Muslims (predominantly Shiite); all of them were Lebanese, and all of them shared in the general unease that had prevailed among those like them since the establishment of the Israeli state in May 1948, when the first Palestinian refugees arrived on Lebanese soil. The DFF and the IDF shared an identical attitude to the PLO, namely one of detestation. The PLO was well aware of this alliance, and each side would shoot at the other, on sight, to kill; arrest and detention were out of the question.

Haddad and I met from time to time, especially when there was a critical situation, and a solution had to be found to prevent the taking of lives. There was such a situation in March 1979 when we agreed to meet on my territory, at the Nepalese Battalion HQ in Blate. The meeting had been arranged by my OGL 'Team Zulu' with Haddad's IDF liaison officer, Lt-Col. Gary Gal, for 1000, but I had to sit waiting at Blate till 1215 when he finally turned up. He reluctantly apologised, seeing that I was furious and looking straight into his eyes. His reason for being late was, to quote his exact words, 'I have been chasing terrorists.' I felt chilled since I could sense exactly what had been going on in those two hours while I had been drinking coffee in Blate. If I had had to wait a few more hours to save the life of that farmer who had been kidnapped and was awaiting punishment on suspicion of being a PLO sympathiser from Tibnin, I would have done so. The DFF's punishment for such 'crimes' could be imagined. Peacekeeping in Lebanon demanded that one should be extremely patient and bury one's pride from time to time, especially when someone else's life hung in the balance. Getting that farmer released into my care not only endeared the Irish troops with their HQ in Tibnin to the local population, but was also seen as UNIFIL's fulfilment of Secco Res 425, even if in a small way.

The situation in South Lebanon had changed since June 1982 with the expulsion of the PLO from the area. Those who were left were Lebanese — Amal, Communists or Hizbollah. It was inconceivable that the South Lebanese Army would have much enthusiam for fighting against its own Lebanese kith and kin just for the sake of

protecting Israel. It appeared treasonable to the Lebanese people and
the Arab world at large that the SLA should fight side by side with an
occupying force of Israelis, and worse still against fellow-Lebanese.
This explains the desertions from the SLA to Amal immediately after
the IDF withdrew from the Awali in June 1985. Serving in the militia
was now a source of employment rather than a way of defending Lebanese soil against the usurping PLO, as it had been in Haddad's time
with his DFF.

We in the UN felt it was time for the Israeli authorities to review
their strategic concept of defending their northern settlements; they
should rather court Amal and abandon their illegitimate surrogates,
the DFF/SLA. Amal was officially acceptable to the Lebanese authorities in both Baabda palace and the Prime Minister's office. Nabih
Berri, its leader, had been given a portfolio in Rashid Karame's
government as a Minister of State, responsible for the south. But Tel
Aviv would not entertain the UN's suggestion for fear that the IDF
might not be able to exercise the same degree of command and control
as it had over the DFF/SLA. Since they had not been able to win Berri
to their side, they had good reason to be wary of the UN's suggestion,
although it had been made in good faith by Brian Urquhart in a letter
to the Defence Minister, General Yitzhak Rabin, in late 1985.

At a meeting with the Israeli Prime Minister (then Yitzhak Shamir)
in Jerusalem in June 1984, the UN Secretary-General Javier Perez de
Cuellar in his wisdom cautioned the Israelis against viewing the
ongoing Iraq-Iran war as serving Israeli interests. He warned Mr
Shamir of the possible disastrous spill-over effect this could have on
their presence in South Lebanon. I am not sure whether Mr Shamir
fully appreciated this warning, but what we have seen since June 1985
when the IDF withdrew from the Awali river to its so-called security
belt vindicates Javier Perez de Cuellar's call for Israel to pull out of
Lebanon completely and let UNIFIL deploy to the 1949 Armistice
Demarcation Line.

The upsurge of hostilities in the south, including Haddad's Christian enclave, against both the IDF and its surrogates the DFF/SLA was
caused partly by the radicalisation of the indigenous Shiites by Iranian
mullahs. In February 1986 a series of visits was made to Tyre and
Sidon by these *mullahs* whose objective is to islamise Lebanon. Since
fighting in Greater Beirut began after the IDF withdrawal, resulting
in the total loss of West Beirut to the Muslims, women have been compelled to wear the black veil (*chador*). Hotels selling liquor have been
ransacked, and two women were reported to have been executed in
early 1986 for drinking alcohol in a hotel in West Beirut. Black veils
were appearing simultaneously in the south. Daoud Daoud, a school-
teacher from Tyre previously known as the moderate Amal leader in

the south, had since 1985 been paying visits to Iran. Nabih Berri could no longer hold back the Lebanese radicals from mounting hostile acts from their own sovereign soil against the Israelis, both inside Lebanon and across the border into Israel.

In February 1986, an IDF/DFF patrol of three half-tracks was ambushed near the village of Kunin. Two DFF soldiers were reported killed and two of the IDF were abducted. The IDF reacted by moving into the entire south, with no less than four motorised battalions, in a search, arrest and destroy operation. Almost all units of UNIFIL came under attack. I felt strongly about IDF's careless shooting at Ghanbatt HQ, and suggested that any senior Ghanaian officer visiting the troops should take up the issue by protesting to the Israeli authorities. This would complement the earlier protests by General Callaghan, UNIFIL Force Commander, to both Yitzhak Rabin as Defence Minister and Moshe Levy as Chief of Staff.

It was normal for visitors to UNIFIL from contributing countries to pay calls on the Israeli authorities, not only to discuss UNIFIL but also to express their feelings about the maltreatment and harrassment of their troops by the IDF. Such confrontations between visiting dignitaries and the Israel authorities helped to boost UNIFIL morale, and I myself encouraged them. Even when I left UNIFIL and moved to Jerusalem as Chief of Staff UNTSO, I still encouraged these visitors to UNIFIL to call at my office for briefing before seeing the Israeli authorities. My job was to give them the ammunition and theirs was to do the firing. Mostly it worked, although the effects on the ground were short-lived.

The IDF and the Israeli General Security Service urged the local population to organise themselves into village leagues to protect their villages with IDF assistance, but the people's response was half-hearted. Some accepted, but others refused; the latter just could not identify themselves with the occupation force and its surrogates who were seen as traitors. I visited the south quite frequently, and on a visit to Shaqra I could see a few old men, women and small children. The able-bodied men had all been thrown out of Shaqra for refusing to raise a village league, and what was worse was the refusal by the IDF to allow food to reach the helpless people who remained. UNIFIL assisted as best as it could. I raised this issue with Brigadier-General Dov Sion, the chief IDF liaison officer, when he later called on me in Jerusalem: I told him that if they wanted to court Nabih Berri and his Shiites in the south, starving the population was obviously the wrong approach. He agreed, but I did not stop there. I raised it again, this time at Foreign Ministry level, though informally, with Gideon Yarden, assistant to Pinhas Eliav, the Director for International Organisation, who had responsibility at the Foreign Ministry for dealing with UN matters. He also agreed. I exhorted both men to use their good offices to do something about the situation and they promised to do so.

Such interventions were necessary for two main reasons. First, for purely humanitarian reasons, it was incumbent on us in the blue berets to help. Secondly—and this I considered vital—, it was my experience while in command of UNIFIL that the IDF Northern Command in Nazareth took certain actions arbitrarily in South Lebanon without the knowledge of either the Defence Ministry or GHQ in Tel Aviv. The Foreign Ministry in Jerusalem only became aware of certain harsh actions carried out by the IDF when their effects assumed political dimensions. It was extremely gratifying when I went back to Shaqra a few months later to find the village bursting with life and its usual activities. This happened to most villages in the south. It is remarkable that all those who joined the village leagues automatically disappeared when the IDF pulled out into their security zone. An example of this occurred at Ath Thamiriyah. The village league militias could not withstand Amal, which had succeeded the IDF in maintaining security in their own villages.

The Israeli presence on Lebanese soil continues to be a provocation to the Lebanese, especially the Muslims. The Israelis trust nobody but themselves to maintain the security of their border with Lebanon, and because the security belt happens to be their only available solution, I cannot foresee any major change in the *status quo*. The principle was applied by the Israeli authorities when they turned down President Reagan's offer in 1983, during the MNF's operations in Beirut, to take responsibility for the security of Israel's northern border with Lebanon. It was less difficult for them to abandon Greater Beirut, the Chouf and the Awali. Abandoning the dream of Dayan would call for a major political decision which any Israeli government, be it Likud coalition, Labour alignment or perhaps a National Unity government made up of both, might find difficult to take. And with the possible return of the PLO into certain areas of the south, Amal joining hands with Hizbollah for more pay if for nothing else, and Baabda or Yarze unable to exert any restraining influence in the south, hostilities in the south are likely either to continue at the same tempo or get even worse.

The numbers of dead and wounded resulting from the 1982 invasion were high, partly because of the major factor that the fighting in Lebanon was non-conventional and required non-conventional tactics. The IDF is a normal conventional force, organised, equipped and trained for conventional warfare, and to my knowledge, it was only when the PLO was thrown out of Khiam in 1976 that the IDF had an abandoned village where it could train in house-to-house clearing.

It would not surprise me if the IDF were to begin serious training in guerrilla warfare and internal security operations for urban or built-up areas.

One of the difficulties for IDF troops in South Lebanon was their insufficient knowledge of the ground. It would take time for new drafts to acquire such knowledge and to become effective. Thus I could never see how the IDF troops, some of them thrown into the area straight from their kibbutzim and employing conventional tactics, could fight against the PLO, most of whom had been born in the area and lived there all their lives, and besides were equipped and trained for guerrilla warfare and highly motivated.

As I watched on my television an IDF foot patrol walking through some of the narrow alleys in Tyre, I wondered what had gone wrong with IDF tactics. Perhaps the IDF thought Nazareth, Ramallah and Hebron were interchangable with Tyre. I felt great pity for those young kibbutzniks and moshavniks. While this was going on, the Knesset (Israeli parliament) and the press back home talked of a war of choice and questioned the value of their boys being in Lebanon. This background spelt non-motivation for the kibbutzniks and moshavniks in Lebanon, and there was no way Israel could win.

17

PRIVATE PEACEMAKING EFFORTS

I had for some time felt very strongly that the Israelis truly wanted peace with their Arab neighbours, and yet at the same time were genuinely concerned with the security of their borders. I also had the feeling that the Israelis believed that the Arabs only understood force, and that its use on a massive scale was the solution to the security problems they had with their cousins at the borders. Like their close associates, the Americans, they always saw or imagined the big things and totally ignored the small ones. Was it possible, I often wondered, for them to see the small things too?

Until the Israelis virtually annexed the Golan Heights in December 1981, family meetings took place fortnightly between the Druze on the two sides of the fence on the Golan that separates Syria proper from Israeli-occupied Syria. This division is one of the many legacies of the June 1967 war between Israel and Egypt, Syria and Jordan. (Alone among the neighbouring Arab countries, Lebanon did not physically participate in the war.) These meetings, organised under the auspices of UNDOF, afforded Syrian Druze families, separated since Syria's loss of the Golan, the chance to meet, sit, chat, picnic and share normal family thoughts. The meetings, which were seen by the UN as a purely humanitarian gesture, also helped to ease tensions between the occupying IDF and the resident Druze. However, following the annexation of the Golan, the Israelis wanted the local Druze to hold Israeli identification cards, which for obvious reasons they refused to do. It was for this unstated reason that the Israelis withdrew their permission for these family meetings.

In the few years following the 1982 invasion of Lebanon, the attitude of the indigenous Shiites of the south towards the IDF had become hostile, an about-turn from what it had been before. I reasoned that if there were peace and quiet in South Lebanon, UNIFIL could make progress in fulfilling its mandate under Security Council Resolution 425. I therefore felt that if I could move the Israeli authorities towards creating those conditions of peace and quiet, I should be doing well as a peacemaker.

I always enjoyed lunches and dinners arranged by Sven Hirdman, the Swedish ambassador to Israel, for at these functions one was sure to meet a good cross-section of the Israeli authorities. It was during a dinner in 1985 for the visiting commander-in-chief of the Swedish armed forces General Llung that I met General Yitzhak Rabin, the

Israeli Minister of Defence, and General Moshe Levy, the IDF Chief of Staff (Rabin had been Chief of Staff in the 1967 war). As is normal at diplomatic social gatherings, I approached Rabin informally and started to chat with him. Of course, in my capacity as Chief of Staff UNTSO and the Secretary-General's representative for peacekeeping activities in the region, I had met him several times, both formally in his office and informally at social functions, and therefore knew him quite well. I asked him what were his thoughts on how to improve the IDF's relations with the Shiite Muslims of South Lebanon, saying that I did not see an end to the Shiites fighting against his men with the IDF pulling back, even to the Armistice Line. There was an inescapable need for Israel to find ways and means of restoring the happy relations that had existed between them before their invasion in June 1982.

He said he accepted my reading of the situation, got a bit more interested and asked me to sit down for a more detailed chat. The following was what I tried to sell to him. At the time of our conversation, the Druze were building their sea-port at Khalde, a few kilometres south of Beirut's international airport, but I emphasised that there was no way this construction could progress without IDF acquiescence, and therefore there should be communication between Israel and Walid Jumblatt. Israel needed the goodwill of the Shiites in South Lebanon, and therefore if the Israeli authorities could restore the cancelled family meetings and thus improve relations with the Druze, the latter could pressurise Berri and his South Lebanese Shiites into changing their present hostile attitude to the IDF back to what it had been before the 1982 invasion.

I said that this was not a UN proposal but a purely personal one — it was essential to make that distinction. Rabin smiled, looked interested in my theory, and wanted me to develop it further; so, in his characteristic baritone voice, he suggested that we move into a secluded corner to continue our talk. He was probably wondering what sort of trap I was laying for him; I believe that the Israeli official mind is by nature suspicious and sceptical, and in this an astute politician and soldier like Rabin would be no exception. Such an initiative as I was making should be coming from a close associate, a friend or colleague, preoccupied, like he was, with the security and defence of Israel and its people. What could the African general of UNTSO, who was paid by the UN, want? Ever since the General Assembly passed a resolution in 1975 equating Zionism with racism, the world organisation has been seen by most Israelis as the arch-enemy of their state. I was thus the chief among the 300 UNTSO military observers whom the IDF have from time to time accused of being spies. General Rabin said that they had made attempts to court Nabih Berri, but so far without success. That was as far as we could go before Ambassador Hirdman came to escort us to our seats in his bomb-shelter dining room. Unfortunately, I was not seated by Rabin and had to drop the subject for the next two hours.

Later I brought it up again, this time with his right-hand man in the field, General Moshe Levy. Again, we knew each other well, even if disagreeing most of the time. In all my twelve years with the UN in the Middle East, there was one important lesson I learnt extremely well, above all with the Israelis. No matter what the issue might be, they always saw it exclusively in their own way. It took a great effort for any good Israeli interlocutor to see any other point of view besides his, and I always had to explain that we in the UN command had to view things from all sides. We had to use our perspective, not theirs.

I introduced the subject in the same spirit and style as I had with his boss Rabin, but Moshe was bewildered and surprised. We discussed my theory for some fifteen minutes, then he had to leave for pressing business at his GHQ, but promised that we should meet and continue our discussion at a later date. Early the following week, Brigadier-General Dov Sion, the chief Israeli liaison officer with the UN, through whose office we channelled all official matters with the IDF, called at my office in Jerusalem to tell me that General Levy wanted to see me at his office in Tel Aviv to continue our *tête-à-tête*. I was delighted and readily agreed. But I made one condition — that no one else should be present. There were several reasons for this. First, I had no mandate from my HQ in New York for my adventurous solo peace-making move; secondly, as at the first meeting, I wanted no publicity; thirdly, I wanted to be unusually open with Moshe about operational activities by the IDF in South Lebanon with which I vehemently disagreed; and finally, I had come to realise that my interlocutors spoke much more freely with me when I was alone with no aide. At most of my meetings, I was accompanied by my senior political adviser, who took notes. I did travel to Tel Aviv with my deputy, Colonel Jacob Ask (Sweden), but he stayed with Dov Sion in his office. I had told Jacob the purpose of my mission to Tel Aviv and he praised my courage.

Moshe Levy and I sat alone in his office for ninety minutes, the longest meeting I ever had with any single official during my whole tour in the mission area. First, I raised the issue of the family meetings, arguing that ultimately it was in Israel's interest to allow them, and restated the reasons I had given at Mr Hirdman's dinner party. He agreed, but said it was a political issue and that he therefore had to take it up with his Minister. I said that I had earlier broached the subject with Rabin, and asked him to follow it up. He said he would. The second subject, a rather more sensitive one, was to do with my impressions of certain aspects of IDF operations in South Lebanon. I had always felt that not only were the local Lebanese Shiite inhabitants of the area being unnecessarily harrassed, but also that the approach of his troops did not promote 'Operation Peace for Galilee', the code-name for the June invasion. Moshe was very attentive. I told him that it was unnecessary to force the shop-owners in Tyre to open their shops at gunpoint when they had decided to close as a demonstration. In the first place, the IDF were not in Tyre to go shopping, and if the closing of the shops posed difficulties to any group, it was the indigenous population who were suffering and not his troops. When he denied that the troops had done this, I referred him to the *Jerusalem Post*. I did not stop there, but added that I always disagreed with the similar tactics they employed in the Arab areas of East Jerusalem and the West Bank, particularly in troublesome towns like Ramallah and Nablus — and it seemed that the IDF had exported those tactics from the West Bank into South Lebanon. In so doing, they ignored the fact that the history, geographical setting and character of the two peoples were completely different. I finished by saying that in all these places the IDF were over-exposed, thus contributing to their own mounting casualties. It was better, I suggested, for them to concentrate on the main entrances and exits, the infiltration routes and their own supply routes. While such an approach would be helpful in realising the objectives of their invasion, their troops would be less exposed, and fewer hostile attacks would be provoked; further, the innocent local Lebanese would be better able to live normal lives and would feel less resentment against their occupation. South Lebanon could thus be a more peaceful and tranquil place, and UNIFIL and the UNTSO observers could relax a little.

Moshe asked me to clarify certain points, which I did. He was well aware that I had spent three difficult years in South Lebanon; that I knew the people and the ground as well as he did; and that I had lived among Jews, Arabs and Palestinians and knew what I was talking about. Naturally he had to defend the Israeli side, but he was grateful for my openness, and as a good commander he promised to look into all the tactics they were using in South Lebanon. We met some more times later, but on those occasions we had all our sides in attendance and so, disappointingly, could not speak out. When I went to say '*Au revoir*' to Moshe on completion of my UN service in May 1986, he gave me this letter, which I reproduce in full:

Dear General Erskine,

I regret to see you leave, both personally and as the Chief of General Staff of the IDF. After so many years of serving alongside each other it is difficult to suddenly part and I am sure that we shall miss your presence on the Mount of Evil Council.

I have always appreciated and respected your views and persuasiveness and will remember fondly the meetings and conversations we held. Naturally, we knew differences of opinion and often held opposing attitudes but these variations did not turn into animosity or negative relationship that could have prevented a dialogue and cooperation between us. We hope that your service in the area made you understand our viewpoint. I guess it was not easy, and often quite complicated to be neutral and still positively disposed. Even if we did not always accept each other's points of view or proposals, I am confident that your suggestions emanated from goodwill and serious concern for the cause of peace and from a desire to promote good relations between us and our neighbours.

I hope that you part from us as a friend and I wish to assure you that this feeling is mutual. We are sure that there is a great future in store for you in the service of peace and in the service of your country. You carry with you a wealth of unique experience and political wisdom that will be a great asset for the United Nations and for your own country and people.

> Yours sincerely,
> MOSHE LEVY, *Lt. General,*
> *Chief of the General Staff, IDF*

To me and my staff it was rather unusual and almost too pleasant to be true, but there it was, with Moshe's own signature. Today I have it framed and hanging on my wall at home in Accra.

18

THE UNITED NATIONS TRUCE SUPERVISION ORGANISATION (UNTSO) AS THE SECRETARY-GENERAL'S FORCE RESERVES

The United Nations operates two main types of peacekeeping mission, the armed force and the unarmed observers. UNEF 1, established in Sinai in 1956 following the Franco-British-Israeli attack on Suez, was the first peacekeeping force established by the UN with armed troops. Later examples have been the UN operation in the Congo (ONUC); the UN Force in Cyprus (UNFICYP); the UN Emergency Force 2 (UNEF 2); the UN Disengagement Observer Force (UNDOF), and the UN Interim Force in Lebanon (UNIFIL). Peacekeeping, as operated today, is an innovation that was promoted by Lester Pearson when Prime Minister of Canada, and UNEF 1 was the 'guinea pig' (it was probably as a special tribute to Canada that the first Force Commander of the first UN peacekeeping force was a Canadian, Lieutenant-General E.L.M. Burns). The composition of contingents of a UN peacekeeping force follows the normal unit order of battle with officers and men carrying weapons.

The second type of UN peacekeeping mission is the observer mission. In contrast to the armed troops, all members of this kind of mission are officers, and they carry no arms of any sort. UNTSO, established on 11 June 1948, was the first UN observer mission. The other such mission still in operation is the UN Military Observer Group in India and Pakistan (UNMOGIP).

UNTSO was established to supervise the Mixed Armistice Agreements — ceasefire agreements — in Palestine between Israel and its Arab neighbours Egypt, Syria, Lebanon and Jordan following the outbreak of armed hostilities on Israel becoming a state on 14 May 1948. Fighting between Palestinian Jews and Palestinian Arabs had gone on continuously while both cohabited in Palestine during the British mandate, which automatically came to an end with the establishment of the state of Israel. Four Mixed Armistice Commissions (MACs) were established: between Egypt and Israel (EIMAC), Israel and Lebanon (ILMAC), Israel and Syria (ISMAC), and the Hashemite Kingdom of Jordan and Israel (HKJIMAC). The Chief of Staff, as the executive head of UNTSO, with his headquarters at Government House in

Jerusalem, was represented by Observers (designated as Chairmen) who headed the four MACs in Cairo, Beirut, Damascus and Amman respectively. UNTSO's main objective was to monitor and supervise the respective ceasefire agreements. Every violation was to be investigated and reported.

The role of UNTSO has naturally undergone various changes with the many developments that have taken place in the mission area. The October 1973 war, between Egypt and Israel in Sinai and between Israel and Syria on the Golan Heights, precipitated the establishment of UNEF 2 and UNDOF respectively. This required changes in the roles of EIMAC and ILMAC. UN Military Observers, UNMOs, from both MACs were assigned to assist UNEF and UNDOF in their operational activities. Observer Group Sinai (OGS) and Observer Group Golan (OGG), carved out from the two MACs, were designed for these new roles. This reorganisation was aimed at preserving the historical nature of the MACs.

When the Camp David Accord came into being, followed by the peace treaty of 1979 between Israel and Egypt and culminating in the establishment of the US-sponsored peacekeeping force known as the Multinational Force and Observers (MFO) which became operational in April 1982, UNEF 2 was disbanded and OGS was transformed into Observer Group Egypt (OGE). Even though MFO functions effectively and efficiently in Sinai, UNTSO continues to maintain a UN presence there with its five observation posts — in El Arish, St Catherines, El Nakhle, El Melize (Bir Gilgafa) and Ismalia (OP 'India', the only post on the west side of the Suez Canal). When I left in May 1986, the sixth observation post at Abu Rudeis was still under construction.

The UN's continued presence in Sinai has been at the express request of the Egyptian government, notwithstanding the operations of MFO. Foreign Minister Esmat Abdel Meguid had asked me personally at a special meeting in Cairo to convey the request to the Secretary-General, Javier Perez de Cuellar. I see the significance of the UN's presence in Sinai in two particular ways. First, it is a passive recognition by the UN of the peace treaty, even though in principle the UN does not accept partial agreements between countries. While the Soviet Union does not recognise the Egypt-Israel peace treaty at all, the other permanent member-countries in the Security Council do acknowledge as a reality the fact that there is a peace agreement between Egypt and Israel. It is also a recognition, an encouragement and a morale-booster for Egypt on the part of the world community through the fact that seventeen countries are represented in UNTSO. In the longer term, with the possibility of MFO folding up due to the cost of maintaining the force proving impossible to sustain, it would be much easier for the UN to assume a full operational role since it would not then have to go through all the Security Council bureaucracies and uncertainties to establish a new mission in Sinai.

All UN missions in the area operate through formal liaison offices established for the purpose by the host-governments. Contacts between the host-governments and the missions are channelled through this liaison system: examples are inspection reports, complaints, requests for meetings, difficulties arising from local conditions, border crossing clearances, vehicle registration, UN flight clearances, airport privileges to facilitate troop rotation flights, welfare visits,and a host of administrative issues. Depending on who were currently serving as liaison officers, I personally found the arrangement quite helpful.

The liaison systems currently operating in the five states within the mission area are the Israel Defence Forces Liaison Office, Jerusalem, and the Senior Israeli Representative (North), Tiberias; the Senior Syrian Arab Delegate; the Senior Lebanese Delegate; the Senior Jordanian Delegate; and the Liaison Services Egypt. These liaison arrangements formed an integral part of the establishment of the Mixed Armistice Agreements, and it was through them that all matters related to the MACs were handled. They still, at the time of writing, perform their original roles and functions.

The working relationship between Observer Group Egypt (OGE) and the Egyptian authorities grew to a height of efficiency and warmth with the appointment of Major-General Farouk Labib as the Chief of the Liaison Services Egypt (CLSE) and Lt.-Col. Franco Ricco (Italy) as Chief OGE and Major Krister Lindholm (Sweden) as senior liaison officer. The difficulties encountered by OGE military observers in crossing the Canal for observation post duties were reduced to an operationally acceptable minimum, and UNTSO's earlier problems in seeking clearances for its Fokker 25 flights almost ceased, as did the excessive bureaucracy one had previously encountered when needing to cross the border at El Arish. The agreeable personalities of General Labib and Colonel Ricco were mutually appreciated, and because of that factor and their great efforts, UNTSO enjoyed a period of happy operations in Sinai. This of course greatly enhanced its efficiency.

UNTSO's military observers, UNMOs, are seasoned, well-trained and mature officers. Some of them come to UNTSO with varied combat experience and senior staff appointments behind them, which are the best preparation for their field duties in the mission area. Their professional qualities, combined with their extended tours of duty with UNTSO (normally two years, as against six months for troops in UNDOF and UNIFIL), make their services invaluable to UNEF,

UNDOF and UNIFIL. Thus they provide the force with a necessary continuity, and provide the experience which is so vital in areas such as Sinai, Golan and South Lebanon.

UNTSO observers have always established the first UN presence in every area newly mandated for peacekeeping: it was so with UNEF 2 in October 1973, with UNDOF in June 1974, with UNIFIL in March 1978, with UNGOMAP (Afghanistan) in May 1988, and again with UNIIMOG (Iran/Iraq) in August 1988. The raising of the UN flag immediately after the Security Council has authorised the Secretary-General to establish a peacekeeping force in an area of conflict is an essential aspect of the peacekeeping mechanism. Such early flag-showing and presence does good to the image of the UN, and fully underscores the involuntarily self-imposed new role of UNTSO as the Secretary-General's peacekeeping force reserve.

UNMOs' experience of the area of operations has always been put at the disposal of newly-arrived contingent and unit commanders. They served as guides for the Swedish, Austrian, Finnish and Irish commanders arriving from UNFICYP with their advance parties to form UNEF 2. As guides for UNIFIL, they led new unit commanders and their troops into their areas of operations, briefed them on the situation in the area generally and on the ground, introduced commanders and officers to some of the indigenous local personalities, and assisted drivers with the techniques they would need in the area, and especially with routes — which to use and which to avoid.

The expertise of UNMOs has been put to full use by Force Commanders at the headquarters level in staff appointments with UNEF, UNDOF and UNIFIL. This was a great asset in providing the force both with expert knowledge and with continuity. For the same reason, Force Commanders have usually chosen UNMOs as their aides-de-camp. The sensitive task of inspecting the Area of Limitation of Forces (ALF) and the Area of Separation (AOS) has always been assigned to UNMOs, who prepare the reports from these inspections — an integral part of the ceasefire agreements between the parties — for the Force Commander. As commander of UNDOF, Major-General Carl Gustav Stahl (Sweden) respected the contribution Observer Group Golan was making towards his force's peacekeeping efforts on the Golan, and this was fully appreciated by UNTSO HQ. He termed OGG his fifth contingent and the observers his officers, a positive outlook which made UNTSO feel wanted.

But there was also a difficult aspect arising from the supporting role UNTSO had to play towards UNIFIL and UNDOF. With the enthusiasm of the UNMOs, we tried in UNTSO to give as much help as we felt was necessary for the effective working of the UN peacekeeping missions in the area, but unfortunately such efforts were not always appreciated, and even appear to have been misconstrued. The very cordial working relationship survived the change in command in UNDOF, when Major-General Gustav Hägglund (Finland) relieved General Stahl in June 1985. General Hägglund, full of youthful exuberance and intelligence, yet eager to learn, also saw in OGG a great wealth of expertise and professionalism among the UNMOs and continued where General Stahl left off. (He was appointed in June 1986 to succeed General Callaghan as Force Commander of UNIFIL.)

The system of joint peacekeeping operations between troops and UNMOs has been effective. It was an experiment which had its roots in UNEF 2, during the second Disengagement of Forces between Egypt and Israel, and was adapted by UNDOF and UNIFIL. In my own assessment, it is a good arrangement which OUSGSPA should adopt as a standing operating procedure whenever feasible. The in-built flexibility of UNTSO's organisation, with its ability to deploy observers at short notice, has gone a long way to enhance the credibility of the Secretary-General's office where its international peacekeeping commitments are concerned, as well as in the maintenance of peace and security. When in June 1984 both Iran and Iraq agreed to refrain from deliberately shelling each other's heavily populated towns and further agreed to the UN sending observer teams to Tehran and Baghdad to supervise compliance, UNTSO was able to plan, prepare and despatch the observer teams to both capitals within forty-eight hours. Whatever may have happened later in that theatre, this was an astonishing achievement which delighted Mr Perez de Cuellar and his Secretariat in New York.*

The Under Secretary-General for Special Political Affairs (Brian Urquhart) and the Secretary-General's Military Adviser (Major-General Timothy Dibuama of Ghana) fully respected the capabilities of UNTSO, which provided the military component when the Security Council set up a special committee for Seychelles in 1983. Major Louis Barbeau (Canada) was a highly successful participant. Again, when a similar committee had to be sent to Angola in 1985, UNTSO was requested to provide an officer to complement the team. This was Major Wat Sliwinsky (Canada), my deputy chief operations officer, who achieved excellent results.

The trust and confidence of the Secretary-General and Brian Urquhart in UNTSO was expressed in another important way. To facilitate the speedy establishment of a UN presence in areas of conflict when so authorised by the Security Council, there was the

---

* The special individual contributions made by my deputy chief of staff, Colonel Jacob Ask (Sweden); chief operations officer, Colonel Tom Fincher (USA); chief military personnel officer, Captain (Navy) Martin Lillevik (Norway); and Chief Administrative Officer Athanase Constantinidis (Greece) should be put in record.

need to have contingency plans for mounting such operations. At the start of the Falklands/Malvinas crisis, when there seemed to be a high probability that the UN would get involved, UNTSO was given the task of preparing the appropriate plans. This was handled down to the minutest detail by my advisory, operations and military personnel and logistical and administrative staff. Since the peacemaking process initiated by Mr Perez de Cuellar and supplemented by the then US Secretary of State Alexander Haig failed to produce a negotiated settlement and the possibility of UN participation evaporated, all UNTSO could do was store the plans. At the request of Brian Urquhart's office, UNTSO had completed and stored similar contingency plans for areas where there had always been potential for UN peacekeeping participation. UNTSO is a repository of UN peacekeeping skill and knowledge, which our colleagues in New York fortunately appreciate and are ready to exploit.

As the Chief of Staff UNTSO during the Israeli invasion of 1982, I was able to witness the impressive performance of the UNMOs and the international civilian staff of ILMAC and its servicing agent Observer Group Beirut (OGB) during the difficult months following the invasion. The situation in Greater Beirut was fraught with all sorts of dangers, and ILMAC, with OGB, had to move its offices from West Beirut in the area of Sabra and Chatila refugee camps, first to the Lebanese army HQ in Yarze, later to the cadet training school, and finally to Hazmieh. We were relocated within Greater Beirut, but for most of the other UN agencies it was either a complete shutdown or the maximum thinning-out. Most embassies reduced their staff, some relocated from Muslim West to Christian East Beirut, some relocated from Beirut to Damascus or Cyprus, and a few closed down completely. All these exercises involved movement through dangerous areas, and the military observers of OGB, with my approval, provided the evacuees with the logistical support they needed to ensure a safe passage.*

OGB even had the singular experience of rescuing Israelis in Greater Beirut. On 31 January 1983 at about 1705 an OGB team near the Galerie Seeman observed two civilian vehicles with Israeli licence-plates, and carrying a total of five IDF soldiers, being stopped at gunpoint by Lebanese army soldiers, who appeared ready to open fire. The OGB team interposed itself between the parties, and succeeded in calming tensions. The UNMOs later escorted the Israeli party to the south along the Saida road.

---

* Letters of appreciation were sent by embassies to the chiefs of OGB, Lieutenant-Colonels Letourneur, Fourrier and Cache (all French), and Field Service Officers Erik Bayerl, Alfred Alleyne and Frank McHugh all made outstanding contributions. Humanitarian service was OGB's watchword during those most difficult times from 1985 in Beirut.

OGB was successful in carrying out these functions because of two main reasons. First, being unarmed, their presence and movement could not present any threat to the armed militias operating in the streets of Beirut, and indeed OGB observers were the only uniformed personnel able to move at night in both West and East Beirut during those difficult periods following the IDF operations in Greater Beirut in 1982 – 3. Carrying no weapons was our strength. Secondly, the friendly disposition of the observers and the nature of the liaison system OGB operated made them familiar with most of the fighting militias and their leaders. Whenever UN or non-UN agencies got themselves entangled in any sort of difficulty with the Christian Lebanese forces, the Druze Progressive Socialist Party, the Shiite Amal, Sunni Murabitoun, Hizbollah, Communists or any other armed group, OGB was the rescue team. It performed a true humanitarian service, and held the UN flag high.

The integrity of UNMOs is essential and critical for the effective and efficient functioning of UNTSO. By its standing operating procedures, UNTSO reports to the Secretary-General are based on physical observations personally made by observers, and not on hearsay or through any other indirect medium. Depending on the Secretary-General's intentions, they may be presented to the Security Council, and they have to be factual, unbiased and dispassionate. Such was UNTSO's report to the Secretary-General on the Sabra and Chatila massacre of September 1982, which no one could have challenged. Thus UNTSO observers have to possess unassailable personal qualities in order to uphold those vital principles of impartiality without which no UN peacekeeping mission could function effectively.

UNTSO has no modern parallel in that it is the only organisation in the world where US and Soviet military — not even civilians — live, eat, sleep and work together. In 1974, when I was with UNEF 2, I became rather curious about this 'peacekeeping chemistry'. The strange thing was that Soviet UNMOs, more often than not, preferred to perform their weekly observation post duty tour with UNMOs from the United States, and *vice versa*. I queried one Soviet observer, then with OGS, about his compatriots' obvious wish to share observation post duties with Americans. 'Yes, General,' he replied, 'we Soviets always want to be with our US colleagues because we know they are CIAs and they know we are KGBs.'

As the Chief of Staff, I tried whenever possible to honour all invitations from senior UNMOs, especially for the celebration of their national days. It was always a pleasure to see the observers and their families in relaxed mood. The Irish celebrated St Patrick's Day, the Dutch their Queen's birthday, the French Bastille Day, Norway the adoption of the Norwegian constitution of 1814, Italy the day when the country was officially declared a republic after a referendum ousted the monarchy; and the United States — like most of the countries that contribute to UNTSO — its Independence Day. For all these festivities good food and drink were served, there was music, and on the whole we all had a lot of fun.

What differed among the countries was the standard of protocol. The Soviets celebrated their Army Day, and I was always with them. On these days the protocol and courtesies they extended to me and my wife were highly impressive, and indeed whenever I and my accompanying staff were passing through Observation Post 'India' at Ismailia on our way to Cairo, we were received with extraordinarily warm hospitality. They extended similar courtesies to UNMOs from other countries.

Since all UN peacekeeping missions were operating without Status of Force Agreements (SOFA) with their host-governments, it was imperative for the missions to establish and maintain viable working relationships with those governments. Even though the Israeli authorities considered the Mixed Armistice Agreement with Egypt, Syria, Lebanon and Jordan to be null and void because of the participation by those countries, in one form or another, in the June 1967 war, UNTSO continued to function with its HQ at Government House in Jerusalem. Furthermore, it maintained a viable and happy working relationship with the Israeli Foreign Ministry in Jerusalem. This had been developed by Jean-Claude Aimé, a Director in Brian Urquhart's office, and his work had been further eased by the warm personality of David Kimche, the Director General of the Israeli Foreign Ministry. The skills, knowledge and tact of Mr Kimche made him respected by Israeli politicians and leading officials and the diplomatic corps alike. From time to time he stood in for his Foreign Minister Yitzhak Shamir in certain important national and international activities. He headed the Israeli delegation which negotiated and signed the 17 May 1983 troop withdrawal agreement between Israel and Lebanon. He also had several outstanding colleagues in the Foreign Ministry — Michael Elitzur, Pinhas Eliav and Gideon Yarden. I personally got on well with all of them, inviting them from time to time to lunches or dinners at Government House and playing tennis if we could squeeze in the time.

This relationship was sustained by Keith Beavan who joined my civilian advisory team in August 1985 as senior political adviser. He had served in UNIFIL as my first chief press and information officer in the early days of the force, and his straightforward personality had then come into conflict with Major Saad Haddad's political ambitions, and confrontation between the two had resulted. For his personal safety, Keith then had to return to UN HQ, New York, but he had performed well as UNIFIL's press officer in those first difficult months after its establishment. In the mean time he had done a tour of duty with UNFICYP as the Force Commander's spokesman, followed by a brief period as Acting Special Representative of the Secretary-General, also in Cyprus, so he was well suited to his new office in Jerusalem, and it was a joy to have him back with me in UNTSO.

Up till Keith Beavan's arrival, UNTSO's ties with the Egyptian Foreign Ministry, though cordial, had not been strong. But his duties as Chief of the Department of Information Publication Services at UN HQ had brought him into contact with many international representatives, including members of the Egyptian Permanent Mission to the UN, and Keith was now to find some of these as senior officials in the Egyptian Foreign Ministry in Cairo. This helped him to redress the previous deficiency in the working relationship between UNTSO and Egypt, so balancing the good relations we had with the Israeli Foreign Ministry and increasing UNTSO's effectiveness.

With the coming of UNIFIL in South Lebanon and UNDOF with its headquarters in Damascus, UNTSO's dealings in Lebanon and Syria have been largely limited to the Lebanese army HQ in Beirut and with the office of the senior Syrian army delegate in Damascus. Its relations with the Jordanian Foreign Ministry assumed a special character due to the special personal relationship between Jean-Claude Aimé and Crown Prince Hassan.

UNTSO continues to provide indispensable services to both UNDOF and UNIFIL. Even though it cannot perform its original role because of political changes in the area over the years, its presence appears to be a critical factor in enhancing the credibility of the UN's peacekeeping and peacemaking efforts there. Its evolved role as the Secretary-General's peacekeeping force reserve has been fulfilled. We have already remarked on the skill and professionalism of UNMOs, combined with their personal qualities; the international and local civilian staff also play a vital role in their administrative and logistical support for the military observers.

The physical and mental wellbeing of UNMOs, the support staff and their families is a critical factor in the maintenance of UNTSO's effective operational alertness. This was the special role of our excellent Austrian medical assistants. And finally, the Swiss government, by providing UNTSO with an aircraft, sustained its air mobility. This was a valuable contribution.

19

GHANA'S PARTICIPATION IN UN PEACEKEEPING: 'OPERATION SUNRISE'

Ghana was among the first few countries to send troops to the Congo in 1960 to participate in the UN's peacekeeping activities there. At the time when President Kwame Nkrumah was despatching his troops to ONUC, I was in England having just left the Royal Military Academy Sandhurst and moved on to a young officers' course at the Royal School of Signals, Catterick Camp, Yorkshire. Because other more seasoned officers were available at home, I was not needed to hurry back to join the Signals Detachment that had been detailed for ONUC. My three Ghanaian intake colleagues, John Kabore, Parker Kwesi Yarney and George Dako, all went to the Congo at one stage or another, and I felt the usual professional jealousy when they came back from ONUC and told of their operational experiences, which made me feel wholly deficient. I suppose every good soldier wants to be exposed to this kind of environment sometime in his military service career. However, there was an opportunity for me to join ONUC as a liaison officer, as I had been earmarked as a replacement for Lieutenant Sosu-Honu, once my fellow-cadet at the Regular Officers Special Training School (ROSTS), Teshie, from March 1958 until we flew together to England later that year. Unfortunately, that never came through and I missed the ONUC exposure.

One of the best institutions that the British colonial administration bequeathed to Ghana was effective and efficient armed forces. Training systems were excellent, and equipment and other logistical items needed to support training and normal day-to-day administration of the units were readily available. The professional training of officers was given meticulous attention: potential candidates were selected with the utmost care, taking all their background and characteristics into consideration.

In my time, selection to ROSTS for secondary school-leavers was based on regional competitive written examinations. I took my examination in Takoradi, invigilated by John Yaw Assassie who was to join me later in ROSTS 10 as a fellow-cadet. Success in the examination qualified the individual to appear before a selection board, centrally held in Accra. My first appearance before the board in February 1958 at the present Ghana Military Police headquarters was a memorable experience. The only Ghanaian officer on the British-dominated board was Major David Anumle Hansen, in his well cleaned and ironed khaki shorts and feathered slouch hat. His immaculate turnout was a major inspiration for me to work harder and get to the military academy.

First, we had to undergo a thorough medical examination. We later had a brief interview followed by an initiative test involving obstacle courses in the field. My group undertook this test at the present Achimota police station. All these elimination processes were meant to leave only the best to enter ROSTS, which was the major elimination testing ground. On completion of the obstacle test, we appeared before the selection board for the final interview, after which the successful candidates finally went to Teshie.

The Ghana armed forces have always had four systems for granting commissions to officers, which I suppose to have been British-inspired, since our organisation, equipment, training and other aspects were largely British. The first arrangement related to my type, those straight from secondary school with 'O' Level certificates. The second category related to soldiers already serving in the ranks, who had worked hard to pass the final stage of the Army Certificate of Education; these soldiers, on strong recommendation from their unit commanding officers, qualified for officer training. Among my fellow-cadets in this category were I.K. Acheampong, later head of state; Charles Tachie-Menson, commissioner for information in Acheampong's administration; Lt.-Col. John Yaw Assassie, director-general of the Ghana Broadcasting Corporation in the same administration and later political counsellor to the Committee for the Defence of the Revolution under Rawlings; Lt.-Col. Sosu-Honu, at one time a regional commissioner, and Major Sam Lamptey, who was still serving with the Signals Regiment at the time of writing. We all completed six months training at ROSTS. From there those of us with 'O' levels proceeded to Sandhurst for two years' further cadet training, and those from the ranks went to Mons, Aldershot, for four months. Others went to Indian and Canadian military academies.

The third category of commission was open to qualified professionals such as medical doctors, dental and eye specialists, engineers, lawyers, priests and others. Their selection was less rigorous and the duration of their training at the Military Academy ranged from six to twelve weeks. On completion of their cadet training they were commissioned and went straight into their various disciplines. Both the second and third categories mentioned were initially granted short service commissions, while the first category became regular officers.

The final category were quartermasters and their like — soldiers who had served for many years in logistics units and were recommended for commission on the basis of their professionalism in this area as against academic qualifications.

ROSTS was unique in the sense that it was attended by cadets from Nigeria, Sierra Leone and Gambia as well as Ghana. Hence we knew one another and such friendship continues. At the time when I went to Jaji, Kaduna, in 1979 and 1980 to lecture at the Nigerian staff college, the ruler of the country was General Olusegun Obasanjo, my one-time mate at ROSTS 10. Another notable Nigerian who had been there with me was Brigadier Benjamin Adekunle, the Black Scorpion. Regrettably, the ROSTS era ceased in 1960 when Nigeria established its own military academy at Kaduna. The Ghana Military Academy then came into being as its successor.

Now back to Ghana and peacekeeping. Even though I had no first-hand experience of the performance of Ghanaian troops in ONUC, I had always heard that it was commendable. This first successful exposure to UN peacekeeping operations had left a pleasant taste also in the mouths of the Ghanaian soldiers themselves, and we all hoped that another such opportunity would arise. This finally came after a wait of nine years in November 1973 when I was commander of the Ghana Army. The news that the Secretary-General had requested our participation in UNEF in Sinai first came through the press, and without even consulting our Chief of Defence Staff, Brigadier Ashley-Lassen, I told the press that Ghana would accept Dr Waldheim's invitation. Feeling ecstatically happy, I went straight to Brigadier Ashley-Lassen and briefed him on the press inquiry and my positive reaction — which, fortunately, he endorsed. Within the next forty-eight hours, the official request came through diplomatic channels, and the government responded positively to the UN secretariat. Late in November, I headed a three-man delegation to UN HQ, New York, to negotiate formally for Ghana's participation (the other two members were Colonel Edwin Sam, Director-General Operations and Plans, and Smyly C.A. Chinery, Principal Secretary, Ministry of Defence). This was my first meeting with Brian Urquhart, who later became such a critical factor for Ghana in our peacekeeping activities in the Middle East.

Ghana's participation in UNEF 2 began with the departure aboard German air force transport planes of Ghanbatt 1 on 3 January 1974, commanded by Lt.-Col. Bruce Konuah; I had felt that the troops should spend Christmas with their families before venturing into the unknown. The senior Ghanaian officer on UNEF HQ staff at the time was Lt.-Col. Daniel Prah (later ambassador in Ivory Coast); his successor was Lt.-Col. Jeff Asmah (later ambassador in Libya).

UNEF HQ was at Heliopolis in Cairo, while the Race Course (Shams

Camp) served as the main logistical base for all the contingents. Camp Fanara served as Ghanbatt HQ in Sinai, but on the west side of the Suez Canal. UNEF HQ and the force's logistical base were relocated from Cairo to Ismailia, a gradual process; it became operational in Ismailia in August 1974, three months after I had joined UNEF as Chief of Staff to Lieutenant-General Ensio Siilasvuo of Finland, the Force Commander. As Chief of Staff, I was responsible for planning the move. Fortunately, the Suez Canal Authority readily agreed to UNEF using its huge complex of apartments both as working and living accommodation. The Poles set up their field hospital within this complex, while Canadian and Polish logistical elements were co-located in the disused Egyptian air force base at El Gala. By the end of 1974, UNEF 2 was fully operational in Ismailia and in the deep sands of the Sinai desert.

In my estimation, 'Operation Sunrise' (the code-name for Ghana's participation in the Middle East) with UNEF 2 was not as critical for the Ghana armed forces as its service with UNIFIL. By June 1979, UNEF 2 had ceased its operations with the failure of the Security Council to extend its mandate, but this was the time when a military-political upheaval took place in Ghana with the first *coup* by Flight-Lieutenant Jerry Rawlings. The ending of UNEF operations was bad in itself for the morale of the troops, and I felt that to send the troops home might act as a catalyst for exacerbating the already difficult and uncertain situation in Ghana. I communicated this assessment to my fellow-countryman Major-General Timothy Dibuama, the Secretary-General's Military Adviser based at UN HQ, New York. We put our heads together to keep 'Op Sunrise' alive, and to send our men, as they were evacuated from Sinai, not to Ghana but to South Lebanon. Timothy raised the matter with Brian Urquhart who was wholly sympathetic. The following month, Brian and one of his directors, Dr James Jonah, visited me in UNIFIL and I seized this golden opportunity to address them, separately, on the need for Ghanaian troops to continue their peacekeeping contribution with the UN. Discussions continued from my HQ in Naqoura to our hotel in Beirut, where they had gone to see the President and government leaders within the context of the peacemaking process. By the time they left for New York, I was confident that Timothy and I had won our point. The only difficulty was the question of UNIFIL's approved strength. By establishment, it was authorised to operate with a ceiling strength of 6,000, and at this time we had about 5,700. A contingent of 300 was not a viable proposition, but Ghanbatt's situation was such that any form of presence in UNIFIL was acceptable. On 1 September 1979 Ghanbatt 11, with Lt.-Col. I.G.M.K. Kpeto in command, became fully operational in the UNIFIL area of operations, with its HQ at Kafr Dunin, where it remained until it was relocated to Marakah in late 1986, on the withdrawal of Frenchbatt.

Little did we expect that UNIFIL's financial constraints would give us the opportunity to boost our strength much higher: by early 1980, we had been able to increase Ghanbatt's strength, due to UNIFIL's general redeployment exercises with some countries reducing their strength, to a full battalion strength of 700 all ranks. It was fortunate that I was on the ground and Timothy Dibuama was at UN HQ to coordinate those efforts. We had a further stroke of luck — in June 1980, when Katmandu temporarily withdrew its troops to help maintain law and order in Nepal during their national referendum. Timothy and I then sought the temporary replacement of Nepbatt by a second full unit from Ghana. Hence for a full year till June 1981 Ghana operated with two full battalions, the second unit head-quartered in Blate. The area around Blate is hilly and I was much concerned that Ghanbatt 15 might suffer severely in the cold winter. However, the Norwegians had greatcoats flown out for them specially from Oslo. Thus we pulled through the cold spell from December 1980 to March 1981, which was a major relief for Timothy and myself. The Nepalese are used to the cold of the Himalayas, but not our men from warm Africa.

Ghana's performance in 'Op Sunrise', especially with UNIFIL in South Lebanon where I kept an eagle eye on the troops, was commendable. Like other units they had their ups and downs, but on the whole, taking the entire difficult and confusing situation of Lebanon into consideration, they did well. Part of their good performance could be attributed to the financial incentives from UN headquarters, through the Ghana government. With their allowances paid to them while in Lebanon, all officers and men were able to purchase all sorts of valuable articles. I have always advised soldiers to think carefully and plan the use to which they will put their financial resources. Such an opportunity does not usually come more than once, and so the maximum use should be made of it.

'Op Sunrise' undoubtedly helped to improve the living standards of our troops. For once they could afford freezers, cookers, hi-fi systems, television sets and all sorts of household items normally too expensive for them. A corn-milling machine — known to the Ghanaian troops as a 'knicker-knicker' — became the status symbol for all troops on 'Op Sunrise'. Almost every soldier bought one, either to use commercially himself or to sell. As I always cautioned them, it did not matter whether they sold the machine or used it commercially, what was important was the use to which they put their enhanced incomes, for their own benefit and the benefit of their families back in Ghana.

The benefits of 'Op Sunrise' to Ghanbatt personnel extended to the government and consequently the entire people of Ghana. Any country's participation in UN peacekeeping operations is based on a contractual agreement between the UN and that country. All UN payments are made direct to the contributing governments, who then pay their troops according to their national terms and conditions of service. The UN has no role in deciding what amounts governments pay their troops. The UN allowances paid to Ghanaian troops by the home government amount to almost half of the total amounts paid by the UN. This is because, for example, clothing is not the UN's responsibility, but that of the home government, and there is other expenditure incurred by home governments which are not reimbursable by the UN. Most contributing governments in Latin America, Africa and Asia pay their troops much less than the governments of the Scandinavian and other European countries. While Western countries lose financially, developing countries gain. I believe that such benefits have been used by governments to procure medicines and other essential items. This, in Ghana's case, is an important contribution to the people by their armed forces, who have often been regarded as a drain on national resources.

The second major beneficiary of Ghana's participation in the UN's Middle Eastern peacekeeping activities has been Ghana Airways, which first became involved in the financially rewarding rotation of troops when I took up my appointment with UNEF 2 in May 1974. I realised that the Canadians, Poles and other contingents were rotating on their own national airlines, and asked UNEF's chief administrative officer why Ghanaian troops were not being rotated by our national airline. He said that if Ghana Airways could put in its bid he did not doubt that it would be awarded the contract; he then briefed me on the UN bidding procedures. I quickly sent a letter home to Wing-Commander Peter Agyekum, then Commissioner for Transport and Communications and an old colleague, advising him accordingly. Ghana Airways won the next contract and has since become part of 'Op Sunrise', initially using its VC-10 to move our troops to and from Sinai. There was a period of interruption when the VC-10 became unserviceable. Ghana Airways had no replacement aircraft of its own, and entered into sub-contracting arrangements with other airlines, but this became too expensive for the UN, with the result that our national airline dropped out completely from this activity. The exercise was reactivated in 1984 when the DC-10 service was introduced.

Recreation and Welfare (R & W) for troops on peacekeeping missions is essential. From time to time, the soldier should be able to get away from the sight and sound of guns to an environment of peace and tranquillity. Until the Israelis invaded Lebanon in June 1982, UNIFIL troops spent part of their leave in Beirut and part in Israel. But when

Beirut was almost cut off from South Lebanon and all road access from the south to the north was blocked by armed militias, Israel became perforce the only country where all UNIFIL troops could go for leave. Ghanbatt troops have been no exception. To cut the cost of hotel accommodation to bearable levels, they normally spend four days in Israel: they enter at the border post of Rosh Hanikra, drive through Capernaum, see the Sea of Galilee, drive past Tiberias along the river Jordan, and arrive in Jerusalem early in the evening. On the second day, they go to Jericho for shopping, visit the area of the Dead Sea and return to Jerusalem. The third day is spent in Bethlehem, visiting the Holy Sepulchre in the Old City, while the Muslim soldiers go to pray in the Al Aqsa mosque and look around Jerusalem. On the final day, they leave Jerusalem by way of Tel Aviv with a stop in Nazareth and back to Kafr Dunin through Naqoura. A few ardent Muslims have been able to make their pilgrimage to Mecca, thus becoming *alhajis* while on 'Op Sunrise'.

From time to time, a few of the officers and men with an interest in agriculture express a wish to visit some *kibbutzim* to acquaint themselves with Israeli farming techniques and know-how, which are well known to be among the best in the world. Such requests have always been warmly received, and arrangements are made by the Israeli liaison staff.

In short, the Ghanbatt participation in 'Op Sunrise' has been immensely beneficial. The troops have benefited professionally by operating alongside so many other national contingents, and the travel to other parts of the world far from home is in itself a great education. Our officers and men went to the Pyramids of Giza, the sands of Sinai and the holy places they had heard of at Sunday School.

I knew that taking leave of Ghanbatt at the end of my tour with the UN was going to be extremely difficult, both for me and for the troops. I was going to miss my periodic visits to Kafr Dunin and their areas of responsibility. While these visits naturally gave me the opportunity to examine how the men were doing on the ground, they were always followed by durbars at which I expressed my candid impressions on their performance and what was expected of them in order to uphold the image of both the UN and Ghana. When the troops came on leave to Jerusalem, they always paid formal courtesy calls on me at my HQ in Government House. On these occasions I gave them my usual pep-talks, again on how to comport themselves and the need for them to take their operational duties seriously so that the UN Secretariat would find it less difficult to invite Ghana to participate in future peacekeeping activities in other parts of the world. Sometimes when UNTSO was organising an evening social function, the Ghanbatt band was made available to entertain the guests, and this especially endeared Ghanbatt to UNTSO personnel.

At times when our contingents were being rotated, I always saw off the departing contingent at the airport and welcomed the newcomers — it gave me the chance to talk to the troops before they entered South Lebanon and took up their weapons to defend UNIFIL's mandate. Thoughts of my occasional logistical rescue operations for the troops during their 'R & W' visits to Israel, the social get-togethers and generally seeing my own people in the mission area, together with much else, weighed heavily on my mind when I went to Kafr Dunin on 18 April 1986 to take my final leave. I knew that Colonel Ben Akafia the contingent commander, Lt.-Col. Alex Ankrah the commanding officer and all the officers, warrant officers, NCOs and men were sorry to see me go. Feeling their emotions, it was difficult for me to control my own. They expressed concern that my absence would mean the removal of what little political cover they had. Ghana's ambassador to Egypt is accredited to Lebanon, but the situation in the area makes it difficult for him to visit the troops. My presence had made his non-availability less important. Their apprehensions were well-founded; in such a confused situation, it was important for senior representatives of the governments of contributing countries to visit the mission area from time to time and show their respective national flags. Also, it boosted morale when a senior national representative came and talked to the troops — officers and men alike. Such visits made the troops feel that their contribution was recognised and appreciated by those who had sent them into the field.

But I knew I was leaving Ghanbatt 25 and subsequent Ghanbatts in mature and sympathetic hands, both in the mission area and at UN HQ in New York. General Bill Callaghan, as their Force Commander, would still be seeing them, though from a different standpoint. I had shared a very close association with Bill for the past decade in UNTSO, where he had served as my deputy and senior staff officer; he had taken over my command both in UNTSO and in UNIFIL. I suspect that Bill's admiration for Ghanaian troops had started in the Congo, where Ghana and Ireland cooperated in the ONUC operations.

Bill showed his care for our men by his frequent visits to Kafr Dunin and Ghanbatt's areas of responsibility, and he always encouraged them in times of operational, administrative and logistical difficulties. As Force Commander, he encouraged and financially supported Ghanbatt Muslims wishing to undertake their *hajj* pilgrimage to Mecca. Finally, he always kept a Ghanaian cook and batman at his official residence in Naqoura. So I was fully reassured that I was leaving the Ghanaian contingent in secure hands and with all the fatherly care they could need.

Bill Callaghan was to be succeeded as Force Commander UNIFIL by the Force Commander UNDOF, Major-General Gustav Hägglund. Gustav had handled UNDOF on the Golan exceptionally well, and I know that neither the Syrians nor the Israelis were happy to see him relinquish his post there to take up the UNIFIL command. I knew he would take good professional care of Ghanbatt.

The complexity of the political and military situation in South Lebanon makes it necessary for the Force Commander to have highly professional and knowledgeable military and civilian staff at the head-quarters. Such staff assistance, when properly extended to the unit commanders, facilitates their operational activities in their respective areas of responsibility. With troops rotating every six months, continuity in this area of support is essential.

UNIFIL's chief press and information officer over a long period was Timur Göksel (from Turkey), who succeeded Keith Beavan in 1979. This well-informed officer went to great lengths to assist unit commanders in their negotiations with the local armed elements as these arose; he knew the leaders of all these groups personally. His political knowledge was also useful to the Force Commander, especially when the substantive senior political adviser was out of the mission area. His briefings on the current local situation for new contingent and battalion commanders was always helpful. In short, he was dedicated to the cause of peace, and made an outstanding contribution to UNIFIL operations. I knew that after my departure he would continue to be a friend to successive Ghanbatts. At UN HQ in New York, Ghanbatt also continued to have well-wishers, including of course Major-General Timothy Dibuama, Military Adviser to the Secretary-General, and himself a Ghanaian, who assured me that he would be monitoring its activities and keeping in close touch with both contingent and unit commanders.

The Military Adviser's office is a rather less familiar wing of the UN peacemaking set-up. Major-General Koho of Finland held the office when I joined UNEF in 1974, and was replaced in 1977 by Timothy Dibuama. As commander of the Ghana armed forces I had sent Timothy to New York immediately following the departure of Ghanbatt 1 to UNEF 2 in January 1974, as Ghana's representative on the Military Adviser's staff. Hence his performance has always been of special personal interest to me. As Force Commander of UNIFIL and Chief of Staff UNTSO, coupled with being the most senior UN officer on the ground in the area in 1981−6, I was in almost daily telephone contact with him. Ghana has reason to feel proud of her torch-bearer on the 38th floor at UN HQ.

I also knew that Brian Urquhart's successor as head of peacekeeping operations, Marrack Goulding, would provide Ghanbatt contingents with the fullest possible support and cooperation. Having come from Angola, where he was British ambassador, he knows something of the African mind and thus understands Ghanbatt's sociological difficulties. So with good commanders and staff on the ground in South Lebanon, and trusted friends and colleagues in New York, I did not feel that my people were being abandoned. Indeed, I could still give them ever-needed support for their morale from Ghana.

To readers from countries outside Africa, it may seem strange that I should emphasise and re-emphasise that participation with UNEF in Sinai and with UNIFIL in South Lebanon has been an inestimable national asset to Ghana. It has, as already mentioned, enhanced the troops' professional expertise and their standards of living — both are important. Perhaps most important of all, it has reduced the risks to Ghana's political stability.

The following is part of a letter I wrote to Brian Urquhart on 22 December 1982:

. . . . The intervening period between Christmas and New Year's Day is, for most Ghanaians, stocktaking time. I am one of those addicts and I am doing precisely that.

In the last few weeks, my senior officers from the Ghana contingent serving in South Lebanon, who are rotating back to Ghana, have come to see me to express their appreciation and gratitude for being able to participate in 'Operation Sunrise'. This feeling of gratefulness among our ranks happens all the time. To you, Sir, and your staff Ghana participation may be normal, but to us, the officers, warrant officers, NCOs and men, 'Op Sunrise' has not only been the major morale-booster but, more importantly, the major activity of military significance in the Ghana armed forces of contemporary times.

Timothy [Dibuama] and I join all ranks of Ghanbatts, past and present, to express our profound thanks, gratitude and appreciation for your continuing support. We all join hands to say 'thank you' with national respect, dignity and pride. To Sir Brian our greatest tribute, highest esteem, respect and admiration.

PART TWO

20
PERCEPTIONS OF THE REGIONAL POLITICAL SCENE

The Arab world feels strongly that if the Middle East is to find peace the Palestinian question must be resolved. The view that it is the crux of the crisis in the region is shared by Western powers, including the countries of the European Economic Community — hence the Venice declaration of June 1980.

Most Arab countries, particularly Syria and Jordan, distrust the mediation efforts made by the United States. This is because of the massive support it gives to Israel, which is the arch-enemy not merely of the Palestinians but of the whole Arab world. US grants and aid to Israel total well over US$2 billion a year, more than any other country receives. Some figures in government circles in Israel feel that the country should reduce its dependence on the United States in the hope of reducing US influence at the same time, and the question of whether Israel can survive without US aid has long been a serious talking-point among Israelis. The proposal made at one time by an Israeli minister of state that the national currency be changed to the US dollar underscores the present dependence.

The United States, in addition to its economic support, gives political support and shelter to Israel in the international arena. For example, it vetoed a Lebanese-sponsored resolution in the Security Council in late 1984 on Israel's occupation of South Lebanon, and the bombing of the US embassy in Beirut has been attributed to this fact. Again the inability of an Arab country to purchase arms from the United States in face of Israeli objections makes the strength of the US-Israeli bond plainly evident. The United States refused to sell much-needed Hawk anti-aircraft missiles and F-16 fighters to Jordan due to the influence of the Jewish lobby. US politicians who denounce Israel suffer a setback in their political careers, and it is strongly felt that Jewish approval is vital for any presidential candidate hoping to enter the White House.

It is for these interlinked reasons that the Arabs feel the United States is a partisan in the conflict and therefore unable to be objective in its mediatory and peacemaking role; hence it cannot function fully as a peace-broker. At the same time, the Arabs are fully aware that without US political clout Israel cannot be moved. It was Eisenhower's influence that got Israel out of Sinai in 1956 and Kissinger's that persuaded it to pull further to the east from the Suez Canal in 1975. Hence the paradox that the Arabs mistrust the United States as a regional peace-broker, but at the same time need the Americans if there is to be peace in the area.

Since the failure of the Multinational Force in Beirut, the Arab countries have been convinced that the United States cannot resolve the region's crisis alone. It has been US policy, supported by Israel, to keep the Soviet Union out of the peace process. But the Soviet Union — and the UN — should be involved, and involved particularly in any international conference on the situation. The Arab position on this international arrangement was stated unambiguously to the Secretary-General, Javier Perez de Cuellar, by Egypt, Syria, Lebanon and Jordan during his visit to the area in June 1984.

Support for an international peace conference, in which all the parties to the conflict including the PLO and the Soviet Union should participate, has always been the UN position; it is also supported by the Arabs but opposed by the United States and Israel. The reasons for Israel's objections to talks with the PLO, and for PLO's direct participation in any peacemaking process are discussed in Chapter 24. Furthermore, Israel insists that the PLO's main objective is not the peaceful resolution of the Palestinian question but the destruction of Israel in accordance with its covenant. Israeli hawks (and in particular the Likud leader Yitzhak Shamir) espouse the psychological minority paranoia. Like the Lebanese Christians fearing that if they give up a little of their political authority to the Muslims they will lose all of it, Yitzhak Shamir is afraid that an international conference could end up requiring Israel to withdraw to the pre-June 1967 borders as a prelude to pulling back to the 1948 Independence borders. At the time of writing, the question whether Israel will annex the occupied West Bank and Gaza strip remains unanswered. The Israelis are well aware of the 'demographic time bomb' of the Palestinians in the occupied territories, and fear that the Jewish character of their state will be destroyed should the West Bank and Gaza be annexed and equal rights have to be extended to the Palestinian Arabs as citizens of Israel.

Even though the United States is opposed in principle to the Soviets becoming involved in the Middle Eastern peace process, the feeling is that the Jewish lobby might influence US policy in the opposite direction should the Soviets relax their policy on Jewish emigration and consider re-establishing their diplomatic ties with Israel which were cut in the wake of the Six Day war in June 1967. US enthusiasm for advancing the peace process slowed down considerably following several notable setbacks in Lebanon. The failure of the MNF with the disastrous loss of US Marines; the abrogation of the 17 May 1983 troop withdrawal agreement, in which Secretary of State George Shultz lost much of his credibility; the subsequent bombing of the US embassy in West Beirut; the constant kidnapping of US citizens; the hijacking of the TWA airliner in 1985 with its passengers being held hostage for seventeen days — all these factors contributed to the negative attitude in Washington.

I attributed part of the difficulties experienced by the Americans in their peacemaking efforts to Washington's lack of a deep understanding of the Arab mind. Regarding the abrogation of the 17 May 1983 agreement in particular, it should have been obvious that Syria would not acquiesce in any agreement relating to Lebanon in which it had not fully participated or on which it had not been fully consulted. Secondly, the terms of the agreement demanded the withdrawal from Lebanon of Syrian as well as Israeli troops. This, of course, could in no way be acceptable to President Hafez el Assad. Furthermore, there was no mention of attempts to resolve the Golan issue as part of a Lebanese-Israeli package deal. Washington should have realised that Syria is a power in the politics of the region, and because of its strong influence in Lebanon, the political shuttles of George Shultz and Morris Draper should have been more intense between Tel Aviv and Damascus than between Tel Aviv and Beirut.

Israel's National Unity government, on the other hand, is not strong enough to take bold decisions on the Palestinian issue — which, in any case, appears to be outside its major priorities. The deep ideological differences between Likud and the Labour Alignment, Israel's two major parties, in their perceptions of the West Bank — which Likud followers call biblically 'Samaria and Judea' — compound the difficulties facing would-be peacemakers.

With the continuing fragmentation of the PLO, whose allegiance is split between President Assad of Syria and Chairman Yasir Arafat (only in the summer of 1988 did King Hussein renounce his claim to control and speak for the Palestinians); and with the continuing power struggle and fighting among the Arab countries, which was compounded by the Iraq-Iran war, peace prospects in the area seem remote.

Potential for an outbreak of major hostilities in the region

If the prospects for peace in the region are so dim, then what is the potential for an outbreak of major hostilities? Here we should turn to what I regard as the paradoxes of the 1982 Israeli invasion of Lebanon.

One of the first major effects of that invasion was the involuntary creation of a no-war mood among the Israeli public. Israel went into

Lebanon ostensibly to protect its northern borders and settlements by destroying the PLO military infrastructure. Hence the code name 'Operation Peace for Galilee'. This was the stated objective, but it is felt that there were certain unstated political aims as well. One of these was to make peace with a second Arab country besides Egypt. Mr Begin, the Prime Minister, was reported to have met Bechir Gemayel, then President-elect of Lebanon, in the northern Israeli coastal resort of Nahariya to demand a formula for a peace agreement. Bechir Gemayel is reported to have refused it. Unfortunately, he was assassinated before he could be formally sworn in, and this act provoked the massacre of the Palestinian refugees in the Sabra and Chatila camps on 14 September 1982. Israel was accused by the world public of being an accomplice in the massacre, and suffered great damage to its national reputation in consequence.

Israel had a further objective, which was to remove the radical Palestinian fighters from Lebanon: it should then be much easier for them to negotiate freely with perceived moderate Palestinians on the West Bank on the Palestinian issue. This has so far not succeeded, since the threat by Palestinian hardliners to eliminate any Palestinian dealing directly with Israel is still actively pursued. The assassination in Portugal of Mr Sartawi is a case in point.

The only tangible benefit of the invasion would have been the 17 May 1983 troop withdrawal agreement, but this had to be abrogated under pressure from Damascus.

After the Israeli final pull-back from the Awali river line southwards to their present forward defended positions in the so-called security belt, re-infiltration of the hardcore PLO into South Lebanon accelerated. The bitter fighting between the PLO and the Shiite Amal movement from late 1986 into the next year clearly indicates that not only had the PLO fighters returned to Lebanon but all those arsenals of heavy weapons confiscated from them on the eve of their exodus from Beirut in August 1982 were also back in full strength. Here again, the stated objective of destroying the PLO military infrastructure was a failure.

Hence Israel had gone back to the same situation as it was in before the invasion. This raises questions whether the war was necessary. The big question asked by the Israeli public is the justification for the cost in human lives in a war which, unlike the wars of survival fought in 1948, 1967 and 1973, was really one of choice for Israel. With over 600 killed and over 4,000 wounded, of whom some are permanently disabled, this will continue to exercise the minds of Israelis for some time.

I have to say that I admired the IDF public information directorate for putting up such an effective information campaign, which succeeded in convincing the general public at home that the security of the state was under threat and that the IDF therefore had to strike at the PLO in Lebanon. It began immediately following the final imposition of the Multinational Force and Observers (MFO) in Sinai at the end of April 1982, and took the form of press, radio and other local media reports of a massive build-up by the PLO of armed bases in South Lebanon and its acquisition of new heavier guns, self-propelled multiple rocket-launchers, rocket-propelled grenades, Grad surface-to-surface missiles and long-range Katyusha rockets, and the influx and concentration of more PLO fighters into the area. Consequently, the air strikes at PLO bases and their main supply routes in early May 1982 must have been welcome by the Israeli public. Little did they know that they were only the prelude to a war, a month later, which they were to condemn.

This war of choice, with its major human losses but with no military or political benefits to the country, created a serious problem of national morale, which explains why Shimon Peres, then the Prime Minister of the National Unity government, was able to get the IDF withdrawn further southwards without much difficulty from the government. Going massively back again into Lebanon or getting seriously involved in any major armed confrontation with an Arab country, particularly Syria, would have needed highly justifiable reasons to convince the Israeli public that their sons from the *kibbutzim* and *moshavim* had an inescapable national cause to defend. Thus the 1982 invasion served as a deterrent against war for the Israelis. This is the first paradox.

Syria is assessed to have lost a quarter of its air force and the same percentage of its best aircrew during the 1982 air battles with the Israelis. This meant quite a long waiting time for re-equipping and, more important, re-training. For Syria to get into any major confrontation with the possibility of heavy losses of Soviet-made equipment would not be good for the image of the Soviets, who are Syria's major arms suppliers. This is the second paradox produced by the 1982 war in Lebanon. It also serves as a factor restraining Syria from going to war, at least for a while.

Jordan will be extremely reluctant to join in any Arab war against Israel. It did not participate in the 1973 war, due principally to its bitter experience in the June 1967 war, which deprived it of sovereignty over the West Bank. Also, war with Israel could destroy the peaceful status of the Jordan valley, and thus affect the economic activity of the West Bank by slowing down the existing traffic between it and Jordan. Egypt is at peace with Israel, and with extensive economic dependence on the United States would find it extremely difficult to go to war against Israel, unless the war were seen as overwhelmingly necessary in order to defend Egypt's sovereignty and territorial integrity. With Iraq slowly recovering from its immensely destructive eight-year war with Iran, which the Arab world financed, it would be extremely difficult for the Arabs to open and support a second front in the region or anywhere else. Leaving other counter-actions aside, the Arab countries are not as rich today as they were before the slump in oil prices. Could this be part of the reason why most Arab governments and Chairman Yasir Arafat are opting for negotiations as against confrontation?

In recent years, we have seen a gradual change in the Arab attitude towards Israel, from aggressiveness to moderation and accommodation. Sephardic Jews from Israel visited Morocco at the end of 1984, obviously with the approval of King Hassan, and Prime Minister Shimon Peres had a meeting with the King in a Moroccan city in July 1986. Saudi Arabia was reported to be buying Israeli-manufactured agricultural equipment. Iraq has re-established diplomatic relations with the United States, a fact which is obviously in the interest of Israel and other moderate Arab countries.

Any prediction of peace or war in the region is hazardous because the situation is so fragile and unpredictable. It is impossible to foresee an environment of total peace in the near future, but it is also difficult to imagine major hostilities like the 1982 invasion breaking out unless the security of a state were seriously threatened and intense public pressure were placed on the government to react.

21

THE LEBANESE CRISIS

Lebanon is gradually disappearing from the map of the Arab world, if not from the map of the world itself. The massive destruction has been caused not only by the Israeli air force's retaliatory bombing raids but, even more, by the indigenous Lebanese themselves. Lebanese Christians have been fighting against Lebanese Muslims; Christians against Christians; Muslims against Muslims; Christians against the PLO; Muslims against the PLO; mainstream PLO Fatah supported by Chairman Arafat against Abu Musah's breakaway PLO faction supported by President Hafez el Assad of Syria; and, perhaps more understandably, Israel against the PLO. In addition, other countries and governments prefer to wage their wars and carry out other forms of hostilities, not in their own countries but by proxy in Lebanon. Israel chooses Lebanon and not even the Golan Heights, which it has occupied since 1967, to wage its war against Syria. Lebanon has provided a stage for the kidnapping of ambassadors and government representatives and the seizure of foreign nationals, either in retribution or as a bargaining instrument for the release of prisoners held abroad for criminal acts and to obtain other forms of political concession. The perpetrators of these inhuman acts escape prosecution, because the anarchy in the country prevents the normal processes of law and justice from being pursued.

Fighting among Lebanese has at times been fierce. Heavy mortars, artillery, tanks and every kind of explosive shell available on the world arms market have been brought into play. I have often been asked how these arsenals of weapons ever get into Lebanon. The pertinent question is not how they get in but how they are financed. As to their entry into the country, this is easy: all the feudal and confessional warlords who command and control the fighters have their seaports which they operate free from any control: the national government just does not have the state resources to exercise its legitimate authority. Hence the proliferation of weapons, providing a catalyst for the ceaseless progressive destruction of the Land of the Cedars since an outbreak of hostilities between the Lebanese Christians and the PLO in 1975 set off the civil war.

In Beirut the large number of destroyed buildings, particularly near the port; the charred remains of famous hotels; the caved-in jewellery market (the *Souk*) and the shell-marks on numerous tall apartment blocks all bear witness to the atrocious fighting and massive destruction that continue to defy sanity. The destruction has spread through-out the length and breadth of the country — the ports of Tyre and Sidon in the south, Tripoli in the north, Sofar, Aley and Bhamdun in the Druze-dominated Chouf mountains, and towns and villages in the Bekaa in the east all bear similar scars. In the midst of it all, UNIFIL seeks to keep the peace in the south.

Muslim-dominated West Beirut presents a much sadder spectacle than Christian-dominated East Beirut. This could partly be because the Palestinian refugee camps, all in West Beirut, also serve as the bases for the PLO from which they fight their wars. Again, because of occasional support given to the PLO against the Israelis by their Muslim armed supporters based principally in West Beirut, the sector west of the so-called Green Line dividing the city into its east and west sectors has been the major target of Israeli air and naval retaliatory raids.

Until the outbreak of the civil war, the main PLO fighting base was Tel Zataar camp, but this was totally destroyed by the Lebanese Chris-tians with the full military support of the Syrian army. It was the then President of Lebanon Suleiman Franjieh, a Maronite Christian, who in 1976 requested President Hafez el Assad to send in his Syrian troops to help destroy the PLO, which at that time appeared to be winning. The Syrian troops, having finished off the PLO, then turned their guns against the Christians.

The civil war has of course resulted in tens of thousands of Lebanese being killed and wounded, and for fear of confessional atro-cities, Muslims have moved away from non-Muslim areas of resi-dence, and Christians have done the equivalent. The displacement of families is most obvious in the Chouf mountain areas of Sofar, Alley and Bhamdun, where Christians had lived as a minority among the predominant Druze for many decades. Families conti-nue searching in vain for their kidnapped relatives. Walid Jumblatt, the Druze leader who reigns in the Chouf, was bold enough in 1984 to tell appealing families that all kidnapped persons who had not been released since being abducted should be considered dead. It was sad, but it was a fact. The killing of the Prime Minister Rashid Karame on 1 June 1987 with a bomb planted in the army helicopter flying him from his home-town of Tripoli to Beirut underscores the gravity of the continuing unstable and unpredictable situation in Lebanon.

Many people have asked me what the fighting in Lebanon is all about, and in particular whether it is a religious war or not. I feel that while it is true that the crisis had religious roots in the 1932 census, followed by the confessionally-based government of 1943, this aspect of the crisis has been overtaken by other considerations.

At the time of going to press, the Maronite President Amin Gemayel is fighting, through the Lebanese army, to sustain Christian authority and maintain the distinct identity of Christians in Lebanon. This survival means the survival of the Lebanese Christian community. The loss of the presidency would mean the end of the National Covenant, and this is something that all Lebanese Christians would fight to maintain. The Muslims would obviously like to see the Covenant come to an end.

The feudal warlords, the *za'ims*, who are the main power-brokers and who call the shots, are fighting to promote and protect their economic interests in the country. Former President Franjieh controls sea and land imports entering Lebanon from the north; the Gemayels control imports coming through their port of Jounieh; the Druze leader Walid Jumblatt has, since 1985, commissioned his seaport in Khalde which he opens to the PLO — if the money is right. Former President Camille Chamoun controlled his own enclave in Christian East Beirut. 'Protection money' — in the form of tax — is levied by these *za'ims* on all residents in their areas of control. If an individual refuses to pay, this normally leaves his shop, hotel or residence 'unprotected', and so people find it safer to pay up for the sake of peace. For the ordinary Lebanese fighting is the only way he knows of earning a living. He has not been to school and has no other skills besides pulling the trigger on the AK47. For the 'have nots' it is matter of survival in a war against the 'haves'.

The Palestinians are fighting because they want to establish a state in Lebanon, which they are unable to do in Palestine, their homeland. Syria is fighting to maintain its influence in Lebanon by ensuring that major decisions on the country, either by the Lebanese or by external powers, are taken in Damascus and not in Beirut. Israel is fighting to protect the security of its northern settlements and in the hope of signing a peace treaty with a second Arab country, if possible. The chaos is further compounded by the perceptions of the dominant powers of East and West of their own 'spheres of influence', 'security' and 'rivalry'. It is important always to recall that all this fighting is taking place on Lebanese sovereign soil.

Was the civil war that broke out in 1975 anticipated by the Lebanese themselves? My own impression has been that they expected it from the period of the French Mandate onwards. With this in mind I have always asked two questions: first, why was Beirut's international airport constructed in West Beirut, a predominantly Muslim sector, and the harbour in East Beirut? The implication here is that in periods of conflict between the Christian and Muslim communities, these two major national centres of communication and economic activity become the main targets for the factions. The second question is why, since its formation when Lebanon first became a state, the Lebanese army has always been weak, to the detriment of national security but to the immense advantage of the feudal warlords and their private armed elements.

Let us look at some of the historical events which may have had an impact on the gradual destruction of the one-time 'Switzerland of the Levant'.

Based on the 1932 census (the only one that has ever taken place in Lebanon) a confessional type of government was formed in 1943 when the country became an independent sovereign state following the end of the French Mandate. By the constitution then established, partly in written and partly in unwritten form (the so-called National Covenant or 'gentleman's agreement'), representation in the government corresponded to religious distribution. The agreed ratio for representation in the Chamber of Deputies (parliament) was 6 Christians to 5 Muslims (in a parliament of 99 deputies, this meant 54 Christians to 45 Muslims). With the Maronite Christians being the largest single Christian entity at the time of the census, the President of Lebanon since 1943 has always been a Maronite Christian, the Speaker of the Assembly (his 'number two') a Shiite Muslim, the Prime Minister a Sunni Muslim, the Army Commander a Maronite Christian, his Chief of Staff a Druze, the Foreign Minister a Greek Catholic, and so on. This rather important aspect of the political structure was not enshrined in the written part of the constitution; it was the part agreed upon by the various confessional leaders in a 'gentleman's agreement'.

With the change that has taken place in the balance of the population since the 1930s, the Muslims claim to be in the majority and so demand a greater share of political authority. The Shiites in particular claim to represent one-third of the total Lebanese population (resident of Lebanon) of around 3 million. The Shiites are the poorest single entity among the Lebanese, and predominate in the south. Logically, the Christians have to give up part of their power and, with it, authority to the Muslims but they are afraid to do so. What is the basis of their fears and apprehensions?

There are ideological differences between the two major religious groups. The Christians are basically oriented towards the West, as against the Muslims who are inclined towards the Arab world; they see themselves more as French and less as Arabs. This could partly explain why President Assad wanted the Lausanne conciliation talks in 1984 to define Lebanon first and foremost as an Arab country. The Christians, being now in the minority, are afraid that if they cede a little of their authority to the Muslims, they may lose everything they have. A Lebanese army officer whom I met in Yarze was frank with me. He said: 'General, look at all the twenty-one countries of the Arab world; it is only in Lebanon that we Christians have authority, and we will die for it.' One could not have asked for a clearer statement. Again, psychologically, there is always the fear of a minority for its survival. Could this be part of the Jewish apprehension and also the fear of President Assad's Alawite minority?

The Shiite political renaissance did not start till 1979 – 80, when their spiritual leader, Imam Musa Sadr, started preaching the gospel of the Shiites' deprivation, repression and underdevelopment. South Lebanon, where most of the Lebanese Shiites live, is the poorest part of the country. I used to travel by road from Beirut to my UNIFIL HQ in Naqoura from time to time. It is nice driving south along the coast road. One can see economic and industrial activity all the way to Sidon and a little beyond. At Zahrani is the oil refinery site, but only a few kilometres further south from there, South Lebanon proper begins, and all evidence of economic and industrial activity disappears. This observation can also be made of the drive from Naqoura on the Mediterranean to the easternmost village of Chebaa. The growing of tobacco and rearing of sheep and goats are all the poor Shiites have. Could this explain why their rate of population growth has outstripped even that of the Druze?

The invasion of Lebanon in 1982 may also have awakened the Druze to certain national realities. They were a good warrior tribe, but locked up in the Chouf mountains without any outlet to the sea and therefore exclusively dependent on their reluctant friends and allies, the Syrians, to make lines of communication available to them for the supply of their war materials. Thus they took the opportunity of the hostilities and confusion after the IDF pull-back from the Chouf mountains to the Awali in 1983 to fight their way westwards to the coast. Walid Jumblatt became fully established on the Mediterranean with his fully operational Khalde seaport, through which come not only his war supplies but also those destined for other factions, who of course pay heavy fees for the privilege. Reports that the PLO use this port to ship heavy weapons into Lebanon cannot be ruled out. After all, Jumblatt allowed the PLO the use of his Chouf grounds to bombard Amal strongholds in Beirut during their serious hostilities in early 1986, when all PLO factions including those under Syrian influence joined arms with Arafat's Fatah to stop Amal decimating the Sabra and Chatila refugee camps. The fact that in 1983 and 1984 Jumblatt's PSP and Amal had fought side by side against the PLO demonstrates the endlessly shifting alliances in the Land of the Cedars with its volatile mixture of politics, religion, local loyalties and the power of money. It is always advisable to expect the unexpected in Lebanon because anything can happen. To be operating his own seaport and thus reducing his dependence on the President of Syria must also be an immense relief for Jumblatt and his Druze clan. For how long could the reluctant alliance with Syria have lasted, in view of contemporary history?

The ability of Jumblatt to construct the Khalde port also raises an unanswered question concerning his relationship with the Israelis. It is undoubted that the Israeli navy is able to exert an immense influence over Lebanon's territorial waters, so the fact that Israel did not interfere with this construction strongly indicates that the IDF has a friendly relationship with the PSP or, more specifically, with Walid Jumblatt. The fact that the Druze in Israel, who serve in the IDF, are of the same stock as the Druze in Palestine, Syria and Lebanon could further explain the ambiguity of Israel's attitude and its relationship with Jumblatt and the Chouf Druze. It cannot be surprising that the Israeli Druze were anxious to go to the aid of their kith and kin in the Chouf during the bitter fighting between the Christian Lebanese forces, predominantly Phalangists, and the Druze PSP following the IDF's withdrawal from the mountains in 1983.

The active presence of thousands of Palestinians, both refugees and active hard-core combatants of the PLO, further compounds the Lebanese morass. The declaration of the Jewish state on 14 May 1948 provoked serious hostilities between Israel on the one hand and Syria, Egypt, Jordan and Lebanon on the other, and this resulted in the first wave of Palestinian refugees — into Jordan, Syria and Lebanon, but not Egypt. The Six Day War in June 1967, resulting in the Israeli occupation of the West Bank, caused the second wave of Palestinian refugees, most of them into Lebanon.

In 1969 came the Cairo Agreement which not only formalised the presence of the Palestinian refugees in the camps but also authorised the carrying of weapons by the Palestinians — later a bone of contention between the Lebanese authorities and the PLO. The Lebanese have always accused the PLO of not respecting the terms of the Cairo Agreement, whereby the Palestinians could carry arms only for the protection of the refugees in the camps. The PLO in fact wielded power and authority, virtually establishing a state within a state in West Beirut, with its own tax system, radio station, police, civil administration and army, which was both efficient and effective. Selim el Hoss, when I asked him in April 1978 the status of the Cairo Agreement *vis-à-vis* Security Council Resolution 425 which established UNIFIL, said that the latter nullified all previous agreements, implicitly including the 1969 Cairo Agreement. However, whenever I questioned the PLO fighters or their commanders as to why they were in South Lebanon, they said it was by virtue of the 1969 Agreement with the Lebanese government. Thus the Cairo Agreement was in

conflict with UNIFIL's terms of reference and created serious difficulties in the operational functioning of our troops. This was a cross
which UNIFIL and all its commanders and troops have had to bear in
their peacekeeping operations in South Lebanon.

Finally came the so-called Black September of 1970, when King
Hussein had to drive the PLO out from Jordan in order to protect the
existence of his own Hashemite kingdom. The PLO's wish to establish
a state in Jordan could now be fulfilled in West Beirut. The Black
September exodus brought into Lebanon the radical hard core of
PLO combatants. Some of them moved to South Lebanon; this was
obstensibly to protect their refugees in Rashidiyah, El Buss and Bourj
el Shamali camps in the Tyre area, but my observations since 1976
have led me to the belief that the PLO's principal objective was to fight
Israel across the border from Lebanese soil. Protecting the camps was
strictly a secondary consideration. The Lebanese — Christians and
Muslims alike — are no lovers of the PLO whom they dislike for taking
their fertile lands and imposing their will on them, whether they like it
or not. Could this perhaps explain why the Lebanese threw rice, as a
welcoming gesture, on the invading Israeli troops when they entered
Lebanon in June 1982 to chase the Palestinians out of their country?

Since 30 September 1986, the Shiite Amal have been locked in bitter
fighting with the PLO. This broke out around Mieh Mieh and Ein
Hilwe refugee camps in Sidon and camps in the Tyre area; it also continued around Sabra, Chatila and Bourj el Barajneh in Beirut. From
these outbreaks it has to be inferred that the PLO is back in Lebanon,
in full force and with a formidable arsenal of heavy weapons. As part
of the August 1982 evacuation package under the auspices of the first
Multinational Force (MNF 1), the PLO were allowed to take with
them only their personal weapons, while their heavy guns were handed
over to the Lebanese armed forces.

The return of the PLO to Lebanon in full force is something that
was bound to stir up strong emotions among Israeli families and
provoke serious questions among Israeli politicians and military
commanders. Yet it had come back only four years after the war and
its expulsion from Lebanon. How then could Israel's heavy losses in the
war be justified? It was a wasted adventure. Paradoxically, the 1982
invasion benefited the PLO: but for the invasion, it would not have
acquired the rare battle experience it now possesses or be able to stand
on its own feet in its quest for return to a state within a state in
Lebanon. It is hard to imagine any radical change in the Lebanese
situation in the immediate future. Part of any durable solution would
have to be the permanent resettlement of Palestinian refugees outside
Lebanon. For as long as the camps exist in Lebanon, fighting between

the PLO and the Lebanese, whether Christian or Muslim, will continue.

There is another frightening aspect of the Lebanese crisis. Those who are holding the AK47s and squeezing the triggers of the myriad of missiles, tanks, mortars, artillery pieces, multiple rocket-launchers and rocket-propelled grenades; pulling the pins from grenades; laying anti-personnel mines and carrying out car-bomb explosions in Greater Beirut, South Lebanon, the Chouf mountain areas, the Bekaa and occasionally the port area of Tripoli — all belong to a very low age-group, roughly between sixteen and an upper limit of twenty-six. This means that those who are sixteen today have known virtually nothing but war and chaos. They have had no education, and are being trained in no skills other than killing and maiming. A big question is what to do with them if there should be peace. For those who are older the story is much the same, except that they may have had some form of education, at best completing their *baccalauréat* exams; perhaps they have seen a better Lebanon. However they have spent much of their adolescence with the gun, have matured in life with it, and may find it extremely difficult to part with that life which, in the eyes of some Lebanese, is flamboyant and honourable. Apart from receiving regular monthly pay, these gunmen steal, rob and commit all manner of criminal acts which supplement their legitimate emoluments many times over. Hence parting with the guns to go to sell bread in Hamra, where they once reigned as kings, would be a nightmare to them. This is a great problem for Lebanon, tomorrow if not today.

There is an inherent characteristics of the Lebanese which is to lay all the blame for their crisis on the outside world. This has got to change. Outside interference certainly contributes to their national problems: they nourish the fear that Israel's ultimate aim is to annex Southern Lebanon and take over the Awali and Litani headwaters, and that Syria's ultimate aim is to incorporate their country within 'Greater Syria'. Nevertheless, these are not the only causes of their problems.

The huge quantities of ammunition that have been expended during different spells of fighting could fully justify their claim that outside powers condone and encourage the crisis. In this connection I vividly remember the major outbreak of hostilities in February 1984. On February 6 alone, more than 2,500 shells of all kinds — tank, mortar and artillery — were fired by the different sides in Greater Beirut. The following week I went on a visit to Observer Group Lebanon, and took the opportunity to discuss the Beirut situation with my Chief OGL, an Australian. He said he could not understand how on one single day the Lebanese could fire that quantity of ammunition

— which represented all the ammunition reserves which the Australian government can afford for its army in a whole year. In one of my regular meetings with General Michel Aoun, the Lebanese army commander, he lamented to me, 'How can Lebanon and the Lebanese afford all these weapons and ammunition that we are using to brutally slaughter ourselves? Where does the money come from?' Of course he did not expect an answer, and I could not give one.

But the Lebanese should concede that part of the crisis is of their own making, and their first move towards resolving the crisis would be to close their ranks. If they only had a united front, then Lebanon would be in a reasonably good position to resist outside attempts to infiltrate and interfere with their peace and stability. But the fighting and internecine atrocities serve the interests of a few feudal warlords, who profit financially from their control of private seaports and their strong and heavily armed private armies. I heard the former Prime Minister Selim el Hoss saying in an address to the American University of Beirut that everyone in Lebanon was making money except the government. Private groups were collecting port taxes and protection money from private enterpreneurs, shops, houses and so on, but the government did not have effective machinery for raising funds legitimately to administer the country and exercise its governmental functions.

However, the resilience of the indigeuous Lebanese, despite all their woes, has always filled me with hope for the future. This quality has kept most of them in Lebanon. During some of the worst times in 1978 – 81, the IDF's heavy artillery was regularly shelling Tyre. As soon as the guns opened up, all the shops in the town would close and everybody, except perhaps the PLO fighters in Rashadiya camp, would run into the shelters. All life would apparently cease. But once the guns fell silent, everything would go back to normal as if nothing had ever happened, except for some new scars on the buildings and roads. Resilience was the essential spirit.

The speed with which the town of Khiam was rebuilt can only be called amazing. After the major hostilities in 1977 between the DFF based in Marjayoun and the PLO based in Khiam, Saad Haddad refused permission for the people of Khiam to return to their homes after his forces had finally driven out the PLO with strong support from the IDF. Khiam, originally a bustling place with over 12,000 inhabitants, became a ghost-town, uninhabited and serving as a training ground in urban house-to-house fighting for the IDF. Every building without exception needed rehabilitation. The only difference between Khiam and the Syrian township of Quneitra on the Golan was that Khiam was at least standing, whereas Quneitra was flattened. However, after the Israeli invasion in 1982 there was a change of heart and the next year the people of Khiam were allowed to return to their homes. The whole town was fully rebuilt and repopulated and soon looked as if nothing untoward had ever happened there. The memory of the first six families coming to their destroyed homes in Khiam to assess the cost of reconstruction will always live with me. They were filled not with bitterness but with the will and joy to come home. I was there because UNTSO maintained a presence in Khiam, with an observation post, during the six years it was deserted. The returnees were happy to see us still flying the UN flag, and I did not fail to make the point that their only hope and source of reassurance is the world body.

There have been other signs that should give us hope. Women and schoolchildren demonstrated in the streets of Beirut in 1985 for an end of the fighting, and in December 1986 both Christians and Muslims joined together to demonstrate against the deteriorating economic situation. In 1988, a large group of severely disabled Lebanese of all communities 'marched' the length of the country, and crossed the 'Green Line' in Beirut, as a demonstration for peace. I believe that the Lebanese Christian and the Lebanese Muslim can live in harmony together. Prime Minister Selim el Hoss, for example, is a Sunni Muslim with a Christian wife.

The Lebanese authorities have not relented in their efforts to resolve their crisis peacefully. There have been reconciliation talks — at Geneva in 1983 and Lausanne in 1984 — discussing among other things equal representation of Christians and Muslims in parliament, the establishment of a Second Chamber headed by a Muslim, and an equitable distribution of government appointments. It is a question of compromise, with the Christians making concessions that are acceptable to all the confessional communities and factions, and of those compromises and concessions being acceptable in Damascus, and not at the expense of Israel's security interests.

Both the indigenous Lebanese and the outside world have to understand that the country's crisis is political and therefore requires a political solution. Were it a military issue, the Israelis could have solved it before the Syrians came on the scene in 1976, and, failing that, the United States could have settled the country's problems with the *New Jersey*'s 16-inch guns in 1983–4.

There remain those soul-searching questions, already alluded to, which none of my Lebanese friends has been able to answer: why were certain vital, sensitive aspects of the political structure left out of the written constitution but agreed only by the National Covenant or 'gentleman's agreement'? Why was Beirut's international airport

located in predominantly Muslim West Beirut and the national seaport in predominantly Christian East Beirut? And why has the Lebanese army been weak ever since independence in 1943? If there is to be
peace in the future, these long-standing anomalies will have to be
eliminated.

22

SYRIA'S GROWING POWER IN REGIONAL POLITICS

Few countries, and certainly not the United States and Israel, fully appreciated the power of Syria in the regional political arena until the abrogation of the US-brokered troop withdrawal agreement of 17 May 1983 between Israel and Lebanon. After the expulsion of Egypt from the Arab League and the severance of diplomatic and economic ties by most Arab countries in the wake of the Camp David Accords, culminating in its peace treaty with Israel in 1979, Syria wanted to be perceived as assuming the role of military leader of the Arab world. This partly explains why President Assad does not want to see Egypt received back into the Arab fold and the Arab League. And it further explains Syria's displeasure at the rapprochement between King Hussein of Jordan and PLO Chairman Yasir Arafat and their partnership with President Hosni Mubrarak of Egypt in seeking an international formula for a solution to the Palestinian/regional crisis.

Syria's perception of Lebanon, which is part of the Lebanese problem and could be part of its solution, is complex. Its forces were invited into Lebanon in 1976 by the then President, Suleiman Franjieh, a Maronite Christian. This was in the midst of the civil war when the Christians needed outside military support against the strong PLO. The presence of Syrian troops was later formalised by the Arab League in Cairo within the context of an Arab Deterrent Force (ADF) in which three other Arab countries, Saudi Arabia, Libya and South Yemen, participated. The Syrians' main objective at this early stage of their armed presence in Lebanon was to finish off the PLO, and this they successfully accomplished. And having expelled the PLO fighters after pitched battles from their strongest camp, the heavily fortified Tel Zataar, they then turned upon the Christians. The reasons for this should be understood. Syria, as a matter of policy, does not want to see any single entity, Christian or Muslim, become too powerful in Lebanon. Such an entity would pose a challenge to it wielding political influence and military power in Lebanon, and would have to be crushed.

Syria's influence on the Lebanese scene can be felt to some extent outside the region. Even though Syria was invited into Lebanon by President Franjieh, President Assad was influential in bringing about Franjieh's exit and the election of Elias Sarkis as his successor. Franjieh very much wanted to continue in Baabda for a while and needed

Syria's support, but this was denied. (The Lebanese Constitution allows a former President to be re-elected but only after stepping down for at least one term following his presidency.)

Major policy issues affecting Lebanon, both political and military, are decided in Damascus and not in Beirut. This process grew stronger during President Amin Gemayel's administration, when not only very senior government officials and other Lebanese dignitaries shuttled between Damascus and Beirut for discussions, negotiations and advice, but the President himself had to do the same. As far as I am aware, President Assad did not return any of these numerous visits.

There are potent reasons why the President of Lebanon, whoever he is, has little choice but to succumb to Syria. First Lebanon's economy is strongly tied in with the Arab countries in the Gulf. Saudi Arabia and other Gulf states had no choice but to boycott Lebanese food products when, following the Israeli invasion of 1982, Israel forced its products on Lebanon, which in turn was compelled to pass them on to the Gulf states. Lebanon is an agricultural country and grows fruit and vegetables in abundance. Syria even depends on Lebanon for its banana requirements. All usable land routes from Lebanon to the Gulf and indeed to the whole outside world (those via Israel obviously being unusable) pass either through Arida in the north or through Chtaura in the east. This is to say that they eventually have to pass through Syria. Huge fleets of freezer containers on articulators can be seen plying daily on the Chtaura-Damascus highway via Jordan towards the Gulf. Thus Lebanon depends on Syria for its economic survival.

Lebanon shares a frontier with only one Arab country, Syria. It is fundamentally weak: it fears its unwanted Palestinian guests, whose objective is to establish a state inside Lebanon; it has no credible national army to defend its sovereignty and territorial integrity; it is even distrustful and apprehensive of its indigenous population who are chronically divided in their loyalties between the Arab world and the West. Thus the Lebanese authorities would find it impossible to ignore their giant neighbour.

Syria perceives Lebanon as part of Greater Syria, and hence does not have formal diplomatic representation in Beirut as other Arab countries do. With a heavy military presence inside the country which participates in Lebanese sectarian and inter-communal fighting either directly or by proxy, Syria unavoidably plays a heavy role in Lebanese politics. If the US Secretary of State, George Shultz, and the Israeli authorities had fully recognised this fact, and talked to Damascus more and to Beirut less, the 17 May 1983 troop withdrawal agreement might have survived. Until Lebanon becomes re-united, with both Christians and Muslims seeing themselves first as Lebanese and only secondly as Christians or Muslims, decisions affecting the

Land of Cedars will continue to be made in Damascus and in Israel.

Syria is assessed as having been the major beneficiary of Israel's invasion in 1982. The United States, with its British, Italian and French allies of the Multinational Force, was forced to pull out in February 1984 under Syrian pressure. It was also under Syrian pressure that the IDF was forced out of Greater Beirut in 1983, and later from the Awali line in June 1985. Israel blamed Syria for most of the attacks directed against the IDF in Lebanon. Syria has also benefited from other US misfortunes. When Lieutenant R.O. Goodman, a US Navy pilot on combat mission, was shot down in the Bekaa in 1983, it was with Syria that the Reverend Jesse Jackson had to negotiate for his release. Syria had a predominant influence in the episode of the TWA Flight 847 hijacked in June 1985 when, after a fearful ordeal of seventeen days, shuttling between Athens and Beirut airports and with US Navy diver Robert Dean being killed in cold blood by the hijackers, Syria eventually got the hostages released and escorted out of Beirut through Damascus. France and other Western powers have had to request Syria's assistance in obtaining the release of their nationals held hostage in Lebanon.

Countries which either exercise political influence in the region or have a political interest in the situation there should be keenly aware that any of their words or actions outside the region which could stir up Arab nationalist sentiment will be extremely likely to have adverse repercussions there, and particularly in Lebanon. Hostage-taking and other hostile acts against nationals of such countries have become a normal means of retaliation or expressing disapproval. This is why it was extremely unwise for the Archbishop of Canterbury's special envoy, Terry Waite, to return to Beirut on 17 January 1987 in pursuit of his peacemaking mission at a time when Britain was having serious political difficulties in the region following an attempt (reportedly masterminded by an Arab national) to smuggle explosives aboard an Israeli (El Al) plane at Heathrow airport, London, in late 1986. Terry Waite was kidnapped by an unidentified group in Beirut ten days after his return to Lebanon. UNTSO's standard practice of putting a temporary ban on the operational activities, especially in Lebanon, of its UN Military Observers who are nationals of countries whose activities at a particular time are perceived as creating an insecure environment for them, is worth consideration.

Syria may never be the undisputed leader of the Arab world — Egypt will always have a strong claim to that role. But any decisions made by the Arab League affecting regional affairs without Syria's full concurrence could be extremely difficult to implement. All regional affairs will almost certainly take the Palestinian issue and the Leba-

Mission with UNIFIL

nese crisis into account, and on both matters Syria's influence is
unquestionable.

Since the coming into force of the Peace Treaty with Egypt in 1979,
Israel has viewed Syria as its arch-enemy, and indeed for as long as the
Golan Heights remain in Israeli hands and the reluctant Syrian Druze
in Majdal Shams remain under Israel occupation, Syria's offensive
posture towards Israel may well continue. Israel is apprehensive of
Syria for another reason: namely, that it finds Syrians difficult to deal
with. In one of my informal chats with my Israeli colleague Brigadier-
General Dov Sion, this issue emerged. Dov felt that the Syrians were
difficult people. I agreed, adding that in this they were like Israelis; I
personally could not see that in their stubbornness they were very different from each other. However, like the Israelis, once an agreement
could be reached with them, the Syrians would be totally committed to
it. Syria's respect for and commitment to the terms of the ceasefire
agreement of May 1974, establishing the Areas of Separation and
Limitation of Forces between them and the Israelis, supervised by
UNDOF and UNTSO observers (Observer Group Golan), has been
total. Even the Israeli government's virtual annexation of the Golan in
December 1981 could not provoke Syria to move a single tank. Even
when political moves in the Security Council and later in the General
Assembly to get Israel to revoke its annexation laws failed, Syria
respected its agreement to keep the Golan quiet and peaceful. I
wondered what was going through President Assad's mind at that time
— knowing, as he did, that Israel had mobilised.

It is my belief (and not my belief alone) that the United States and
Israel cannot completely achieve a peaceful situation in the region
without the Soviet Union — and Syria. President Assad's Syria may not
be able to achieve peace on its own, but Israel cannot do so either. For
any meaningful negotiations with Syria on a peaceful resolution of the
continuing crisis, the question of the Golan Heights has to feature
prominently. The 'bottom line' is that to ignore Syria's power and
influence in the politics of the region is to guarantee failure.

23

THE REGION'S MOST STABLE
ARAB STATE

Prince Charles, heir to Queen Elizabeth II, has said that it is the people who make the king (or the queen for that matter). This is the essence of monarchy in the modern age, and is perhaps especially true of King Hussein of Jordan who has reigned since he was seventeen years old in 1953. He has been successful because he is the people's king. He is down-to-earth with his Beduin people and the Jordanian Palestinians, the latter group constituting more than 60 per cent of the total population of the Hashemite kingdom. All his energies have been geared towards building up Jordan and improving the quality of life of his subjects.

Whenever I went to visit my small UNTSO outstation, the UN Liaison Office (UNLO), in the Jordanian capital Amman, I could see improvements — new hotels, shopping centres, highways and residential areas had been springing up at an unusually fast rate. A new international airport became fully operational in 1985. Western Europe, the United States and Japan have been investing in Jordan because they sense an atmosphere of political stability and direction. Some Arab countries have also transferred some of their financial assets from Beirut to Amman because of the continuing warfare in Lebanon — thus incidentally weakening the Lebanese economy still further. Tourism is a major economic activity for Jordan, contributing greatly to its GNP. The understanding between Jordan and Israel on sharing tourism by simplifying crossing procedures for tourists at the Allenby Bridge is pragmatic and sensible; Moshe Dayan wisely advocated an 'Open Bridge' policy in 1967. The situation between the West Bankers and the occupying Israeli authorities would have been worse without this outlet.

I learnt from my Iranian troops in UNIFIL that the total isolation of the Shah from his people contributed to his downfall. He was too elevated to know his people on the ground, and consequently his people, apart from the few beneficiaries of his wealth, power and authority, did not know him. King Hussein sees his grassroots subjects frequently — in their homes, at school, at work, on project sites and when they are in hospital. Whenever he can find time, he prays with them in the mosque on Fridays. He gets to know them at social functions where he mixes freely. They love and respect him.

The Jordanian army is most loyal to the monarchy as an institution and to King Hussein personally. As supreme commander-in-chief of the Jordanian armed forces, the King regularly visits military installations, attends manoeuvres, and sees his army commander and chief of staff in their offices at the Ministry of Defence. When he is out of Jordan on official or private visits and on his endless peacemaking tours of Egypt, Saudi Arabia, Iraq, Kuwait and the United Arab Emirates, among other countries, his younger brother Crown Prince Hassan takes his place. The Crown Prince happens to be an excellent speaker, and it is a joy hearing him speak at functions.

King Hussein and Crown Prince Hassan are building Jordan with their hearts and minds and with minimal resources. The country has effective and efficient armed forces, but it is disappointing to the King and indeed to most Jordanians that they cannot acquire military hardware from the United States to boost their capability. In this, of course, Israel has always stood in Jordan's way.

When I was with UNEF in Sinai in 1974, I never at any time received a salute from an Egyptian soldier. I went to Syria on a visit to UNDOF, and no Syrian soldier would salute me either. I spent four days in Israel, and the IDF, not used to saluting its own commissioned officers, could be excused for treating me in the same way. But when I drove to Jordan, the Military Police sergeant instantly understood the two stars on my car, called his men to attention and gave me my first salute from a non-UN soldier. It was a British-type salute, reflecting the British style of training and discipline the King, himself Sandhurst-trained, has given to his army.

Jordan portrays three significant images — towards Israel, towards the Palestinians and towards the Arab world in general. As regards the first, the country continues to ensure that the Jordan valley, separating it from Israel, remains quiet, and consequently has always viewed violations from its own side, interfering with the *status quo*, with serious concern. UNLO's office — within the spirit of the Hashemite Kingdom of Jordan-Israel Mixed Armistice Commission (HKJIMAC) — has always served as the line of communication with Israel to discuss such issues. Because of the bitter experiences of the June 1967 war, Jordan did not participate in the October 1973 war with Israel, as we have already mentioned. It supports the Israeli 'Open Bridge' policy linking the two countries for economic and social activities. Other bitter experiences with the so-called 'Black September' of 1970, and the desire to protect the Hashemite monarchy, also contribute to Jordan's interest in coexisting peacefully with Israel.

Jordan has, understandably, not been able to respond to Israel's calls to it to follow in Sadat's footsteps and contract a formal peace treaty. I do not believe that the country has the political, economic and military stature to withstand the effects that such a move might provoke, especially from the Arab world. President Sadat's strong personality, buttressed by the historical pride of the Egyptians in being of Pharaonic stock and in their present military might made it possible for Sadat to withstand the wrath of Syria, Libya and the other Arab states in his pursuit of peace with Israel.

I am confident that if it ever came to a question of Israel giving Jordan military protection against Syria, this would readily be done. When Jordan convened an Arab summit at Amman in 1982 and Syria made military threats, Israel gave the feeling that it would not sit by to allow this kind of disturbance of the *status quo* in the region. Such an Israeli move would definitely create serious confusion in the Arab world, but its possibility should not be ruled out. Keeping the peace in Jordan could be seen as among Israel's prime security interest.

As regards Jordan and the Palestinians, until Israel occupied the West Bank in 1967, it had been administered by Jordan as successor to the British mandatory power (the British administration ended on 14 May 1948 when Israel became an independent state). Thus Jordan has a particular territorial and sociological concern for the West Bank and its Palestinian population. Most West Bank Palestinians have been permitted to hold Jordanian passports, and Jordanian law is used in part by the Israeli authorities to administer the area. However, they would mostly have pledged their loyalty not to King Hussein but to Arafat and the PLO as their spokesman and representative, thus making any peace process difficult for both Jordan and Israel, as well as for the United States without the PLO's active participation. Jordan continues to support West Bank businessmen financially, and all West Bankers who were in employment during the Jordanian administration are still receiving their salaries monthly from Jordan. Jordan readily accepted almost a battalion strength of PLO fighters expelled from Beirut in August 1982, and King Hussein was present at Amman airport to receive them. With this background, one can understand why the King for so long found it impossible to accept the 1974 Rabat Declaration, claiming the PLO as the sole legitimate representative of the Palestinians. He only moved officially from that position with his major policy reorientation in mid-1988.

Also after the exit from Beirut in 1982, King Hussein agreed to the PLO establishing its political headquarters in Amman. Tunis remained the military HQ. Chairman Yasir Arafat and his most senior aides, particularly Abu Jihad (assassinated in Tunis in April 1988) and Farouk Kadoumi the PLO's foreign affairs representative, were regular visitors to Amman and were frequently received by the King, the Crown Prince, the Prime Minister and senior government officials.

The rapprochement between King Hussein and Chairman Arafat grew strong enough for both to defy President Assad by convening the Palestine National Council—the Palestinian parliament-in-exile — in Amman. They sealed their new alliance by signing an accord following the PNC conference on 11 February 1985.

However, the relationship between the PLO and Amman subsequently cooled, and in mid-1986 the PLO office in Amman was closed. The chill in relations has been attributed to King Hussein's disagreement with Arafat's unyielding position on Security Council Resolutions 242 and 338 which see the Palestinian issue only in the context of refugees. Arafat and the PLO, including the splinter groups (notably PFLP, DFLP and DFLP-GC), are all united in wanting these Resolutions updated to reflect the Palestinians' national aspirations and right to a homeland. With Arafat's acceptance of 242 and 338 when he proclaimed the independent state of Palestine on 15 November 1988 in Algiers, the cool relationship between him and the King should warm up considerably.

Finally, as regards Jordan's relations with the Arab world as a whole, it was the first Arab country to re-establish diplomatic relations with Egypt, in late 1984. King Hussein, President Mubarak and Chairman Arafat are perceived as the Arab moderates who are serious in their search for a peaceful solution to the Palestinian and Jewish problems through negotiations. This explains the frequent meetings between the three in recent years in Amman, Aqaba, Cairo and Alexandria. King Hussein has been intensely active in his peace-making visits to the Gulf countries, where at the same time he has solicited petrodollars to sustain his Jordanian people and the Palestinians on the West Bank and, since 1986, in Gaza. Jordan cannot subsist on its only natural resource, phosphates from the Dead Sea, which it shares with Israel.

Jordan is the only Arab country that took a strong and unequivocal stand on the Gulf War in support of Arab Iraq against the Islamic fundamentalist regime in Iran. In the early stages of the war King Hussein, who has family links with Iraq, sent a considerable number of Jordanian volunteers there to help President Saddam Hussein's war effort. This loyalty to the Arab cause was seen as boosting the King's image. By the same token, Syria and Libya could be perceived as being out of step with the Arab world because of their strong support for Iran.

24

THE VIEW AHEAD

At the time of writing, prospects for peace in the Middle East seem remote. Efforts to resolve the Palestinian-Israeli problem continue to be made, and both the UN Secretaries-General under whom I served, Kurt Waldheim and Javier Perez de Cuellar, visited the area and met heads of state and government, foreign and defence ministers, parliamentarians, senior officials and diplomats, and influential private citizens to discuss and share views. Follow-up contacts with the parties were always sustained by the Secretary-General through his Under-Secretary General for Special Political Affairs. To complement the UN's efforts, the United States has also involved itself actively in the peacemaking process. Special Presidential envoys have shuttled in the area, discussing ways and means of containing conflicts and tirelessly probing the possibilities for a just and lasting solution to the problem. Philip Habib, Morris Draper, Richard Murphy and Robert McFarlane have all played parts in this seemingly unending exercise.

Until it became trapped in the Multinational Force tragedy in Beirut in August 1982, the United States, with unqualified self-confidence, made Arab countries believe that Washington was the sole legitimate peace-broker in the area. This conformed with its unstated policy of keeping the Soviets out of the peace process — a policy difficult to achieve because not only Syria and its fellow confrontation-states but also Saudi Arabia and most other Arab countries are still buying large quantities of their ever-needed arms and ammunition from the Soviet Union. A further step towards peace was taken when, on 17 May 1983, Israel concluded a troop withdrawal agreement with Lebanon. That agreement was abrogated by President Amin Gemayel and Prime Minister Rashid Karame under intense pressure from President Hafez el Assad of Syria.

The problems, as I see them, are as follows. First, on the Palestinian side, Chairman Yasir Arafat (Abu Ammar) may control the mainstream PLO Fatah, but his authority does not extend to Georges Habash's Popular Front for the Liberation of Palestine (PFLP), the Democratic Front for the Liberation of Palestine (DFLP) commanded by Nayef Hawatmeh, the Popular Front for the Liberation of Palestine — General Command (PFLP-GC) under Ahmed Jibril (a former Syrian army captain and graduate of Sandhurst), or the Palestine National Salvation Front under Abu Abbas, formerly an assistant to Ahmed Jibril. Abu Abbas was alleged to have masterminded the hijacking of the Italian cruise liner *Achillo Lauro* in 1986, and was actively sought by the US authorities with a view to criminal charges being brought against him.

Most of these PLO factions are based in Syria and come automatically under the influence of President Assad. Up till now, Assad and Arafat have not been the best of friends; the animosity between them is said to be personal, and to date back a long time. Just as Assad does not want to see a single strong faction in Lebanon which could be perceived as a challenge to his authority, he also finds it difficult to see Arafat wielding total power over the PLO — which he, Assad, would like to control himself. The serious fighting in Tripoli in late 1983, which saw Arafat's final exit from Lebanon, clearly demonstrated Assad's bitterness. The upshot of this is that Arafat and his breakaway colleagues cannot establish a common basis of approach, a unified front to tackle their Palestinian national problem. Great credit should be given to Arafat and his PLO colleagues for compromising their opposing stands to accept Security Council Resolutions 242 and 338, recognising the state of Israel and proclaiming their own Palestinian state. It must remain the hope of the peace-loving world that this spirit of compromise prevails at the peace-table, when the time comes.

Syria, seeing itself as the leader of the confrontation states in the Palestinian struggle against Israel, is furiously opposed to any Arab state or organisation moderating its position towards Israel in the effort to resolve the Palestinian issue, especially in situations where Syria is not involved as a principal in the negotiations. The abrogation of the May 1983 troop withdrawal agreement is a case in point. Also, in any peace process where the question of the Golan Heights is not on the agenda, Syria is bound to be uncooperative. This explains why from time to time King Hussein refers to the Golan Heights in his efforts at peacemaking. This is the major difficulty facing the Palestinians in their peace-seeking efforts.

These factors make a unified Palestinian approach almost unobtainable. Arafat is seen by the Western world as a moderate. The Israelis probably see him in the same way; and I believe a similar assessment would be found in the Soviet Union and among the countries of Eastern Europe. He speaks the UN language of more negotiation and less force while his colleagues in the Syrian camp still talk of armed confrontation to liberate Palestine from the Jews.

The second problem is the totally disunited and disintegrated nature of the Arab world. During the twelve years that I served in the region, never for even a brief moment was there total Arab unity such as could have brought about an Arab consensus on the Palestine issue. Syria continues to see Egypt as left out on a limb, and Libya and Egypt

continue to hate each other. The divisions were further exacerbated
by the Gulf war, which, as we have seen, split the Arab world into two
well-defined camps, with Syria and Libya on the Iranian side and the
rest supporting Iraq. It is noteworthy that up till the outbreak of hostilities with Iran, Iraq was totally opposed to Egypt for making peace
with Israel in the Camp David Accord; indeed, the delegation that
went to persuade President Sadat to withdraw from the peace accord
had met to plan its mission in Baghdad. That delegation, headed by
my friend Selim el Hoss the Prime Minister of Lebanon, had to return
to Baghdad without even having had a meeting with Sadat.

Arab attitudes towards the Palestinians and the peace process
continue to differ, again causing a split into several camps. Since the
PLO were thrown out of Tripoli in late 1983 by the uncoordinated but
joint efforts of Syria and Israel, there has been a gradual rapprochement between Egypt, Jordan and the PLO. King Hussein accepted
some of the PLO fighters back into Jordan. Watching the event on
Jordanian TV in Jerusalem, I could see the emotion among the
Jordanian hosts and the Palestinian guests as King Hussein shook
hands with each of the arriving PLO fighters at the airport. Surely the
King and the PLO were thinking of the same thing — Black
September in 1970.

President Hosni Mubarak on the Egyptian side provided a naval
escort for Arafat and the fighters who remained with him to ensure
that they arrived safely at their final destinations — which included
Tunisia and South Yemen. Jordan and Egypt, both of which are seen
by the West as moderates, have a consensus on the Palestinian issue.
King Hussein and President Mubarak get together from time to time,
in both Jordan and Egypt, to deliberate on the Palestinian and other
regional problems and the peace process. One can only hope for a
well-established compromise between their position, which favours an
international conference (also favoured by most Arabs) with the
Soviets and the PLO participating, and the US-Israeli position which
objects to Soviet participation unless the Soviets renew their diplomatic relations with Israel and relax restrictions on Jewish emigration.
With the successful peacemaking reconnaissance through the Middle
East by the Soviet Foreign Minister Eduard Shevardnadze in February
1989, it could be inferred that the United States and Israel are
prepared to compromise on this stand.

From the foregoing, one can readily conclude that the Arabs are
disunited, and there is neither a Palestinian nor an Arab consensus on
the approach towards peace in the region. Arab and Palestinian backs
are still up against the walls of peace. And what about the Palestinian
Jews?

The Israeli National Unity government, as structured at the time of going to press, is perceived as lacking the normal governmental strength and clout to take major political decisions. The Likud coalition did not permit Shimon Peres to make any serious political moves during his term as Prime Minister which ended in October 1986, and it is difficult to see how the Labour Alignment could avoid following in the same path. The fact remains that in normal times, as before 1984 when the National Unity government came into being, these two major parties saw the Palestinian issue from completely different angles. Thus the peace process cannot be expected to advance significantly while it governs the country.

Likud takes an extreme line on the issue, viewing it from a purely biblical standpoint. There are some hard-core 'hawks' like General Ariel Sharon and General Rafael Eitan who have gone so far as to say that the Palestinians already have a home and that is East Jordan—in other words, Hussein's Hashemite kingdom. With its extremist supporters, Likud holds that any Jew should be able to settle in any part of Palestine including the West Bank. It was General Eitan who, in earlier years as IDF Chief of Staff, reportedly called the Palestinians 'cocroaches in a bottle'. The serious disturbances that erupt periodically in towns like Hebron, Nablus, Ramallah, East Jerusalem and Bethlehem and in the Universities of Bir Zeit and Bethlehem are rooted in such Israeli statements.

The Labour Alignment, on the other hand, is assessed as rather moderate by Likud's standards. Shimon Peres and his colleagues mainly feel that it is not necessary for Jews to settle in every part of Palestine, and they are vehemently opposed to Jewish settlements in heavily-populated Arab townships. Labour's thinking that areas of importance for national security could be settled by Jews sounds reasonably sympathetic and accommodating in the eyes of Western countries. Again, Shimon Peres when Prime Minister stated on some occasions that a Labour government would be willing to trade land for real peace with the Arabs.

Thus it is difficult for Israel to sit down in Washington, Cairo, Amman, Damascus, Moscow or Geneva to negotiate for peace because of the lack of a well-defined and acceptable Israeli consensus on a basis for resolving the Palestinian question. Hence, we have problems with the Palestinians, the Arabs in general and with the Jews.

The mode of negotiation also poses a difficult dilemma for both Israelis and Arabs (including the Palestinians). Israel wants direct talks with the Arabs, particularly Jordan. However, for the Arabs direct talks would imply recognition by them of the state of Israel, which has concluded a peace treaty with Egypt. For Israel, direct talks with Jordan on the Palestinian issue would be an encouraging sign of progress towards procuring a second peace treaty with an Arab country, and this could strengthen Egypt, which for a long time has been out of step with the rest of the Arab world because of its peace treaty with Israel.

The Arabs, on the other hand, advocate an international forum, a Geneva-type conference, in which the PLO and the Soviet Union would be participants. Israel objects to any forum in which the PLO would participate for two principal reasons. First, it would give recognition to the PLO and make it more acceptable to the international community as the true and sole representative of the Palestinian people, as declared at the Rabat Conference in 1974. And secondly, such international recognition would not be in Israel's interest, since it insists on seeing the PLO only within the context of terrorism. Participation by the Soviet Union in the peacemaking process would be agreeable to the Israelis on the two principal conditions already mentioned.

Even though Israel might talk to the PLO now that it accepts Security Council Resolutions 242 and 338 concerning its recognition as a state, it is apprehensive of such a move by the PLO because it interprets these Resolutions as implying changes in the post-1967 borders. Hitherto Chairman Arafat and the entire PLO, including all the splinter-groups, balked at accepting Resolutions 242 and 338 which the PLO hierarchy sees as putting the Palestinian issue in a perspective that only takes account of the refugee aspects. The PLO tried — without success — to obtain amendments to 242 and 338 which would reflect the political and social aspirations behind the Palestinian issue.

For other, purely practical reasons — some already alluded to — Israel would want to deal directly with Jordan. Sharing a common border, the two countries are bound to be close to each other in many ways, and direct contact is merely a human phenomenon. Their common interests include the Jordan river and the phosphate resources of the Dead Sea, both of which they share, and the economic activity which takes place via the Allenby Bridge is mutually beneficial. Peace and security in the Jordan valley are in the interests of both. Hence Israel feels it could influence Jordan when they finally sit down face-to-face at the same table. Israelis know King Hussein and he knows them, and there have been direct secret contacts with him and his representatives. Israel knows that he does not favour an independent Palestinian state but rather a Palestinian political unit in confederation with Jordan.

It is worth noting that the United States undertook, as a condition for Israel agreeing to the Second Disengagement Agreement of 1975 (by which Israel withdrew further eastwards from the Suez Canal into Sinai), not to deal direct with the PLO for as long as it did not

accept Security Council Resolutions 242 and 338, with a new adden-
dum requiring that the PLO renounces the use of force and terrorism.
When Andrew Young, then US Permanent Representative to the UN,
was reported to have met a PLO representative, albeit informally, in
New York in apparent breach of this condition, he was obliged to
resign. Hence the reversal of the policy of a US-PLO dialogue, engi-
neered by Henry Kissinger when US Secretary of State in President
Nixon's administration, as a reaction to Arafat's declaration on 15
November 1988 is in fulfilment of Washington's policy undertaking.
Although it accepted the PLO's assistance in escorting US nationals
from Beirut to Damascus during the flare-up of fighting in Lebanon in
1976–7, the US administration could not be flexible on this agreement with Israel until the PLO's change of heart.

Some political and social analysts hold the view that the Israelis will
destroy themselves and Israel will fall apart with the achievement of
peace with its Arab neighbours. It could be true that Israelis might be
afraid of peace because they have never known it, but there are strong
contrary arguments. Their nationalism has its roots in the ancient
Jewish religion, which is too potent to be destroyed. Jewish
nationalism, furthermore, was tempered by the pains of the Holocaust
and the shame of a stateless diaspora. This is a particularly strong
force behind the foundation of their state. Having founded it, they will
sustain and keep it at all cost. But I feel particularly close to those
Israelis today who feel, as I have always felt, that they are particularly
well qualified to sympathise with those who are now a stateless
diaspora as they once were, and should therefore be the torchbearers
in bringing their Palestinian cousins and neighbours back to their
home in Palestine.

The key to peace in the area (as elsewhere) continues to rest in the
hands of the superpowers. However, the unstated United States policy
of keeping the Soviets out of the regional peace process is viewed by
most of us who are acquainted with Middle East politics as unrealistic
and impracticable. As the major supplier of arms and military hardware to Syria, Jordan and most other Arab countries, the Soviets
unquestionably have an indirect presence in the region. They continue to have advisers in Syria; the SAM-5s they are reported to have
installed in 1984–5 in northern Syria are manned by Soviet crews;
and they were quick to re-equip the Syrian air force when it lost almost
a quarter of its fighting power during the 1982 air battle with the
Israelis in the Bekaa. The Soviets may not control Syria, but they exercise influence there, and Syria, as we have emphasised, is a major,
unavoidable force to reckon with in the politics of the region, simply
by virtue of its contiguity with Jordan and Israel and its influence in
Lebanon. Hence the extreme lack of realism in ignoring the Soviets

and keeping them out of the quest for peace in the region. The Soviets are the counterbalance to the Americans, and for as long as the United States stays in the region for the sake of the Israelis, so will the Soviets stay to support the Arabs. A lasting peace needs a strong and broad political base with many countries involved.

The 1979 peace treaty between Israel and Egypt is a case in point. The Israelis have come to complain that the peace itself has gone cold. They rightly wish to see the real elements of peace freely demonstrated by Egypt: they want considerable improvements in trade and tourism, frequent official visits at a high governmental level, and regular meetings between the Egyptian President and the Israeli Prime Minister. But the peace arrangements between them continue to be fragile. For example, terms for conciliation and/or arbitration over the insignificant Taba issue took a considerable time for the two countries to resolve. It also took Egypt four years to reinstate its ambassador in Israel after his withdrawal from Tel Aviv following the Israeli invasion of Lebanon in 1982. The chargé d'affaires, Mohammed Bassiouny, who had taken charge of the mission, was promoted ambassador and presented his credentials in September 1986. The Israeli government complains from time to time of Egyptian press attacks and would like to see a more congenial, mature and peaceful relationship between their countries.

Again, if Washington is to continue its superpower role of peace-broker in the region, it must endeavour to restrain Israel from deep military incursions into Lebanon. No Arab country can afford to be seen co-existing with Israel while it is subverting another Arab country. The four-year absence of the Egyptian ambassador to Israel is a precedent which most Arab countries in the same position would follow. The Israelis are certainly well aware of the political constraints on President Mubarak. As an Arab leader, he is rightly fighting to get back into the Arab fold where he pre-eminently belongs. At the same time, he needs all the money he receives from the United States to provide his 50 million Egyptians with the basic necessities of life. Egypt may still be paying its war debts to the Soviet Union with cotton exports. Even before Camp David, when subsidies were coming from the Gulf oil states such as Saudi Arabia and Kuwait, that was not enough to meet the debts Egypt had incurred as a result of its participation in all the wars that had been fought on behalf of the Palestinians — in 1948, 1956, 1967 and 1973.

By maintaining its peace with Israel and not returning to the pre-Camp David 'no peace no war' situation, Egypt can afford to utilise the sizeable income it derives from the Suez Canal, its relatively modest oil resources in Abu Rudeis (both on- and off-shore) and the remittances from its nationals working in Libya and the Gulf on more pressing national needs. The US government's financial aid to Egypt since the peace treaty is reckoned to be the largest to a single country after Israel, and Egypt would surely prefer that to the scanty aid it received from its Arab brothers in the Gulf. Furthermore, with dwindling income from nationals working abroad due to difficulties with Libya, Egypt may try to keep the peace treaty in being as an insurance for continuing US aid.

Politics and logic are often strangers, but Sadat's peace overture to Israel did follow a logical path. I had figured this out as early as 1975, after one of our fortnightly inspections of the Area of Limitations on the Israeli side in Sinai. As the Chief of Staff and Deputy Force Commander of UNEF, I would join the UNTSO observers on such trips from time to time to ensure that the terms of the agreement were being respected to the letter and that our observers were carrying out their inspections professionally. I happened to meet Colonel Shimon Levinson, then chief of the Israeli liaison office, charged with all UN matters related to Sinai. We had a chat and, like most of my Israeli colleagues, he was suspicious and pessimistic, and expected the worst to happen at any time. I think that militarily this is a good mental posture, but I told Shimon he was wrong and gave my reasons why Sadat would not want to go to war again.

I propounded my theory as follows. President Sadat won a psychological victory in the 6 October 1973 war, reversing the embarrassments of the June 1967 war. He did what his predecessor President Nasser had failed to do. He started the war on Yom Kippur thus catching the Israelis unprepared, uprooted them from their seemingly inpregnable Bar Lev Line strongholds, and pushed them back across the Canal. This has provoked the Security Council eventually to organise a cessation of hostilities and create a situation where it had no choice but to fly in international troops from UNFICYP in Cyprus under the authority of Security Council Resolution 338, which formalised Egypt's few gains, to defuse tension and stabilise the area. I could not see Sadat going to war with Israel again. With his few gains, he had restored the confidence of the Egyptian armed forces and the pride of his people to their highest point since before the Six Days War. Sadat, the Egyptian people and the armed forces had gained international respect, and that was possibly one of the few achievements Sadat wanted. His own personal stature had been established and recorded in history. He knew that another attempt to fight the Israelis might result in the misery of losing all those gains, so what could be the point of it?

Shimon nodded reluctantly as I went along with my theory, saying little, but I realised that he was taking in all I said. He assured me we would meet again, and we did: he was still chief of the IDF liaison office with the UN when I went to Lebanon in March 1978 to establish UNIFIL. He left the service in early 1979 and, as with most of them, he and his family have become close friends of myself and my family. I always told Shimon that he was a bad Jew because he understood the UN cause and our limitations and difficulties in the area and was reasonably sympathetic to us.

The story has no ending. Over the years, well-considered plans have been put forward for solving the crisis in the region: the Allon Plan (1967), the Rogers Plan (1969), the EEC's Venice Declaration (1980), the Fahd Plan (1981) and the Reagan Peace Initiative (1982), among others. It would serve little purpose to analyse them in detail here. The hour is late, and although the danger of frustration and hatred producing a major conflagration is perhaps increasing the longer the crisis remains unsolved, yet there is hope in the fact that the conditions for a meaningful solution become clearer all the time. They are that full account must be taken of the problems of the Lebanese, the Palestinians and the neighbouring Arab countries on the one hand, and of Israel's security concerns on the other. A formula has to be reached that is equally acceptable to Israel, the Palestinians of the West Bank and Gaza, and the other Arabs. The Israelis cannot keep all that they have got, and the Arabs cannot have all that they want. Consensus, conciliation, concession and compromise are absolutely necessary. Because a just and lasting peace needs to have a broad political base, the eventual resolution of the crisis and the achievement of peace could well lie with the United Nations. At the time of writing, this seems a more hopeful prospect than for many years past.

APPENDIXES

A

RESOLUTION 425 (1978)

*Adopted by the Security Council at its 2074th meeting
on 19 March 1978*

The Security Council,
Taking note of the letters of the Permanent Representative of Lebanon
(S/12600 and S/12606) and the Permanent Representative of Israel (S/12607),
Having heard the statements of the Permanent Representatives of Lebanon
and Israel,
Gravely concerned at the deterioration of the situation in the Middle East, and
its consequences to the maintenance of international peace,
Convinced that the present situation impedes the achievement of a just peace
in the Middle East,
1. *Calls for* strict respect for the territorial integrity, sovereignty and political
   independence of Lebanon within its internationally recognized boundaries;
2. *Calls upon* Israel immediately to cease its military action against Lebanese
   territorial integrity and withdraw forthwith its forces from all Lebanese
   territory;
3. *Decides*, in the light of the request of the Government of Lebanon, to
   establish immediately under its authority a United Nations interim force for
   southern Lebanon for the purpose of confirming the withdrawal of Israeli
   forces, restoring international peace and security and assisting the Government of Lebanon in ensuring the return of its effective authority in the area,
   the force to be composed of personnel drawn from States Members of the
   United Nations;
4. *Requests* the Secretary-General to report to the Council within twenty-four
   hours on the implementation of this resolution.

B
REPORT OF THE SECRETARY-GENERAL ON THE IMPLEMENTATION OF SECURITY COUNCIL RESOLUTION 425 (1978)

1. The present report is submitted in pursuance of Security Council resolution 425 (1978) of 19 March 1978 in which the Council, among other things, decided to set up a United Nations Force in Lebanon under its authority and requested the Secretary-General to submit a report to it on the implementation of the resolution.

Terms of reference

2. The terms of reference of the United Nations Interim Force in Lebanon (UNIFIL) are:
(a) The Force will determine compliance with paragraph 2 of Security Council resolution 425 (1978).
(b) The Force will confirm the withdrawal of Israeli forces, restore international peace and security and assist the Government of Lebanon in ensuring the return of its effective authority in the area.
(c) The Force will establish and maintain itself in an area of operation to be defined in the light of paragraph 2 (b) above.
(d) The Force will use its best efforts to prevent the recurrence of fighting and to ensure that its area of operation is not utilized for hostile activities of any kind.
(e) In the fulfilment of this task, the Force will have the co-operation of the Military Observers of UNTSO, who will continue to function on the Armistice Demarcation Line after the termination of the mandate of UNIFIL.

General considerations

3. Three essential conditions must be met for the Force to be effective. Firstly, it must have at all times the full confidence and backing of the Security Council. Secondly, it must operate with the full co-operation of all the parties concerned. Thirdly, it must be able to function as an integrated and efficient military unit.
4. Although the general context of UNIFIL is not comparable with that of UNEF and UNDOF, the guidelines for these operations, having proved satisfactory, are deemed suitable for practical application to the new Force. These guidelines are, *mutatis mutandis* as follows:
(a) The Force will be under the command of the United Nations, vested in the Secretary-General, under the authority of the

Security Council. The command in the field will be exercised by a Force Commander appointed by the Secretary-General with the consent of the Security Council. The Commander will be responsible to the Secretary-General. The Secretary-General shall keep the Security Council fully informed of developments relating to the functioning of the Force. All matters which may affect the nature of the continued effective functioning of the Force will be referred to the Council for its decision.

(b) The Force must enjoy the freedom of movement and communication and other facilities that are necessary for the performance of its tasks. The Force and its personnel should be granted all relevant privileges and immunities provided for by the convention on the Privileges and Immunities of the United Nations.

(c) The Force will be composed of a number of contingents to be provided by selected countries, upon the request of the Secretary-General. The contingents will be selected in consultation with the Security Council and with the parties concerned, bearing in mind the accepted principle of equitable geographic representation.

(d) The Force will be provided with weapons of a defensive character. It shall not use force except in self-defence. Self-defence would include resistance to attempts by forceful means to prevent it from discharging its duties under the mandate of the Security Council. The Force will proceed on the assumption that the parties to the conflict will take all the necessary steps for compliance with the decisions of the Security Council.

(e) In performing its functions, the Force will act with complete impartiality.

(f) The supporting personnel of the Force will be provided as a rule by the Secretary-General from among existing United Nations staff. Those personnel will, of course, follow the rules and regulations of the United Nations Secretariat.

5. UNIFIL, like any other United Nations Peace-keeping operation, cannot and must not take on responsibilities which fall under the Government of the country in which it is operating. These responsibilities must be exercised by the competent Lebanese authorities. It is assumed that the Lebanese Government will take the necessary measures to co-operate with UNIFIL in this regard. It should be recalled that UNIFIL will have to operate in an area which is quite densely inhabited.

6. I envisage the responsibility of UNIFIL as a two-stage operation. In the first stage the force will confirm the withdrawal of Israeli forces from Lebanese territory to the international border. Once this is achieved, it will establish and maintain an area of operation as defined. In this connexion it will supervise the cessation of hostilities, ensure the peaceful character of the area of operation, control

movement and take all measures deemed necessary to assure the effective restoration of Lebanese sovereignty.

7. The Force is being established on the assumption that it represents an interim measure until the Government of Lebanon assumes its full responsibilities in southern Lebanon. The termination of the mandate of UNIFIL by the Security Council will not affect the continued functioning of ILMAC as set out in the appropriate Security Council decision (S/10611).

8. With the view to facilitating the task of UNIFIL, particularly as it concerns procedures for the expeditious withdrawal of Israeli forces and related matters, it may be necessary to work out arrangements with Israel and Lebanon as a preliminary measure for the implementation of the Security Council resolution. It is assumed that both parties will give their full co-operation to UNIFIL in this regard.

Proposed plan of action

9. If the Security Council is in agreement with the principles and conditions outlined above, I intend to take the following steps:

(a) I shall instruct Lt. General Ensio Siilasvuo, Chief Co-ordinator of United Nations Peace-keeping Missions in the Middle East, to contact immediately the Governments of Israel and Lebanon and initiate meetings with their representatives for the purpose of reaching agreement on the modalities of the withdrawal of Israeli forces and the establishment of a United Nations area of operation. This should not delay in any way the establishment of the Force.

(b) Pending the appointment of a Force Commander, I propose to appoint Major-General E.A. Erskine, the Chief of Staff of UNTSO, as Interim Commander. Pending the arrival of the first contingents of the Force he will perform his tasks with the assistance of a selected number of UNTSO military observers. At the same time urgent measures will be taken to secure and arrange for the early arrival in the area of contingents of the Force.

(c) In order that the Force may fulfil its responsibilities, it is considered, as a preliminary estimate, that it must have at least five battalions each of about 600 all ranks, in addition to the necessary logistics units. This means a total strength in the order of 4,000.

(d) Bearing in mind the principles set out in paragraph 4 (c) above, I am making preliminary inquiries as to the availability of contingents from suitable countries.

(e) In view of the difficulty in obtaining logistics contingents and of the necessity for economy, it would be my intention to examine the possibility of building on the existing logistics arrangements. If this should not prove possible, it will be necessary to seek other suitable arrangements (*f*) It is proposed also that an appropriate number of observers of UNTSO be assigned to assist UNIFIL in the fulfilment of its task in the same way as for UNEF.

(*g*) It is suggested that the force would initially be stationed in the area for a period of six months.

Estimated cost and method of financing

10. At the present time there are many unknown factors. The best possible preliminary estimate based upon current experience and rates with respect to other peace-keeping forces of comparable size is approximately $68 million, for a force of 4,000 all ranks, for a period of six months. This figure is made up of initial setting-up costs (excluding the cost of initial airlift) of $29 million and ongoing costs for the six month period of $39 million.

11. The costs of the Force shall be considered as expenses of the organization to be borne by the Members in accordance with Article 17, paragraph 2, of the Charter.

C
RESOLUTION 426 (1978)

Adopted by the Security Council at its 2075th meeting on 19 March 1978

The Security Council

1. *Approves* the report of the Secretary-General on the implementation of Security Council resolution 425 (1978) contained in document S/12611 dated 1978;

2. *Decides* that the Force shall be established in accordance with the above-mentioned report for an initial period of six months, and that it shall continue in operation thereafter, if required, provided the Security Council so decides.

D

SOME PROBLEMS FACING THE COMMANDER OF A PEACEKEEPING MISSION

The major problems facing the commander of any UN peacekeeping force or mission are directly associated with the weaknesses that are organic to the UN itself as a world body. Thus, in effect, the commander's problems derive from the Organisation's own drawbacks.

Political. As a body, the UN passes resolutions. These can be, and sometimes are, flouted or ignored with impunity. The UN's authority has been challenged, but it does not have the power to enforce that authority and in particular its resolutions. The basic weakness in its system is that it deals with member-countries that have sovereign rights, while it does not have those rights itself. This defect is strongly felt in a UN force dealing with interested parties — mostly member-countries — which are free to choose whether to implement UN resolutions or to defy them. This is the situation that both the Secretary-General and the UNIFIL Force Commander continually face in getting the force's mandate executed.

Lack of unanimity of Security Council members. A strong UN force should at all times enjoy the full support and confidence of the Security Council. However, since Security Council members have various national interests of their own in a mission area, there is bound to be less than total unanimity on certain vital decisions affecting the mission.

A case in point is the length of UNIFIL's mandates, which has at different times been six, five and four months. The Secretary-General recommended six months, but the Security Council had to accept four and five months as a compromise for the extension of UNIFIL's first and second mandates respectively. Not only did this affect the administrative and logistical planning and financial support of the mission, but politically it created a feeling of uncertainty over the continuing presence of UNIFIL in South Lebanon and of a lack of total commitment by the UN. Such a lack of unanimity could also embarrass the Secretary-General who by the terms of the mandate is directly responsible for the mission and keeps the Security Council informed of its functioning, but whose recommendations can be rejected by the Security Council. Lack of unanimity also weakens the mission, and so jeopardises the effectiveness of command in the field.

Cooperation and support from parties.   Against this background, no
UN mission can succeed unless it enjoys the full support, cooperation
and goodwill of the participating countries and all other parties
involved in the conflict. The PLO chairman, Yasir Arafat, pledged to
the Secretary-General his full support for and cooperation with
UNIFIL, assuring him that the PLO would not stand in the way of it
fulfilling its mandate. But in reality, this cooperation was not forthcoming: whatever reasons Arafat may have had for not cooperating
fully with UNIFIL, this compounded the force's problems. UNIFIL
also did not enjoy the desired political cooperation from the Israelis.
This was partly because Israel viewed UNIFIL's objectives as being in
conflict with its own military and political interests in Lebanon.

To execute its mandate fully, UNIFIL needs to deploy right to the
international borders, taking Lebanese authority along with it so that
it can exercise the normal governmental functions of a sovereign state.
For the time being, this seems unacceptable to Israel, and thus the
mission's progress is stalemated. Since 13 June 1978, no further
progress in deployment has been made. Ever since the establishment
of the force in 1978 the Security Council has held no less than two
formal meetings each year, when the mandate has been extended, to
discuss the issue of deployment to the border, but the problem has
remained. Everybody seems angry, but Israel is adamant: as a
sovereign country with sovereign rights, it cannot be pushed around by
the Security Council. Invoking enforcement action under Chapter 7 of
the UN Charter is completely out of the question.

The situation is similar to that in Namibia where the Security
Council has passed Resolution 435 to establish the UN Transition
Assistance Group (UNTAG), which is opposed by South Africa
because its objectives are in conflict with South Africa's own political
and economic interests. Hence the protracted stalemate until positive
developments in 1988 (ten years after 435 was passed) ushered in fresh
hopes for UNTAG.

*Contributing countries' national political biases — effect on
command.*   In a highly politically charged mission, such as that in
Lebanon, national political considerations and biases can have both
positive and negative effects on command. All contingent commanders take instructions from home, and some are instructed to
report daily to their home authorities. This practice is tantamount to
interference in command, but when properly exploited it assists the
commander in critical situations. For example, when our three Dutch
soldiers were abducted on 9 May 1979 from Observation Post 'Hin'
with threats to kill them in revenge for the death of a militiaman, we
sought help from The Hague through the Dutch ambassador in Israel.

The ambassador received instructions to intervene and we got our men back. This was certainly a helpful contribution.

Political constraints on command. Responsibility for any UN mission is vested in the Secretary-General under the Security Council's authority. The command in the field is exercised by a force commander appointed by the former with the consent of the latter. Hence the force commander is directly responsible to the Secretary-General, who may invite him to attend Security Council meetings when important matters affecting the mission are discussed, and indeed I attended all Security Council meetings on the extension of UNIFIL's mandate. A force commander's presence at the Security Council meeting helps the Secretary-General to clarify certain issues which may be required by members of the Council. This highlights the sort of political responsibility a UN force commander shoulders. But the main difficulty is that there are a lot of things which, as a soldier in field command, a force commander cannot do on his own because of political constraints, even though militarily they may be sound.

UN missions as pressure points. As a pressure point to be manipulated, a UN mission such as UNIFIL has been subjected to harassment from time to time. UNIFIL operates against the Christian militia (the DFF) in the south — Lebanese who, some time earlier, received their full pay and emoluments from the government in Beirut. These were later cut off or suspended, and as a consequence UNIFIL troops were periodically harrassed, our supply routes were blocked, our freedom of movement was restricted, our troops were kidnapped, and so on. All these things were done as expressions of the DFF's displeasure at the severance of their pay. Whenever there was conflict or tension between the Syrians and the Christians in Beirut and its suburbs, we felt the effects in the south; this was the Christians' way of drawing the attention of the world body to the situation in Beirut.

The Lebanese authorities blamed UNIFIL for the deteriorating situation in the south, knowing very well that it was mostly outside the mission's control. The point was that someone had to be held responsible; someone had to carry the blame as a scapegoat, and that someone was always the UN, the ready and easy target. When tension mounted in the area as a result of IDF military incursions, the Lebanese National Movement, the Rejectionists and other armed groups fired on us, hijacked our vehicles, and much else, in revenge. This should not have happened, but there it was. Naturally it was a serious handicap for the force commander.

World opinion as the UN's strength

Against all these difficulties, a UN peacekeeping force derives its strength from world public opinion. That strength lies not so much in the weapons we have as in how the world reacts to what is being done to us. Hence the significance of press coverage of the mission's activities. Contributing countries should not fail to raise their voices when things go wrong and jeopardise the safety and security of the troops, and members of the Security Council should do the same. When troops in the field know that the world cares about them, their morale goes sky-high.

Because it was afraid of adverse world opinion, the IDF reluctantly agreed to withdraw its battalion-strong task force which on 9 May 1978 insisted on passing through the UNIFIL area of operations to chase supposed terrorists in the town of Shaqra. I warned the task force commander, Brigadier Amos Baram, that his request to use our area of operations was not acceptable and that any attempts to push his way into it would be resisted with force. I further warned him that should anything happen to UNIFIL troops, Israel should be prepared to take the full responsibility. At least for once, Israel showed an awareness of world opinion and backed down.

INDEX